D1572647

Due on or before the latest date stamped below	

FROM A TINY CORNER
IN THE HOUSE OF FICTION

FROM A TINY CORNER
IN THE HOUSE OF FICTION

CONVERSATIONS WITH IRIS MURDOCH

EDITED BY GILLIAN DOOLEY

University of South Carolina Press

© 2003 University of South Carolina

Published in Columbia, South Carolina, by the
University of South Carolina Press

Manufactured in the United States of America

07 06 05 04 03   5 4 3 2 1

Library of Congress Cataloging-in-Publication Data

From a tiny corner in the house of fiction : conversations with Iris Murdoch / edited
by Gillian Dooley.
    p. cm.
  Includes bibliographical references (p.) and index.
  ISBN 1-57003-499-0 (alk. paper)
   1. Murdoch, Iris—Interviews. 2. Novelists, English—20th century—Interviews.
 3. Philosophers—Great Britain—Interviews. 4. Philosophy in literature.
 5. Fiction—Authorship. I. Murdoch, Iris. II. Dooley, Gillian, 1955–

  PR6063.U7 Z657 2003
  823'.914—dc21
                                       2002154231

To my parents with love

I feel like somebody who's living in a great big house and just occupies a tiny corner of it.

Murdoch to W. K. Rose

CONTENTS

Acknowledgments / xiii
Major Works by Iris Murdoch / xv
Introduction / xvii

1. HAROLD HOBSON
Lunch with Iris Murdoch, 1962 / 1

2. FRANK KERMODE
Interview from "The House of Fiction: Interviews with Seven
English Novelists," 1963 / 9

3. Speaking of Writing XII, 1964 / 14

4. W. K. ROSE
Iris Murdoch, Informally, 1968 / 16

5. SHEILA HALE
Interview from "Women Writers Now: Their Approach and Their
Apprenticeship," 1976 / 30

6. STEPHEN GLOVER
Iris Murdoch Talks to Stephen Glover, 1976 / 33

7. MICHAEL O. BELLAMY
An Interview with Iris Murdoch, 1977 / 44

8. JACK I. BILES
An Interview with Iris Murdoch, 1978 / 56

9. JEAN-LOUIS CHEVALIER, EDITOR
Closing Debate, *Rencontres avec Iris Murdoch*, 1978 / 70

10. CHRISTOPHER BIGSBY
Interview with Iris Murdoch, 1982 / 97

11. RUTH PITCHFORD
Iris Murdoch—Set to Music, 1980 / 120

12. JOHN HAFFENDEN
John Haffenden Talks to Iris Murdoch, 1983 / 124

13. WILLIAM SLAYMAKER
An Interview with Iris Murdoch, 1985 / 139

14. SIMON PRICE
Iris Murdoch: An Interview with Simon Price, 1984 / 148

15. JO BRANS
Virtuous Dogs and a Unicorn: An Interview with Iris Murdoch,
1985 / 155

16. RICHARD TODD, EDITOR
Discussions from *Encounters with Iris Murdoch*, 1988 / 167

17. BARBARA STEVENS HEUSEL
A Dialogue with Iris Murdoch, 1988 / 194

18. JONATHAN MILLER
My God: Iris Murdoch Interviewed by Jonathan Miller, 1988 / 209

19. JEFFREY MEYERS
Two Interviews with Iris Murdoch, 1990 & 1991 / 218

20. ROSEMARY HARTILL
Flight to the Enchantress, 1989 / 235

21. MICHAEL KUSTOW
Boundary Breaker and Moral Maker, 1992 / 241

22. JOANNA COLES
The Joanna Coles Interview: Duet in Perfect Harmony, 1996 / 245

23. ROBERT WEIL
Memories of Iris, 1999 / 251

References / 257
Index / 259

ACKNOWLEDGMENTS

I would like to thank Professor Peter Conradi for his constant encouragement and advice from the very beginnings of this project, and Professor John Bayley and Ed Victor Ltd. for granting permission for the overall project to go ahead. Janfarie Skinner kindly provided me with her transcripts of several broadcast interviews, one of which ("My God" by Jonathan Miller) I have included in this book. I would also like to thank Barry Blose at University of South Carolina Press for making this publication possible.

I am grateful to the following for permission to reproduce copyrighted material:

Times Newspapers Limited for "Lunch with Iris Murdoch" by Harold Hobson, *Sunday Times* (London), 11 March 1962, copyright © 1962 Times Newspapers Limited; Professor Frank Kermode for "The House of Fiction: Interviews with Seven English Novelists" by Frank Kermode; Times Newspapers Limited for "Speaking of Writing XII," *Times* (London), 13 February 1964, copyright © 1964 Times Newspapers Limited; Professor Eugene A. Carroll for "Iris Murdoch, Informally" by W. K. Rose; PFD on behalf of A. S. Byatt and Sheila Hale for "Women Writers Now: Their Approach and Their Apprenticeship" (first published in *Harpers and Queen,* October 1976), © 1976 A. S. Byatt and Sheila Hale; Stephen Glover for "Iris Murdoch Talks to Stephen Glover"; University of Wisconsin Press for "An Interview with Iris Murdoch" by Michael O. Bellamy, *Contemporary Literature* 18, no. 2 (1977), © 1977 University of Wisconsin Press; the editors of *Studies in the Literary Imagination* and Mrs. Edith Biles for "An Interview with Iris Murdoch" by Jack I. Biles; the University of Caen's Centre de Recherches de Littérature et Linguistique des Pays de Langue

Anglaise for "Closing Debate," in *Rencontres avec Iris Murdoch,* edited by Jean-Louis Chevalier; Professor Christopher Bigsby for "Interview with Iris Murdoch" by Christopher Bigsby; Professor John Haffenden for "John Haffenden Talks to Iris Murdoch"; the editors of *Papers on Language and Literature,* Vol. 21, no. 4, 1985, and William Slaymaker for "An Interview with Iris Murdoch" by William Slaymaker; the editors of *Omnibus* and Simon Price for "Iris Murdoch: An Interview with Simon Price"; Jo Brans and the editors of *Southwest Review* for "Virtuous Dogs and a Unicorn: An Interview with Iris Murdoch" by Jo Brans; Free University Press for *Encounters with Iris Murdoch,* edited by Richard Todd; Barbara Stevens Heusel for "A Dialogue with Iris Murdoch" by Barbara Stevens Heusel; Granada Television Limited for "My God: Iris Murdoch Interviewed by Jonathan Miller" by Jonathan Miller; Jeffrey Meyers for "The Art of Fiction CXVII: Iris Murdoch" by Jeffrey Meyers, *Paris Review,* no. 115 (1990) and "An Interview with Iris Murdoch" by Jeffrey Meyers, *Denver Quarterly* 26, no. 1 (1991); Rosemary Hartill for "Flight to the Enchantress," in *Writers Revealed,* by Rosemary Hartill (London: BBC, 1989); Guardian Newspapers Limited and Michael Kustow for "Boundary Breaker and Moral Maker" by Michael Kustow, © 1992 Guardian Newspapers Limited; Guardian Newspapers Limited and Joanna Coles for "The Joanna Coles Interview: Duet in Perfect Harmony" by Joanna Coles, © 1986 Guardian Newspapers Limited; and Robert Weil for "Memories of Iris" by Robert Weil.

MAJOR WORKS BY IRIS MURDOCH

1953	*Sartre: Romantic Rationalist*
1954	*Under the Net*
1956	*The Flight from the Enchanter*
1957	*The Sandcastle*
1958	*The Bell*
1961	*A Severed Head*
1962	*An Unofficial Rose*
1963	*The Unicorn*
1964	*The Italian Girl*
	A Severed Head (play cowritten with J. B. Priestley)
1965	*The Red and the Green*
1966	*The Time of the Angels*
1968	*The Nice and the Good*
	The Italian Girl (play cowritten with James Suanders)
1969	*Bruno's Dream*
1970	*A Fairly Honourable Defeat*
	The Sovereignty of Good
1971	*An Accidental Man*
1973	*The Black Prince*
	The Three Arrows and The Servants and the Snow: Plays
1974	*The Sacred and Profane Love Machine*
1975	*A Word Child*
1976	*Henry and Cato*
1977	*The Fire and the Sun: Why Plato Banished the Artists*
1978	*The Sea, the Sea* (winner of Booker Prize)
1980	*Nuns and Soldiers*
1983	*The Philosopher's Pupil*

1984   *A Year of Birds: Poems* (with wood engravings by
        Reynolds Stone)
1985   *The Good Apprentice*
1986   *Acastos: Two Platonic Dialogues*
1987   *The Book and the Brotherhood*
1989   *The Message to the Planet*
1992   *Metaphysics as a Guide to Morals*
1993   *The Green Knight*
1994   *Joanna Joanna: A Play in Two Acts*
1995   *Jackson's Dilemma*
        The One Alone
1997   *Existentialists and Mystics: Writings on Philosophy and
        Literature* (edited by Peter J. Conradi)

INTRODUCTION

The great critic Frank Kermode, Iris Murdoch's exact contemporary, whose brief but essential interview is included in this collection, once wrote that her novel *Bruno's Dream* was "disappointing only by the fantastically high standards it contrives to suggest."* Indeed, as a novelist she was always an idealist, and her artistic ambitions reflected the modified Platonism that her philosophical works espoused. Her idealism was equaled by her humility, which continually shines forth in these interviews. It was essential for her to aim for high ideals—the creation of free, independent characters in realistic social settings—however far away she felt she was from attaining them. As she said in 1964, "Any novelist worth his salt knows very clearly what is wrong with his work before it is ever published: why else, after all, would he be writing his next novel except to correct in it the mistakes of his last?"

These interviews have a unique place in the study of Murdoch's life and work. Although she often wrote about literature in her essays, she never discussed her own work. Therefore, interviews are particularly precious: a skillful interviewer could prompt her to talk about specific aspects of her novels. But the dynamic nature of conversation poses inbuilt dangers to its reliability. Where there appears to be sympathy between Murdoch and an interviewer, she is, on one hand, perhaps more likely to have answered questions openly and without constraint; on the other hand, there may also be an element of wishing to please, or not to offend, the interviewer. Modesty did not prevent her from making it clear, politely but with occasional asperity, when she found

* Frank Kermode, "*Bruno's Dream*," in *Iris Murdoch,* ed. Harold Bloom (New York: Chelsea House, 1986), 25.

an interviewer's approach unsympathetic—when Barbara Stevens Heusel applied Bakhtinian theory to her novels, for example, or when Stephen Glover suggested that "there is something too middle-class about the modern English novel." The slight antagonism in these cases may have influenced her responses, giving her opinions unwarranted emphasis. Thus some of the apparent contradictions that arise from time to time on topics—for example, the role of philosophy in her novels—might result only from different responses to different interviewers.

On the whole, Murdoch was a courteous and cooperative interviewee. Only once did she refuse outright to answer a question: Haffenden asked her to give an example of one of her dreams, and she replied, "I don't think I will." More often she seemed preoccupied, as if she were still dwelling on an earlier question, and responded to a new one absently before amplifying an earlier answer. A frustrating example occurred during a discussion of *The Black Prince* with Jack Biles. He proposed that "there is no way in the world to know what really did happen. Which is what you were aiming for," to which Murdoch replied, "Yes, yes," and continued, "I should say just one thing about this matter of symbolism. . . ." Her affirmative answer not only contradicts other statements, such as that made to Bigsby—"The thing is *The Black Prince* has got its own inbuilt mode of explanation"—but goes against her consistent belief in the stability of truth, especially in a work of art, which "must have authority over its victim, or client or whatever you can call the person who is meeting it." Occasionally the way she answered, or did not answer, a question changed the direction of the discussion. Bellamy, for example, asked her about one aspect of *A Fairly Honourable Defeat*—the connection between art and morality—but she replied with an explanation of the "theological myth" underlying the novel, which did not address his question directly.

Despite these reservations, these interviews, taken in context, give a clear overall picture of Murdoch's beliefs on a wide range of topics and her intentions and techniques as a writer. Many of her opinions remained stable over the years. However, it is important to remember that fame, with its consequent media and academic attention, came to her relatively late in life: her first novel was published when she was thirty-five, and the first interview included here was conducted in

1962, when she was forty-three. By then, youthful infatuation with Marxism was long past and her Left-leaning views were becoming more moderate. In 1962 she told Hobson that she was a member of the Labour Party even though she disagreed with its education policy: "One doesn't necessarily support a party because of its record or because of very explicit things in its policy. One may support it because in general it has good sense and goodwill about things one thinks matter." Even this qualified approval for the Labour Party had disappeared by the late 1980s, and she admitted to having voted Conservative: "Margaret Thatcher's government has done a number of good things," she told Rosemary Hartill in 1989.

She was fairly constant in her belief that the novel was not the place for expression of social or political comment: she told both Rose and Bellamy that she felt plays were better vehicles for propaganda than novels. Her two plays *The Three Arrows* and *The Servants and the Snow* are indeed more political in nature than her novels, although she also claimed in the Bellamy interview that "in a quiet way, there is a lot of social criticism in my novels." Strong political and social beliefs usually underlie a desire for justice, which she seems not to have had: she told Hartill that "the concept to hang on to is truth. Let justice look after itself"; and she regarded a desire for revenge as "the opposite of freedom." Satire, that vehicle of the political propagandist, has little place in her work, and when Heusel asked Murdoch whether she considered herself a satirist, she was predictably answered in the negative.

One subject on which Murdoch's views were forthright was women's education, although concerning other aspects of the feminist movement she was less than supportive. She said to Bellamy, "I'm not interested in women's problems as such, though I'm a great supporter of women's liberation—particularly education for women—but in aid of getting women to join the human race, not in aid of making any kind of feminine contribution to the world." At the French symposium she asserted, "I disapprove of 'separatism' as a mode of liberation: women's studies, black studies, and nonsense of that sort. The main point is to join the great main stream of thought and art."

In Murdoch's novels women are often depicted in the very feminine predicament of being controlled, enslaved, or even imprisoned by the will of egotistical males. Jo Brans brought this matter up, citing as examples Hannah in *The Unicorn,* Dorina in *An Accidental Man,* Crystal in *A Word Child,* and Hartley in *The Sea, The Sea.* Understandably, Murdoch protested that there were significant circumstantial differences which resisted generalization among these cases; but Brans certainly had a point: men are less likely to be enslaved in these ways by women in Murdoch's fiction. Other examples are early characters such as Anna in *Under the Net* and Rosa in *The Flight from the Enchanter,* as well as later ones such as Franca in *The Message to the Planet,* Jean in *The Book and the Brotherhood,* and even Morgan in *A Fairly Honourable Defeat,* although Morgan's enslaver, Julius, has become reluctant to continue in that role.

In the novels there is a conflict between the egotism of men who justify their adultery by their imagined need for more than one sexual partner, and the resulting suffering of their respective wives and mistresses. These situations would not be plausible if the sexes of the parties were reversed. In any event novels such as *An Unofficial Rose, The Sacred and Profane Love Machine,* and *The Message to the Planet* seem quite explicitly concerned (inter alia) with "women's problems as such." The fact that women and men in her novels are seldom equivalent and equal is perhaps a reflection of Murdoch's impulse to depict life as it is rather than as it should be.*

Some of the questions most commonly asked in these interviews concern the relationship between Murdoch's philosophy and her fiction, and although her answers often seem contradictory, she consistently rejects the title of "philosophical novelist." For example, Hobson asked in 1962, "Do you express a philosophy in your novels?," to which she replied, "In the strict sense, certainly no. But having thought about philosophy, especially moral philosophy, does sometimes affect the way I set a problem up in a novel." Rose brought up the question of the double career in 1968, and she commented that "more philosophy seems to be getting into the novels." In 1977, however, she told Biles,

---

* The contrast between her own chaotic love life, as revealed in Peter Conradi's biography, *Iris Murdoch: A Life* (London: HarperCollins; New York: Norton, 2001), and the more conventional lives of most of her female characters would make a fascinating study, but that is well beyond the scope of this introduction.

"I don't want philosophy, as such, to intrude into the novel world at all and I think it doesn't. I find really no difficulty in separating these activities. I mention philosophy sometimes in the novels because I happen to know about it, just as another writer might talk about coal mining; it happens to come in." Talking to Meyers in 1988, she said, "The consideration of moral issues in the novels may be intensified by some philosophical considerations, but on the whole I think it's dangerous writing a philosophical novel."

Given the above examples, it seems her position was ambiguous. On the one hand philosophy was a subject like coal mining (she mentioned coal mining to Glover, Hartill, and Biles as one of the subjects she would have liked to know about as a novelist). On the other hand it was a basic element of her "moral orientation" and as such naturally affected her fictional writing. It is certainly an important feature of her work that in a novel "one sees the moral problem in a real context" (as she said in the 1978 French symposium). Her novels are full of theorists whose theories fail when tested against reality, Rupert in *A Fairly Honourable Defeat* being perhaps the clearest example.

The concept of freedom was of continuing interest to Murdoch from the time she wrote her book on Sartre. Rose asked her whether freedom were her main subject, and she replied, "No, not now. I think it might have been in the past. No, I think love is my main subject. I have very mixed feelings about the concept of freedom now. This is partly a philosophical development. I once was a kind of existentialist and now I am a kind of platonist." The interview with Slaymaker focuses on her understanding of freedom, expanding on the position that she "would connect freedom with knowledge and with the ability to discipline emotion and to love and to live in some more disciplined and better way," rather than taking the existentialist view, in which "freedom is often identified with casting off of bonds, with emotional unrestraint, with various kinds of unbridled conduct." She explains the important difference between "political freedom as opposed to or as contrasted with intellectual, emotional or spiritual freedom." This difference is central to the understanding of, for example, Morgan in *A Fairly Honourable Defeat,* who believes she is or can be free but for whom freedom is an impossibly distant goal, and Ludwig in *An*

Accidental Man, who exchanges his political and personal freedom for the freedom of acting in the way he sees as right.

The question of religion was also a popular one among these interviewers. Murdoch's position as a Christian fellow traveler without a belief in a personal god or in the supernatural aspects of religion was apparent as early as the Hobson interview: Christianity, she said then, contains "all the wisdom one requires." An interest in Buddhism came later. She told Meyers in 1988, "I've been very attached to Buddhism. Buddhism makes it plain that you can have religion without God, that religion is in fact better off without God."

Jonathan Miller's 1988 interview concentrates on her religious attitudes and examines some of the difficulties inherent in some of her beliefs, such as that children should be brought up understanding religion even if their parents are nonbelievers. She said, "I have no children, but if I did have children I think I would put them into the situation of learning about Christianity and regarding it as religious." Miller replied, "But you were told by people who actually held these beliefs rather than someone who, as it were, is going to pretend to hold these beliefs in order to introduce the child to religious views." To this she could answer only, "Well, I think that a knowledge of Christianity in childhood is very important."

In the Biles interview she said, "The disappearance of prayer from people's lives, the disappearance of any sort of practice of religion, is, in any case, a sad phenomenon." She told Brans that meditation techniques should be taught in schools to make up for this absence. The more dangerous aspects of religion, touched upon by Brans, are rarely acknowledged. When Brans described her own childhood "in a fundamentalist religion, scared of hell for years, nightmares about hell," Murdoch responded, "You must have felt you'd gotten out of something when you broke free. It's an awful thing to bring up young people like this. But if one has some religion, if one is in any sense at home there even as a lapsed believer, this probably can help, because one has the idea of how to pray." This position requires considerable moral sophistication; behaving as if there is a transcendent reality, while believing there is not, is unlikely to be a viable path for people who have not been conditioned by Murdoch's particular upbringing and education.

Many of the literary interviewers favored questions concerning their subject's opinions of other writers. Murdoch's admiration of Samuel Beckett waned over the years: both Hobson and Glover asked her whether she admired him, and her answers were, in 1962, "Enormously. But why did he stop writing in the best language?" and, in 1976, "I don't think I admire and love him as much as I used to." Otherwise her literary pantheon remained the same—Homer, Shakespeare, Austen, Dickens, Tolstoy, Dostoevsky, Proust, and with reservations, Henry James and Sartre. Her position on Sartre remained very much as set out in her 1953 book, *Sartre, Romantic Rationalist.* She told Bellamy, "I'm not very interested in his later philosophical development. . . . I think he's a marvelous man and his whole career is very interesting. . . . He's a heroic figure and perhaps a great writer."

James is a more interesting case. In the 1968 interview with Rose, Murdoch said, "The only person I'm certain has influenced me is Henry James, though I think he's less good than some of the people I've mentioned just now"—Jane Austen, Emily Brontë, Dickens, Tolstoy, and Dostoevsky. However, in the 1986 symposium John Bayley commented, "I think, though Iris is not influenced by him at all, that she likes Henry James very much." Murdoch did not correct him; whether this betokens a change of attitude or a moment of matrimonial inattention is a matter for conjecture, but in 1988 she told Meyers that she loved James, without mentioning whether she still felt his influence. (Bayley has not done any serious critical work on his wife's novels and occasionally in the memoirs makes a factual error—for example, referring to Fanny Peronett [misspelled "Peronet"] as the heroine of *An Unofficial Rose,* when she has died immediately before the action of the novel begins.*)

George Eliot was mentioned often with approval, although Murdoch admitted to Hale that "George Eliot is not somebody who touches my heart terribly although one must admire her." D. H. Lawrence, although he was "a great writer and a genius," was often cited as an example of a writer who failed in the fair treatment of his characters, especially in his portrayal of Clifford Chatterley in *Lady Chatterley's Lover:* "This is not a house of free characters; I mean this

---

* John Bayley, *Elegy for Iris* (New York: St. Martin's Press, 1999), 155.

is not a novel where these people have any kind of self-determination," she said to Bigsby.

Her two favorite fictional characters were Achilles in Homer's *Iliad* and Mr Knightley in Jane Austen's *Emma*. Her own reading habits were centered on the classics, and only in 1964 did she say that she was reading modern fiction. Bayley confirms this in *Elegy for Iris:*

> She hardly ever read a contemporary novel, except when a friend or the friend of a friend had written one and asked if she could bear to give an opinion, whereupon she would read every word of it conscientiously. Having done so, she was very often enthusiastic; sometimes, it seemed to me, if I also read the work submitted, disproportionately so. I think this came not only from the warmth and loyalty of friendship but from a kind of innocence: she had no experience of what novels today were like, and was impressed by what I could have told her was just the current way of doing it, a mere imitation of contemporary modes and fashions.

The most detailed information about her habits and techniques of composition is to be found in Jeffrey Meyers's *Paris Review* interview from 1988. Bellamy's 1976 interview gives a good overview of her aims and ideals as a writer. Her practice was to compose her novels completely before she began to write, and she remained more or less content with that technique. She did say in 1964, however, "I sometimes think that I may plan too much in advance; I have never yet begun a book without knowing exactly how it would turn out and where I was going in it. I know other writers work that way, but I can't imagine myself doing it; still, people whose opinions I respect tell me I ought to try, and perhaps I will." She told Bellamy, "There is a great deal of experimentation in the work, but I don't want it to be too evident. I am happy in the tradition."

Several times she used Henry James's famous "house of fiction" metaphor: she told Rose that she occupied only "a tiny corner" of the house, and Glover that it was a "very big house as it were, the novel, within which all sorts of things can happen and a lot of experiment can take place without the reader being necessarily disturbed." Her criticism of D. H. Lawrence's failings was not withheld from her own writing. She believed in the ideal of free characters in realistic settings but acknowledged the difficulty of achieving this: she told Kermode in 1962, "One starts off . . . hoping every time . . . that a lot of people who are not me are going to come into existence in some wonderful way. Yet often it turns out in the end that something about the structure of the work itself, the myth as it were of the work, has drawn all these people into a sort of spiral, or into a kind of form which ultimately is the form of one's own mind."

Biles and Meyers both asked her if she were content with her work, and she answered in the negative. The paradox inherent in her need to control the novels in order to make them free of her subconscious mind was discussed with Haffenden: "A strong form tends to narrow the characters. . . . The idea of the myth and the form have got to be present, but one has brutally to stop the form determining the emotion of the book by working in the opposite direction, by making something happen which doesn't belong to the world of the magic." Similarly, in the Bigsby conversation she said:

> art comes out of the unconscious mind and there are bound to be personal obsessions and images which are around the place. If there isn't any force from the unconscious you haven't got a work of art so that the force is something you must thank the Gods for if it is there. The rational intellect is also involved. I have got no shortage of the stuff from the unconscious; it is rather a matter of sorting it out and preventing it from following patterns which it wants to follow. So the intellect comes in very much to prevent it, say, from being too coercive, to prevent the plot from being coerced by unconscious forces.

As for the status of her intentions in the interpretation of her work, she believed that although a certain amount of leeway could be allowed to readers, "if the reader or observer can do anything he likes with the thing then one result, of course, is that he becomes bored." She also said, "I would want mystification to be something of a further intensification of the story: not a contradiction of it, but a kind of shadow hiding the story which people could see if they could unveil it." Intentional mystification and indeterminacy were not within her usual artistic ambit.

Drama and the theater played an interesting if minor part in her career. She collaborated on two plays adapted from her novels *A Severed Head* and *The Italian Girl*, and she later adapted *The Black Prince* for the stage. She also wrote two original plays, *The Three Arrows* and *The Servants and the Snow*, and *Acastos*, two dialogues based on *The Fire and the Sun*, the genesis of which was recounted in the 1992 interview with Michael Kustow. As she told Biles, "I don't actually *like* the theater very much. But I would like to write for it, which is a paradox." She explained this more fully to Bigsby: "I don't know how to write a play and therefore of course it interests me because I like to learn." She told Haffenden that she liked working in the theater because it was less lonely than writing novels, but she said to Bigsby that, as with her novels, she wanted to maintain authority over her plays in performance. Her collaboration with J. B. Priestley on *A Severed Head* worked well—"Jack had a bottle of whiskey, and somehow or other it happened!"—but *The Italian Girl* was not such a happy experience: "I am not pleased with that. I was told that nothing would happen until I was satisfied with the version, but in the end I was hustled and it was a botched job." According to the interview with Pitchford in 1980, she enjoyed her collaboration on *The Servants*, an opera based on her play *The Servants and the Snow*. It is clear, though, that she never really thought of herself as a playwright and was happier giving her principal energies to the novel form, where she was more confident of artistic and critical success.

Her attitude toward literary critics was even more ambivalent. In "The Idea of Perfection" she wrote, "the most essential and funda-mental aspect of culture is the study of literature."* Her husband, John Bayley, is an eminent literary critic. However, these interviews are pep-pered with statements such as "One never learns anything one doesn't know from critics"; "This is critics' talk and as such may not be very important"; "Artists must be left alone, the critics must leave them

---

* Iris Murdoch, "The Idea of Perfection," in *Existentialists and Mystics*, ed. Peter Con-radi (London: Chatto and Windus, 1997), 326.

alone too"; and "It's very unlikely that one would learn something deep from a critic." She was, nevertheless, apparently willing to engage in discussions with critics. She and Bayley would often do "a joint discussion and a question-and-answer session. . . . We always enjoyed such outings" (*Elegy* 121); the Chevalier and Todd symposia are examples of these occasions. Perhaps the distinction to make is between the usefulness of critics to writers, which she believed was minimal, and the pursuit of criticism as an end in itself, or as a means of interpretation to other readers. In a talk entitled "Structure in the Novel," delivered at another symposium, she said, "The critic is engaged as a whole man exercising many talents and many kinds of knowledge in the attempt to exhibit something densely concrete and particular to his reader."* Obviously she felt that some critics with whom she had dealings did not conform to this ideal: her impatience became palpable in statements such as "I'm just a novelist and critics are critics. If people want to explain something by saying that it is like something else then okay. Anyway we can't stop them, so they will." There is surely some sarcasm implicit in the phrase "just a novelist."

Despite her reservations about critics, she often appeared to enjoy discussing her work. At the beginning of the Chevalier symposium she said, "it's a great feast of egoism for me to listen to your thoughts"; but she remained modest about her achievements. One particularly disarming illustration of her modesty arose when symposium participants were discussing the character Morgan in *A Fairly Honourable Defeat*: she cut in with her own "simpler view . . . that she's just not a very successful character" and proceeded to discuss what she saw as her shortcomings in creating characters. One might say she was taking control of the conversation here, but she was steering it firmly in the direction of self-criticism. In the earlier symposium she started to criticize herself for failing to make the rhetorical position of *A Word Child* part of the novel in the way she had with other first-person books such as *The Black Prince* and *The Sea, The Sea*. But in that case she talked herself

* Iris Murdoch, "Structure in the Novel," in *Structure in Science and Art: Proceedings of the Third C. H. Boehringer Sohn Symposium Held at Kronberg, Taunus, 2–5 May 1979*, ed. Peter Medawar and Julian H. Shelley (Amsterdam: Excerpta Medica, 1980), 103.

out of her self-criticism: "now I come to say it, I don't see why one shouldn't use that convention."

These symposia afforded her opportunities for viewing her work objectively, which she seemed to find useful and stimulating. Among the other detailed discussions of her work, Christopher Bigsby's interview is particularly exciting to read because he encouraged her to talk at her own pace about the issues of freedom, morality, and politics. It also includes a wonderful analysis of the character of James in *The Sea, The Sea* and detailed discussions of the morality of several of her novels. She often explained to interviewers the religious allegory underlying *A Fairly Honourable Defeat,* while maintaining that "it doesn't matter if nobody sees this." And she seemed oddly determined to reveal the identity of the narrator in *The Philosopher's Pupil,* which is deliberately left vague in the novel. Unprompted, she told Heusel that "he [the narrator] might well be the psychiatrist Ivor Sefton," and she also brought the matter up at the 1986 symposium, as if she found the indeterminacy she obviously intended to leave in the novel too frustrating to maintain. There is something appealing about her eagerness to share this secret with the world.

Interviewers were sometimes disconcerted by Murdoch's habit of turning their questions back on them, but this could demonstrate her engagement with other people and her interest in their opinions. She would ask whether her interviewer had written novels, sometimes perhaps to imply how little the practice of writing relates to literary theories, but in other cases to encourage writing. Her own theories of the novel were sometimes expounded in detail: for instance, her ideal of a novel with no central characters, with all the characters peripheral and equally important—a notion which, thankfully, she never carried out in practice.

Her personality, as revealed in many of these conversations, was engaging and sometimes quirky. "Spiders are my friends," she told Meyers; and dogs, unlike cats, can be "images of human virtue," she said to Brans. Talking to Simon Price about classical literature, she admitted to reading Horace "in a selfish kind of way"—without explaining what that might mean—and deplored the fact that her Latin style was more Tacitean than Ciceronian. She reported to both Rose and

Meyers that she spent part of every day doing housework, which contradicts John Bayley's claim that "neither of us felt any need to keep the house clean" (*Elegy* 80). Jo Brans challenged her about the "horrifying filth" of Tallis Browne's kitchen in *A Fairly Honourable Defeat*, to which Murdoch replied, "I must say, I don't mind filth as much as you do." Her tolerance for filth might be explained by the fact that, as Bayley said, she had no sense of smell, with the result that "her awareness of others is transcendental rather than physical" (*Elegy* 66). But if that were true, what can be made of her statement to Glover that she found the smell of foreign countries such as India and Japan exciting?

As much as was possible, the interviews were reproduced in the form in which they were originally published. Most of the major academic interviews and the two symposium debates have been reproduced more or less complete, but some of the press interviews have been shorn of repetitious details and fascinating but inessential descriptions of setting and dress.* Ellipses in brackets indicate where cuts have been made. The interview with Jonathan Miller was transcribed from a television program, and some slight textual editing was undertaken, though not enough to remove the long sentences and idiosyncrasies of her speech. These are also evident in the Bigsby interview.

The final two interviews were not cut. They show Murdoch at the beginning and end of her decline into Alzheimer's disease, which I refrain from calling tragic—she would not have approved of this word to describe such a contingent state of affairs. Joanna Coles visited the North Oxford house in September 1996, before the disease was diagnosed or at least publicly acknowledged, and found Murdoch in what she herself described as "a very, very bad, quiet place." Robert Weil, John Bayley's American editor, movingly describes his friendship with her in her last few years—still sweet-tempered in spite of her mental deterioration. These two pieces necessarily include John Bayley and testify to his devotion to his wife that is so evident in his two books *Elegy for Iris* and *Iris and Her Friends*.

As Weil points out, to pay too much attention to Murdoch's last years would be "a horrendous trivialization of a remarkable career."

---

* An important interview with Bryan Magee is excluded here, as it is to be found in *Existentialists and Mystics*, 3–30.

I hope this collection will help to focus attention on that career, a life spent aspiring to the courage and truthfulness that, as she told Meyers, are the characteristics of all great art.

FROM A TINY CORNER
IN THE HOUSE OF FICTION

1

HAROLD HOBSON

Lunch with Iris Murdoch

Sir Harold Hobson (1904–92) was the theater critic for the *Times* of London from 1947 to 1976. This interview was first published in the London *Sunday Times* on 11 March 1962.

After meeting in the comfortable Ladies' Section of the Union Club in St. James's Street, Hobson and Miss Murdoch moved a few hundred yards north for lunch.

HOBSON: I hope you hadn't any difficulty in finding your way here. I couldn't direct you very well, because I don't know the Union Club myself. At the Athenaeum there's no room at present for women. We're building new quarters for them.

MURDOCH: They're not allowed in the Club itself?

HOBSON: Good heavens, no. What an extraordinary idea. Now in "Who's Who" you describe yourself as "Novelist and lecturer" in that order. You think that novelists are more important than scholars?

MURDOCH: I'm not responsible for that description, but I suppose I could change it if I wanted to, and I haven't done so. I don't know whether novelists are more important than scholars. But I suppose they are more influential than scholars.

HOBSON: In what way?

MURDOCH: In altering people's sensibility, altering the kind of light in which they see the world. Novelists are partly symptoms and partly causes. One can see these changes of light more dramatically perhaps in other arts—in painting, for example. But literature is the strongest, and in my view the most important, of the arts because it's made of words—and words are connected with our highest rational activities. It's dangerous to become careless about words, and literature should always be seeing to it that we don't. Though unfortunately not all modern writers love words as much as they ought.

HOBSON: Changes of sensibility? What kinds do you see in present-day literature?

MURDOCH: An obvious one is a sort of sense of disintegration of personality. Novelists seem to find it harder to create "characters" now, and I suppose this is a symptom of a general *malaise* about the nature of persons. It's in this way, through the novel, I mean, that a lot of what was originally highly theoretical stuff becomes diffused into the general consciousness. By now, through literature, Freud has reached us all. Another related aspect of the modern scene is a failure of belief in society. But I seem now to be talking precisely about what's wrong with modern novels. No characters and no significant relation of persons to social background.

HOBSON: You think a novelist should be able to deal with both?

MURDOCH: Well, the great novelists did. It's much more difficult now to say something really truthful about the social scene and remain within the bounds of art: and in so far [*sic*] as we can't it's a very serious loss.

HOBSON: Why is it more difficult?

MURDOCH: I imagine for a lot of obvious reasons concerned with the greater instability of societies and the world, and disappearance of the idea of progress, and the fright which people like Freud have given us. Or maybe there just happen to be fewer talented writers now than there used to be!

HOBSON: What about philosophy? Are you not the only well-known novelist who is a trained philosopher?

MURDOCH: In England, maybe. But abroad, no. Sartre and Simone de Beauvoir, for instance.

HOBSON: Simone de Beauvoir taught philosophy in a secondary school. That's hardly what I meant by a philosopher.

MURDOCH: But she *is* a philosopher, a real one out of the Ecole Normale Supérieure! I admire her very much indeed. I've tried to meet her, but never managed it.

HOBSON: You've met Sartre?

MURDOCH: Once, long ago. He seemed a gentle, donnish man. He gave most careful attention to a series of quite unimportant young people, including me, who were dying to talk to him without having anything much to say.

HOBSON: Do you express a philosophy in *your* novels?

MURDOCH: In the strict sense, certainly no. But having thought about philosophy, especially moral philosophy, does sometimes affect the way I set a problem up in a novel. In *The Bell*, for instance, there is an obvious and fairly explicit theoretical background to the different moral attitudes of the main characters.

HOBSON: People sometimes say you tend to leave "moral questions" unresolved in your novels. Do you agree?

MURDOCH: It depends on the novel. In *The Bell* I offer three extremely clear types of moral reaction to a certain situation and I indicate to the reader which is the right one. I don't know what more he wants.

HOBSON: Should a writer have a "philosophy" in some sense of the word?

MURDOCH: I suppose a good writer can't help having a philosophy in some sense of the word, in that he has wisdom about the human condition. Great literature is morally great and involves making judgments on the way human beings go on. But it may be very hard to say *what* a writer's philosophy is apart from just pointing at his work. Eliot implies somewhere that Dante is greater than Shakespeare because Dante has a richer and more coherent philosophy behind him. But Eliot must be wrong. I would argue another way. Shakespeare is greater than Dante, so it can't be essential for a writer to have a coherent philosophy behind him. What is Shakespeare's "philosophy"? And these are the two greatest writers in the world.

HOBSON: What about the Bible? "Belshazzar the king made a great feast to a thousand of his lords and drank wine before the thousand."

MURDOCH: All right, I suppose one must allow a few competitors, but there aren't many!

HOBSON: You rate poetry very high, evidently.

MURDOCH: Poetry is the most important thing in the world. Poetry in the sense of *Dichtung*. It is our understanding of ourselves, us human beings, at its most subtle and truthful and beautiful. Words again. We must look after words.

HOBSON: We have spoken rather generally of literature. What about branches of literature? Do plays interest you?

MURDOCH: Apart from Shakespeare and the Greeks I don't know much about them. I've hardly seen any modern plays. Except for *Waiting for Godot,* which I would gladly see a dozen times.

HOBSON: You admire Beckett?

MURDOCH: Enormously. But why did he stop writing in the best language? I discovered Beckett long ago, at the beginning of the war. I remember being in an Oxford pub and hearing someone recite the passage from *Murphy* which begins: "Miss Counihan sat on Wylie's knees . . ." I was immediately enslaved. I got the book and read it. There was one copy which circulated in Oxford, which I think belonged to Denis Healey. The influence of that book, together with Queneau's *Pierrot,* upon *Under the Net* should be obvious. I imitated these two great models with all my heart. Samuel Beckett is the only person I've ever written a fan letter to.

HOBSON: What about music? Does that interest you?

MURDOCH: I know very little about it. I like to hear the few things I know over and over again. I have no intellectual grasp of music and it attacks my emotions directly. Tears will roll down my cheeks at practically any piece of music. It affects me with a sort of desolation. This shows I don't really understand it.

HOBSON: Wittgenstein could whistle whole concertos. I don't know whether they made him miserable. The cinema?

MURDOCH: I hardly ever go. I haven't time. I'd rather talk to people. Anyway, the cinema upsets me terribly when it's sad. Life is sad enough without that too. Crying at music is a kind of pleasure, but in the cinema I just get filled with a dangerous sort of self-pity. The only films I go to now are Danny Kaye's.

HOBSON: How disconcerting the tastes of you deep thinkers are! Jean-Paul Sartre and Simone de Beauvoir prefer dance bands, and

Wittgenstein liked Carmen Miranda and Betty Hutton. You say you admire Simone de Beauvoir. It seems to me that in *Le deuxième sexe* she postulates the inferiority of women to men, because their biological function is reproduction, whilst the Existentialist philosophy insists on the virtue of change, development, advance. Do you too accept the superiority of the male?

MURDOCH: Of course not.

HOBSON: It must be admitted that the achievement of women in the arts is less than that of men.

MURDOCH: But naturally it is. The emancipation of women is only just beginning—and there are signs of reaction against it already. Did you see all those letters in *The Times* recently saying that girls ought to be educated for marriage and the home? This is nonsense. Girls ought to have as tough an education, academically speaking, as their talents will allow—otherwise, as human beings, they are being cheated, they are being made smaller and less free. Any intelligent person can learn home management quite quickly at any age, from practice and out of books. But if you don't learn Greek and mathematics at school you'll probably never learn them.

HOBSON: Surely you exaggerate when you say that men are still trying to suppress women?

MURDOCH: Oh no, I don't. Look at *you.* You're trying to do it yourself.

HOBSON (Petrified with astonishment): Never!

MURDOCH: Oh yes, you are. The very first thing you said to me was that you thanked heaven because women were kept out of the Athenaeum.

HOBSON: That was a joke.

MURDOCH: Are you sure?

HOBSON (Defeated): Not altogether. Perhaps you're right.

MURDOCH: Clubs are a special case. I suppose men can have the Athenaeum if they want to. But the notion that women are inferior is deep, very deep, even in our fairly sensible society, and it does nobody any good. Men and women are still thought of as having stereotyped parts to play, regardless of their temperament. But any individual is a mixture of masculine and feminine and would be best employed just being himself and treating other people as individuals, too.

HOBSON: I suppose that holds in education too. Yet I have the impression that you think that the aim of education is to produce scholarships to the university. Don't you prefer Demoyte, who wanted scholarships, to his clergyman successor in *The Sandcastle,* who thought more of the average boy than the brilliant?

MURDOCH: No, there's just a contrast between them, that's all. It must be very painful to feel deprived of one's full intellectual development at any level. It's important that the less clever should not be made to feel inferior. But there's much more danger just now of the clever not getting the full treatment. There seems to be no tendency in this country to overrate the intellect.

HOBSON: You yourself were at a public school, Badminton School, weren't you? What do you feel about the Labour Party's views on public schools?

MURDOCH: I am a member of the Labour Party, but I don't feel happy about its education policy. I think clever children should be segregated and not condemned to be slowed down by the dull ones in the interests of brotherhood. And I don't think we should sacrifice existing high standards in education to a hasty plan for making education democratic. Standards in education can be easily destroyed and not so easily set up again. Our independent schools are a very precious possession. But in fact neither of our great political parties seems to have much sense about education. If I were Prime Minister I would raise school teachers' salaries to some astronomical level. I can't think of anything which would do the country more good.

HOBSON: Would you agree that in other matters, foreign policy for instance, the Labour Party hardly differs from the Conservative?

MURDOCH: Well, no. Anyway, one doesn't necessarily support a party because of its record or because of very explicit things in its policy. One may support it because in general it has good sense and goodwill about things one thinks matter. I think the Labour Party has good sense and goodwill about important things such as racial policy, for instance. And the bomb. I am a unilateralist myself, and although Labour is not yet officially with me, I think the Labour Party is more likely to be able to think clearly on this issue than the Conservatives. [. . .]

HOBSON: [. . .] You are Irish, aren't you? You were born in Dublin?

MURDOCH: Yes, my mother is a Dubliner, but my father came from Belfast.

HOBSON: Protestants?

MURDOCH: Yes. I was baptised and confirmed in the Church of England, but I don't believe any more. Though in a sense one is never outside Christianity if one has been caught up in it. Nor would I altogether want to be. There is all the wisdom one requires there, if one can get hold of it.

HOBSON: People often divide your novels into two categories, both equally striking, but different: *Under the Net, The Flight from the Enchanter,* and *A Severed Head* they describe as belonging to the world of fantasy, and *The Sandcastle* and *The Bell* as tending more to realism. Are they right in doing so?

MURDOCH: If fantasy and realism are visible and separate aspects in a novel, then the novel is likely to be a failure. In real life the fantastic and the ordinary, the plain and the symbolic, are often indissolubly joined together, and I think the best novels explore and exhibit life without disjoining them.

I suppose there is some justice in dividing my novels as you suggested, though the ones you called "realistic" certainly don't aim at realism as something opposed to fantasy.

HOBSON: Which are your favourites?

MURDOCH: I confess I like *The Flight from the Enchanter* and *A Severed Head* best, but that's just because they are myths and more organically connected with myself. They are more full of me. Probably they are for that reason less good. I agree with Eliot that the artist's task is the expulsion of himself from the work of art. In other books I have at least made the attempt, though not very successfully, to create persons other than myself. As in philosophy, the direction of attention should be outwards. It's said of Wittgenstein that he had a special way of saying "Let's see" when sitting down to consider a problem which expressed this absolutely truthful and selfless direction of attention. And Socrates obviously affected people in the same way.

HOBSON: A willingness to follow the question wherever it leads. Surely that's a philosophical but not a religious attitude. A Christian knows where it leads before it starts.

MURDOCH: I should be sorry for any religion which had no place for "Let's see." It can after all be an expression not just of curiosity but of love. And this is what the novelist needs in order to create characters. God, if He exists, is good because He delights in the existence of something other than Himself. And that is the condition to be aimed at.

2

FRANK KERMODE

Interview from "The House of Fiction: Interviews with
Seven English Novelists"

Sir Frank Kermode (born 1919) has held professorships at University
College London, Cambridge, and Harvard. One of his generation's
foremost literary scholars, he has written books that include *The Sense
of an Ending, The Genesis of Secrecy,* and a memoir, *Not Entitled.* At
the time of this interview he was in the English department at Manchester University. Sir Frank has told me that the published version of
this interview was seen and approved by Murdoch at her request. The
other novelists included in this article are Graham Greene, Angus Wilson, Ivy Compton-Burnett, C. P. Snow, John Wain, and Muriel Spark.
This interview has appeared in *The Listener* (30 August 1962), the *Partisan Review* (Spring 1963), *Abstracts of English Studies* (February
1964), and *The Novel Today,* edited by Malcolm Bradbury (Glasgow:
Collins, 1977).

These conversations are abridged from longer talks; they were entirely
free and unprepared. In cutting them I have naturally preferred to
leave out whatever seemed most remote from the center represented
by the title. If this seems a somewhat abstract topic, I can only say that
it proved reasonably easy to keep the mind of the contributors fixed
upon it. Clearly it is a relationship that they all think about in a more
or less abstract way, as well as handling it daily in terms of technique.
　　[. . .] It seemed to me that a recent article by Miss Iris Murdoch
expressed most of the issues we wanted discussed in a clear, usable

way.* Most of the contributors did in fact find her terminology convenient, so we began with what she said about it. The antithesis of "crystalline" and "journalistic," plot and myth, will in fact echo through the conversations.

I first asked Miss Murdoch to enlarge on one of her points, this distinction between "crystalline" and "journalistic" modes:

MURDOCH: It's one of these epigrammatic distinctions which are probably themselves rather inexact. This distinction was suggested to me in a way by worrying about my own work and about what was wrong with it. There is a tendency, I think, on the one hand, and especially now, to produce a closely coiled, carefully constructed object wherein the story rather than the people is the important thing, and wherein the story perhaps suggests a particular, fairly clear moral. On the other hand, there is and always has been in fiction a desire to describe the world around one in a fairly loose and cheerful way. And it seemed to me at present in the novel that there was a flying apart of these two different aims. Some ideal state of affairs would combine the merits of both.

KERMODE: You spoke of the consolation of the form in your article as being a deceptive presentation of reality. Is this a certain kind of form? It doesn't apply to the sort which combines crystalline and journalistic, but only to the crystalline sort?

MURDOCH: This is a delicate question. It's almost absurd to say that form in art is in any sense a menace, because form is the absolute essence of art. But there can be a tendency too readily to pull a form or a structure out of something one's thinking about and to rest upon that. The satisfaction of the form is such that it can stop one from going more deeply into the contradictions or paradoxes or more painful aspects of the subject matter.

KERMODE: You didn't want myth to the degree that it interferes with the representation of character in a rather old-fashioned sense?

MURDOCH: Yes, this is perhaps my main thought in that article you referred to. I think that it would be coming back to character in the

---

* Iris Murdoch, "Against Dryness," in *Existentialists and Mystics,* 287–95. This essay originally appeared in *Encounter* 16, under the editorship of Kermode, in January 1961.

old-fashioned sense which would save one from being too readily consoled.

KERMODE: You also say that writers write what they can and not what they should. May I ask you whether in work that you perhaps have in hand there's any attempt to carry out this program?

MURDOCH: I always attempt to carry it out but I find it very difficult to do so.

KERMODE: Because of the strength of the myth?

MURDOCH: This sounds pretentious, as if one were thinking of one's work in a rather grandiose way, but yes, I suppose it is. Another way of putting it would be just that one isn't good enough at creating character. One starts off—at least I start off—hoping every time that this is going to happen and that a lot of people who are not me are going to come into existence in some wonderful way. Yet often it turns out in the end that something about the structure of the work itself, the myth as it were of the work, has drawn all these people into a sort of spiral, or into a kind of form which ultimately is the form of one's own mind.

KERMODE: Yes. And in so far [sic] as they are absorbed into that, they lose identity.

MURDOCH: I think this tends to happen.

KERMODE: So that the myth is a sort of safety net under the tightrope?

MURDOCH: Well yes, if you put it so, it's a form of safety. I don't take a low view of it. I think it can be important and beautiful; but I think it comes more easily to writers now than the other thing.

KERMODE: Yes. And although myth is in itself, as you say, a high matter, if it is ultimately something that distorts reality, then it is the enemy, however dignified, of the kind of novel that you feel ought to be written.

MURDOCH: Well, not altogether the enemy. It should be present also. It's perhaps the thing which at the moment one should guard against giving in to.

KERMODE: One of the more sensible definitions of myth in this connection would be one which allowed it to look after itself, wouldn't it?

MURDOCH: Yes.

KERMODE: May I now bring the discussion a little closer to your own books? Would you feel free to say that in your books since *Under the*

Net there has been any movement towards the kind of fiction that you say ought to be written?

MURDOCH: It's very hard to say. Leaving aside the question of whether they're better or worse or anything—well, I don't know that you can leave this question aside quite, but trying to leave it aside—I think they oscillate rather between attempts to portray a lot of people and giving in to a powerful plot or story. I think the last one, *A Severed Head,* probably represents a giving in to the myth; and the previous one, *The Bell,* has more people in it; and the one I've just written now [*An Unofficial Rose*] I think again has more people in it. But it's always rather a problem. Given that one hasn't achieved the kind of synthesis which I think is desirable and which would make one's stuff of some use, there is a tendency to oscillate between achieving a kind of intensity through having a very powerful story and sacrificing character, and having the character and losing the intensity.

KERMODE: It might seem, perhaps, using myth in too crude a sense, that there was more of it, or that it was more openly to be met with in *The Bell* and *The Severed Head* than in *Under the Net,* for example.

MURDOCH: *Under the Net* has in fact got its own myth, but I think it probably just hasn't emerged very clearly in the story.

KERMODE: Is it a philosopher's novel?

MURDOCH: In a very simple sense. It plays with a philosophical idea. The problem which is mentioned in the title is the problem of how far conceptualising and theorising, which from one point of view are absolutely essential, in fact divide you from the thing that is the object of theoretical attention. And Hugo is a sort of non-philosophical metaphysician who is supposed to be paralysed in a way by this problem.

KERMODE: And you set this novel quite deliberately in places which are given a good deal of actuality, in London and Paris, for example, as I remember rendered in some detail.

MURDOCH: That was just self-indulgence. It hadn't any particular significance.

KERMODE: The technical excursions which we all like so much in your novels, how a car turns over, or how you get a bell out of a lake and so on, are they also self-indulgence under this very strict definition?

MURDOCH: Yes. That is just a kind of fascination with completely theoretical amateur mechanics.

KERMODE: Well, someone will come along and call them a myth all the same.

MURDOCH: Of course the bell itself has significance, and is quite explicitly used as a symbol by the characters. But I think the majority of my "technical excursions" are pure play.

3

Speaking of Writing XII

This anonymous interview was published in the *Times* of London on 13 February 1964.

[. . .] "I do not begin the actual writing until a fairly late stage of creation. First of all I plan out a novel in great detail—characters, scenes, the overall structure—and only when I have the shape of the book and the people in it very clear in my mind do I begin writing: after which I write as a rule two drafts of the whole thing, and maybe three or four of particular scenes. I sometimes think that I may plan too much in advance; I have never yet begun a book without knowing exactly how it would turn out and where I was going in it. I know other writers work that way, but I can't imagine myself doing it; still, people whose opinions I respect tell me I ought to try, and perhaps I will. One of the troubles of having everything planned out in advance is keeping the thing alive while one is writing it; but if one's creativity is functioning properly, the very act of writing engenders its own excitement—something starts working inside the language itself, bringing up all sorts of new qualities and ideas unforeseen in the initial plans."

How much fiction by other writers did Miss Murdoch herself read, and how far did she feel that what she read influenced her own practice as a novelist?

"I read quite a lot of current fiction, for one reason or another, and I read and reread the classic novels, though according to my mood at the moment rather than to any plan: if I feel in the mood to reread some Dickens, say, or George Eliot, then I do, but on the other hand there are quite a number of accepted great novelists—Balzac, for example—whom I have never found very sympathetic and would certainly not persevere with from a sense of duty. As for influences, well, of course, one would like to think one was influenced by all those great writers who because of the unique qualities of their greatness could not possibly exert any definable influence: perhaps, though, Homer and Shakespeare can be influences in that they may inspire one with the hope of expanding oneself to a comparable imaginative scope, even if that hope remains only a remote aspiration. More immediately, I would like to think that something of the spirit of Jane Austen, whose work I love dearly, had entered into my work. But the only writer I am really sure has influenced me is Henry James: he is a pattern man too."

Evidently, at least, Miss Murdoch was not influenced by her critics, since she never reads them? "No, it seems to me a waste of time. One never learns anything one doesn't know from critics. Any novelist worth his salt knows very clearly what is wrong with his work before it is ever published: why else, after all, would he be writing his next novel except to correct in it the mistakes of his last?"

4

W. K. ROSE

Iris Murdoch, Informally

William Kent Rose (1924–68) held a master's degree from Stanford University and was professor of English at Vassar College for the last fifteen years of his life. His edition of Wyndham Lewis's letters was published in 1963. This interview has been published in *Shenandoah* (Vol. 19, no. 2, 1968), *London Magazine* (June 1968), *Abstracts of English Studies* (1968), and *Harper's Bazaar* (May 1969).

Iris Murdoch lives with her husband, John Bayley, in a village outside Oxford. She comes to London for two or three days in the middle of each week and teaches pupils from the Royal College of Art and University College. At the time of this interview, initially made on behalf of the American magazine *Shenandoah,* she was also commuting to Bristol for rehearsals of the play based on her novel *The Italian Girl.*

ROSE: How is the play going?

MURDOCH: I hope it will be all right. I'm doing it with a young playwright called James Saunders. I'm quite involved in this one, as I was in *A Severed Head.* I enjoy it, but theatre people like to work in a rush, and it's been rather a rushed job.

ROSE: Have you ever done anything in the theatre on your own?

MURDOCH: No. I think I might some time [*sic*]. It's not a medium that's very natural to me. I like writing prose and I don't feel I could explore the things I want to explore very easily in the theatre. If I could do it without terrible difficulty, I would like to write some propaganda plays, plays which were really pamphlets. People used to do that in the 1930s much more than they do now. But if I thought of a good plot, I think I should want to write it as a novel.

ROSE: The dramatization of *A Severed Head* had a much lighter effect than the novel. Was it your intention to play up the comic side?

MURDOCH: No. It was just that the dialogue is fairly comic, and in so far [*sic*] as the novel has other aspects, they're not really carried by the dialogue. The same thing has happened with *The Italian Girl*. It's turned into a kind of funny object; the novel is a half-funny object anyway. It's very interesting seeing the two dramatizations now and comparing them. In both cases the main burden of the narrative is borne in the play by the person who is the narrator in the novel. The new one, too, turns out to be a kind of funny play, in the form of a poor, rather gullible, confused man stumbling on from one awful blow to another. This is a comic form which is quite familiar.

ROSE: How does the collaboration work?

MURDOCH: Unfortunately, the time-table has been so rushed on this occasion that James Saunders and I haven't been able to collaborate as much as I would have wished, because I had hoped to learn a lot from this operation. I learnt a lot from working with Priestley, whom I knew before; and James Saunders, whom I had not met before, is a very good dramatist, and I would like to have had more time to discuss the text with him.

ROSE: What would you write a propaganda play about?

MURDOCH: Well, I would like to write one about Vietnam, of course.

ROSE: In your book on Sartre you discuss his views on the novel of commitment.* What is your own feeling about the novel and society? I know you don't stand where he does.

MURDOCH: No, I don't, and I think less and less. I mean I don't think that an artist should worry about looking after society *in his art*. That's why I said "propaganda plays." I wouldn't regard this quite as being my job as an artist, but as an alternative to another method of making people pay attention. I think as an artist, one's first duty is to the art you practice, and to produce the best kind of work that you know how.

* Iris Murdoch, *Sartre: Romantic Rationalist* (Cambridge, UK: Bowes & Bowes, 1953).

I think every artist knows roughly how this should be done. A novelist working well and honestly, and only saying what he knows and what he understands, will in fact tell a lot of important truths about his society. This is why tyrannical societies are often frightened of novelists. I think it's a novelist's job to be a good artist, and this will involve telling the truth, and not worrying about social commitment. I think social commitment, in so far [sic] as it interferes with art, is very often a mistake. It can make the novelist nervous and anxious and not able to open himself to the whole of reality as he understands it.

ROSE: But you do feel that the artist ought to speak out on social questions?

MURDOCH: Yes. But I don't suppose I will ever actually do a propaganda play. I don't think I probably could do it; art might get in the way, and one would simply hate the result. But I certainly think that one ought to write pamphlets. I feel strongly about a number of things and don't say enough. I think, after all, it's the job of any intellectual in society to make comments.

ROSE: Would you favor a complete withdrawal in Vietnam, if America had the opportunity of saying simply, "We get out now, with no strings attached"?

MURDOCH: Yes, but that's non-feasible politically. I think it's a very great pity that this business began at all. I think that nothing very serious would have happened if the whole situation had been left alone. Now, what will happen afterwards may be very much worse. This notion of containing Communism is wrongly thought out anyway. These national groups need to be left alone, to work out their own destiny. The fact that some label like Communist is attached doesn't alter the fact that these people are very separatist and want to run their own show. The notion that there's going to be some great big kind of world conspiracy is very outdated. It would be much better to let these people work things out for themselves as they will have to in the end. For a country like Vietnam, although a Communist régime is not what I would choose to live under myself, it may be a necessary stepping-stone to some kind of rational form of government. And the Vietnamese, one may be sure, would have their own brand of Communism, just as the Yugoslavs do.

ROSE: Let's talk about you. You were born in Ireland and educated here?

MURDOCH: Yes, I was born in Dublin and educated in England.

ROSE: Do you feel you have a nationality?

MURDOCH: Well, I feel Anglo-Irish. I went to Ireland a great deal as a child for holidays, but I never really lived there; I grew up entirely in London. But I feel a very emotional attachment to Ireland, of a rather obscure, half-annoyed kind. I also feel a tremendous attachment to England.

ROSE: You've no Celtic blood, then?

MURDOCH: No. It's all settlers' blood, but both sides of my family have been in Ireland for several centuries—at least for two or three centuries—so that they regard themselves as Irish. They regard themselves as *the* Irish, in fact.

ROSE: I was thinking of your delight in the fantastic as having, possibly, Celtic roots?

MURDOCH: About this fantasticalness of Irish writers, when you look and see who's doing it, it's very often an *Anglo*-Irish writer. Perhaps it's the climate.

ROSE: Was writing an early impulse with you?

MURDOCH: Yes. It was very early. I knew as a child that I wanted to be a writer. I always knew that I would do something else as well. But I started writing stories when I was about 9 or 10, and I always knew that this was what I wanted to do—though I was never certain that I would get anywhere. And I went on writing; I wrote a lot of stuff before I ever published anything.

ROSE: I suppose the "something else" turned out to be your career as a philosopher.

MURDOCH: Yes. But that was pretty unforeseen actually. I grew up into the war, and I saw the war coming, as most of us did. This thinking about the future had a very odd feeling in the 1930s. I was a very left-wing Socialist, and I joined the Communist Party at Oxford. I thought I might do politics or social work or international work of some kind. I certainly wanted to get a good education, and I enjoyed my academic work very much. I did classics, philosophy, and ancient history at Oxford; but I didn't really think of being a philosopher until rather later. During the war I was a civil servant and then I went into UNRRA, doing relief work after the war. I was in Belgium for a short time; after that I was in some displaced persons' camps in Austria. But when I was in Belgium immediately after the war, everyone was in a state of frenzy about existentialism. It was the first moment of being able to get hold of books by Sartre and people. It was during this strange period that I became so excited about this world of ideas that I decided to go back to philosophy.

ROSE: How does it work as a double career? Would you say it's complementary or conflicting, or both?

MURDOCH: It's conflicting in a purely time sense, that one is leading a sort of double life. One doesn't have enough time, and it's the philosophy side that I give up, and increasingly give up. I have stopped teaching philosophy at Oxford, though I teach a little bit in London and enjoy that very much. I write philosophy quite regularly—lectures and so on—but it's a game that needs an immense amount of time. It really needs a lifetime of thinking about nothing else, and I do, if I've got to choose, choose the other game. I think in other ways they are, for me, perhaps increasingly complementary. I felt a little worried about this for a while, but I think that I am not now so worried. More philosophy seems to be getting into the novels. The reason, I think, is that I have now got a philosophical viewpoint, a more organized position than I had earlier.

ROSE: Is this more organized position explained in your recently published Leslie Stephen lecture?*

MURDOCH: Yes, I suppose that is the most up-to-date expression of what I think. It's very short and condensed, however, and by no means as clear as I would wish.

ROSE: How would you relate yourself to the Oxford analytical school?

MURDOCH: I am certainly connected with it. In so far [sic] as I had a professional training, that's it. And I think that as a basis for looking at any other philosophy whatever, it's ideal. It's tremendously critical

* Iris Murdoch, "The Sovereignty of Good over Other Concepts," in *Existentialists and Mystics,* 363–85.

and exacting, anti-woolliness and anti-emotion. I think this is necessary in philosophy, where one can so easily lose one's grip. But I am not a linguistic analyst in the sense of thinking that there isn't any positive content to philosophy, that it's all critical in this particular way. I think there is positive content, at least in moral and political philosophy, the area which I'm interested in. But one has to state it with very great care and without jargon. I think that philosophy should—in the tradition of Hume and Locke—be written in ordinary language.

ROSE: In the book on Sartre, you say: "He brings to the novel, together with a remarkable literary gift, his typically philosophical self-consciousness. Whether this awareness helps or hinders him as an artist will have to be considered."* In your own case, I gather, you think that there is now more help than hindrance?

MURDOCH: I am a little worried about how far one should let the philosophy come in. I think that sometimes it comes into the very center of the plot, as it did in *The Time of the Angels*. But more often, I think, it comes in through a character wanting to talk in a kind of metaphysical way. This might have a chorus-like effect, or some sort of dimension-changing effect, in relation to the activities of the non-philosophical characters.

ROSE: Would "The Silencer" in *Under the Net* be an example?

MURDOCH: Yes. Only that was more sharply separated from the rest of the book than in some later things. In *The Nice and the Good* there's a certain amount of metaphysical conversation, of a non-technical but definitely philosophical kind, between two of the characters from time to time throughout the book. This may be seen as a kind of interpretation of the activities of the other characters.

ROSE: Once I heard William Golding make a division between two kinds of novelists. One starts with experience and lets the meaning come with the characters and situations as they develop in his imagination: Dickens was Golding's example. The other sort, of which he said he was one, has an idea and then discovers a myth to embody it; then in the writing the myth takes over, acting as a guide and a spark

---

* Murdoch, *Sartre* (1953), 9. This passage is part of the introduction to the first edition, which was replaced in the 1987 edition by a longer introduction.

to the writer's imagination. The end product might not be vastly different, but the differing origins will mark the two kinds of novels. Does this interest you as a distinction?

MURDOCH: I think it's an interesting contrast, but trying to relate it to my own work, I don't feel it quite fits. I don't think I am either kind, exclusively, though I would like to be like Dickens. In a way one is just a slave of one's unconscious mind; but in so far [sic] as one can push one's work one way or another, I am always pushing myself towards a starting-point in experience. The other stuff is pretty automatic with me; I don't have to look for myths or philosophical ideas. What I feel my work needs, what makes it less good, is that I'm not able to present characters with enough depth and ordinariness, and accidentalness. This has always been a problem for me—my characters get cramped by my story. I certainly always attempt to start with experience. That is, I start with two or three people in some kind of situation—except, as I say, in one or two cases, in *The Unicorn* and *The Time of the Angels,* for instance, where there was a kind of religious or metaphysical conception at the very root of the idea. I would much rather start with something very much more ordinary—that is, experience in some quite ordinary sense—and people, without thinking of them as playing any special role. I sometimes think that if I could have a novel which was made up entirely of peripheral characters, accidental people like Dickens' people, this would be a very much better novel. One might even go so far as starting to invent the novel and then abolishing the central characters.

ROSE: In your novels there seems to be a division between the *Sandcastle* sort, which is written in the traditional mode of realistic fiction, and the *Severed Head* sort, where one is more in a world of patterns and of artifice, or coincidence and arrangement. Is this a difference you have in mind as you are planning the novel, or is it something that happens after you've started composing?

MURDOCH: I see there's a kind of alternation between a sort of closed novel, where my own obsessional feeling about the novel is very strong and draws it closely together, and an open novel, where there are more accidental and separate and free characters. I would like to write the second kind. *The Nice and the Good* is a pretty open one,

I think—perhaps the most open one I've done yet. But the one I'm writing now [*Bruno's Dream*] turns out to be the other kind, unfortunately.

ROSE: What about symbolism? In an open novel, like *The Bell*, one recognizes that the bell is more than a bell; yet it seems to be quite different as a symbol from some in the more closed novels, like the slicing of the napkins in *A Severed Head*. Is that a fair distinction?

MURDOCH: This business of symbols is rather confusing. I am not, I think, a symbolic writer in any allegorical or complete sense. Symbols come in, perhaps more in some novels than in others. I would want them to come in in a completely natural way, through the characters. That is, being a symbol-maker is not a kind of odd thing which artists are; it's something which everyone is. One notices in any kind of family situation or love affair, people invent symbols, all sorts of things become symbolic. This kind of pattern-making, although it may be connected with art in some genetic way, is not just an effect of art; it is something one spots if one looks around at human beings. I think my symbolism is of this kind—in *The Bell*, for instance, people with different temperaments take the bell differently as a symbol. And in *The Unicorn* the characters take the plight of the imprisoned woman in different ways. I would feel nervous of having too much symbolism if it became part of the structure of the work. If it comes in in a natural, subordinate way, it is absolutely O.K. and perfectly realistic. This is different, of course, from the way in which symbolism comes in when it's connected with a dominating myth—which has happened in some of my novels.

ROSE: For example?

MURDOCH: Well, *The Unicorn*. The symbolism is rather fundamental there, I suppose. In the case of *The Italian Girl*, the myth is so familiar that it hardly seems to us like a myth. But the Oedipus myth is fairly fundamental in that book, and that again is what I feel nervous of.

ROSE: I take it that the Oedipal theme extends through the two generations in *The Italian Girl*. Could one consider David Levkin and his sister *children-by-adoption*, as it were?

MURDOCH: One could look on them as sort of demon children. The notion of the demon child is one that interests me—the sort of changeling that suddenly appears and alters the destiny of the people round about. But I don't think there's anything quite as close-knit there. I needed some kind of outsiders, and these two presented themselves. I was thinking about, well, I'm always thinking about Russia—but I mean something to do with the homeless emigré Russian, the counterforce to the very deep-rooted hominess of the rest of the scene. It is a story about home and mother, coming back to mother and settling down with mother and so on, and these homeless people passing through, and then something tragic happening: they are not really children and this is not really their home, and they are banished. And the notion of returning to the truth was also involved. In the end it's quite right for David to go back to Russia; he has to live in his own place, as he puts it. But this sounds rather artificial in relation to the book, and I think it's not a very successful book. I think the idea of the substitute mother was a good one; I think Otto and Edmund and Isabel are quite real, but Maggie and the Russians are not real enough to carry the plot.

ROSE: Are the two Poles in *The Flight from the Enchanter* as comparable figures to the two Russians?

MURDOCH: Yes. They're very much more sinister, of course, and I suppose mysterious, in a sense which means that they're not quite complete characters. They *are* demons. The notion of the intrusion of demons—well, I feel this is something that happens in life. Not necessarily that people really are demons but that they play the role of demons for other people. This is one of the themes of *The Flight from the Enchanter,* the way in which people make other people play the role for them of gods and demons.

ROSE: Would this apply to Honor Klein?

MURDOCH: Yes. Mischa Fox and Honor Klein are both power characters. They are gods who are deified by their surrounding followers.

ROSE: Do you mean that people can assign, as it were, demonic energy to their chosen masters, or do you see certain persons as being endowed with it anyway?

MURDOCH: I think there is in some sense, which I don't mean to be religious or metaphysical, demonic energy and that there is a great deal of spare energy racing around, which very often suddenly focuses a situation and makes a person play a commanding role. People are often looking for a god or ready to cast somebody in the role of a demon.

ROSE: Then the demon *must* wait for his victims to choose him, or at least for his time?

MURDOCH: No. I think people possessed of this kind of energy do come in and generate situations. One's seen it happen in life. But then too there are always victims ready to come forward. Rose is so placed *vis-à-vis* the Poles and Mischa in *The Flight from the Enchanter.*

ROSE: Would you say that freedom is your main subject?

MURDOCH: No, not now. I think it might have been in the past. No, I think love is my main subject. I have very mixed feelings about the concept of freedom now. This is partly a philosophical development. I once was a kind of existentialist and now I am a kind of platonist. What I am concerned about really is love, but this sounds very grandiose. One is also telling a story, making jokes, and so on. I think the novel is a comic form. I think tragedy is a highly specialized and separate form. Doubtless it's the highest of all art forms, but it depends on certain limitations which a novel can't have. The novel is always comic.

ROSE: How do you see love, or more specifically, sex, as relating to demonic energy in your novels?

MURDOCH: Everybody, I imagine, agrees that sexual energy is something so enormously diffused and so various in form that it covers all kinds and aspects of human life. Certainly it is connected with this sort of worshiping and extension of power, with the way in which we make other people play roles in our lives—dominating roles or slave roles. So this sort of drama is a fundamental expression of sex, though it has other aspects connected with power in what seems to be a much more primitive sense. Very often this appears as a kind of animal situation, so fundamental that even sex in any recognizable sense is not present.

ROSE: Often in your closed novels the characters all link up via sexual encounters that seem almost mechanistic, or like steps in a ritual. Is your concern here for larger meanings or formal effects, or do you see sex as working this way in life?

MURDOCH: I think sex *does* these things in life. Part of the drama in those closed-up, rather obsessional novels is the struggle between love and sex. Love obviously in its genesis belongs with sex, but it's able to transcend sex—I don't mean in any sense of moving away from carnal expressions of sex but simply that sex is a very great mystifier, it's a very great dark force. It makes us do all kinds of things we don't understand and very often don't want to do. The kind of opening out of love as a world where we really can see other people and are not simply dominated by our own slavish impulses and obsessions, this is something which I would want very much to explore and which I think is very difficult. All these demons and so on are connected with the obsessional side of one's life, which in a sense has got to be overcome. In *The Flight from the Enchanter,* Rosa is enslaved; the outsider, Peter—not a particularly real character, I'm afraid, represents an open world, a world which is not a world of slavery. This would be a theme too in one or two of the other novels.

ROSE: Would you say that most of the characters in *A Severed Head* are slaves?

MURDOCH: Yes. In *A Severed Head* there's no resolution. Martin is just lucky—or is he lucky?—in his relationship to one of his enslavers. Equally there isn't really any resolution in *The Unicorn.*

ROSE: Would you say then that the mechanical love-making in some of these closed novels is an *effect* of compulsion?

MURDOCH: Yes. I think in some of these relationships, in *A Severed Head,* say, that the mechanicalness of it is an aspect of the dreariness of this unenlightened world. But I think *The Unicorn* is a much better novel than either *The Flight from the Enchanter* or *A Severed Head* or *The Italian Girl.* It's about the ambiguity of such relationships when they get mixed up with notions of redemption and other religions notions. In a way it is about the ambiguity of the spiritual world itself, the curious connections there are between spirituality and sex.

ROSE: One gets this in *The Bell* too.

MURDOCH: Yes—how people get lost in this sort of labyrinth; and how in a quite genuine way the motive power for our activity is sexual. This doesn't mean that great saints are in any way discredited. It's just that it is very difficult to become a great saint.

ROSE: You don't follow Freud on religion then?

MURDOCH: No. I'm not Freudian. I think Freud discovered a lot of things, but I think this whole business of sexuality and spirituality is very much more ambiguous and hard to understand.

ROSE: What has been your own experience with regard to religion?

MURDOCH: I was brought up as a Protestant Christian and I am still very much connected with Christianity, though I'm not a believer in any conceivable sense. I am very interested in religion.

ROSE: Can we talk about writing habits and the way you compose a novel? Do you begin writing soon after a subject forms itself in your mind, or is there a period of gestation?

MURDOCH: I am not neurotic about writing. I don't wait for inspiration; I just go ahead and work office hours, as it were. But I spend a great deal of time planning what I am going to do. I need a very long time to brood on the subject and the plot and the characters, and to let them sort themselves out in a kind of automatic way, without actually starting to write anything except notes. The longer one can prolong this stage of creation, I find, the better. By the time I start to write, the thing is practically finished; there's nothing to do except write it. Then, of course, one modifies it a great deal in the writing.

ROSE: How does that go?

MURDOCH: I always write at least two drafts. I write a first draft, which is often a bit muddled in places. Then I write an entire second draft, and very often for a particular part, I might write it ten times.

ROSE: And after the second draft is completed?

MURDOCH: I take as much care as I can, but then I want to get rid of the damned thing—because the next one is already sort of around.

ROSE: Do you do a daily stint when you are working on a novel?

MURDOCH: Yes. I am not a nocturnal worker. I start at nine o'clock in the morning, when I feel most intelligent, and go on till one or so. In the afternoon I do some sort of manual work; I've got a house to run as well as other jobs one does. I wash up in the afternoon, and so on. Then about four o'clock I start again and go on to about half-past-seven. That's a day's work.

ROSE: Do you read much contemporary fiction or poetry?

MURDOCH: No. It's partly a matter of time, partly that I don't think we're as good as people of the past. One is so rewarded by going on and on reading nineteenth-century fiction, particularly English and Russian writers—and Proust I read a lot—that really I'd rather read them.

ROSE: Which of the early novelists do you go to most?

MURDOCH: I read Dickens and Jane Austen. I'm very attached to *Wuthering Heights*. And I read Tolstoy and Dostoievski. And Henry James I feel a good deal of affinity with. I just re-read the big things at intervals.

ROSE: Do you think any of these writers has had a formative influence on you?

MURDOCH: The only person I'm certain has influenced me is Henry James, though I think he's less good than some of the people I've mentioned just now.

ROSE: Have you ever been interested in Jacobean or Restoration drama?

MURDOCH: Yes, I have had this interest. But speaking of contemporary writers, I have in fact been influenced, at least in my earlier work, by two contemporary writers whom I'm very fond of—Raymond Queneau and Samuel Beckett. I knew about Beckett long before anybody'd ever heard of him. I'm an old, old Beckett fan.

ROSE: Of the novels or the plays or both?

MURDOCH: Of the novels, particularly those in English. He's a marvellous master of English, and it's slightly different in French. It's marvellous but doesn't seem to me quite as good.

ROSE: Was it Beckett's language or the whole thing that attracted you?

MURDOCH: The whole thing really. *Murphy* and *Watt*—particularly Murphy. It's a kind of ancestor of *Under the Net*.

ROSE: What about Queneau?

MURDOCH: Well, he's a sort of post-surrealist novelist. I don't think *Zazie dans le métro* is his best work. Again I like his earlier novels better. He writes in a kind of argot about characters wandering round Paris. It's wild stuff, but also very poetic.

ROSE: Do you admire Genet?

MURDOCH: I think he is a marvellous writer, full of beauty and poetry. But I think his work can't help being hurt by its subject matter, I haven't ever settled down to thinking about Genet; but the author's attitude towards the subject does pull the thing apart in a way.

ROSE: It's a kind of miracle of self-indulgence, isn't it?

MURDOCH: Yes. I don't think one can get away with something as extreme as that, with such extremes of self-indulgence, however beautiful the object is which you're making. But I think this is a very difficult point.

ROSE: You're not going to write a *Pale Fire* or a *Naked Lunch*?

MURDOCH: No. God forbid—at least in the case of the latter. No, I don't think so. One can't see very far ahead really. I feel that I want to drive my writing in the other direction, that I would like to drive it back towards a much simpler kind of realism. I would like to be thought of as a realistic writer, in the sense in which good English novelists have been realists in the past. I want to talk about ordinary life and what things are like and people are like, and to create characters who are real, free characters. Whether one could use experiment in the interests of this is something I have wondered about. But I don't at the moment see any big break with the way in which I have been writing.

ROSE: So you're not one of those who find the novel a restrictive form?

MURDOCH: No. I think it's a great big form. The only restrictions are my restrictions, or my limitations. I feel like somebody who's living in a great big house and just occupies a tiny corner of it.

5

SHEILA HALE

Interview from "Women Writers Now: Their Approach and Their Apprenticeship"

Sheila Hale was editor of *Harper's Bazaar* in the 1960s. She has written travel books, and her new book *Beyond Words* is due to be published in 2002. This interview was published in *Harpers and Queen,* October 1976, as part of a feature on ten women writers. Sheila Hale conducted the interviews with the writers, while A. S. Byatt evaluated their work.

One of the unpleasant consequences of literary fame for a woman is, in Iris Murdoch's view, the obligation to talk about being a "woman writer." Humble though she is about her own work, which she dismisses as "small stuff," she is too much the intellectual mandarin to wish to be associated with "the market in which women write consciously for other women."

She avoids interviews. Although she gave up teaching philosophy many years ago, my own meeting with her was more like a tutorial with a rather shy don. And she made it clear from the start that she "dissents from the thesis" that gender, whether of author or of imagined audience, is of the slightest importance in serious fiction. "And my own characters are often androgynous, yes, because I believe that most people are androgynous: there is certainly no difference in terms of mental make-up. There are fewer women in public life, men are better educated; but there are not different kinds of mind."

As the author of a Black Paper on education, does she really believe that inferior education has no effect on the way women write?*

"The problem for women is the way they think about themselves. Education is fundamental to their socially conditioned behaviour of inferiority. The wretched girls are demoralised at each age by fobbing off with soft subjects; and unless there is a positive move for women's education, there is no hope. But is education important for a writer? I'm told that it's not."

Nevertheless, Iris Murdoch's literary pantheon appears to be largely, if not quite exclusively, masculine. She mentions Tolstoi and Conrad with special admiration; doesn't care for the French novelists, apart from Proust. She acknowledges the influence of Henry James on her earlier novels; and wishes she *could* be influenced by Shakespeare and Homer: "I often read one or the other when I am writing in the hope that will happen. Shakespeare has everything a novelist needs: magic, plot, characters, construction. Unfortunately somebody that great hasn't got a style you *can* imitate.

"The greatest writers have an evasive tone, they are open to the world. There is a largeness of vision which is lacking in most contemporary fiction, a freedom which allows characters to grow and develop independently of point of view and structure. Without this freedom there can be no great fictional characters. Jane Austen had it even though her world was so restricted. I haven't got it: too obsessive about plot. And I don't know that anyone has since Conrad, or perhaps Lawrence. The Russians are an exception—Solzhenitsyn and Pasternak—but that is a case of arrested development. They are still writing as though it were the nineteenth century: and of course they have a *subject.*"

There are many women writing now who have a subject: female sensibilities and feminist politics. Might it be because they are over-concerned with the feminine predicament that none writes with the larger political vision of, say, a George Eliot?

"There was simply more drama in being a woman in the nineteenth century. George Eliot is not somebody who touches my heart terribly

* Iris Murdoch, "Socialism and Selection," in *Black Paper 1975: The Fight for Education,* ed. C. B. Cox and Rhodes Boyson. (London: Dent, 1975), 7–9.

although one must admire her. She was *driven* to develop an intellectual vision through reaction to her situation as a woman. Now women are supposed to be liberated but of course they're not, and that does have a deadening effect. But then who are the contemporary male George Eliots? I'm afraid the excitement has gone out of everything at the moment, for everybody—except a few Scottish Nationalists. There is the disillusion with socialism and a sort of dull anti-religious feeling. In the Thirties, when I was beginning to grow up, there was a sense of drama, a tension: it was as though great lights of hope and fear were falling on the world. Now we are afraid, but even our fear is dull."

The only woman you have mentioned spontaneously so far is Jane Austen. Is there one writing now whom you respect?

"Simone de Beauvoir is someone I admire enormously. *The Second Sex* is a very good book and makes me like her as a *person,* although I've never met her. (I wrote to her once when I was in Paris. She answered, saying she couldn't see me, in a note written on graph paper which I somehow thought very significant. I don't suppose she's ever heard of me: the French are so pleased with themselves.) But although I, too, am prejudiced on behalf of the downtrodden group to which I belong, the subject bores me in a way. Women who think of themselves as something separate are joining a kind of inferiority movement, like women's clubs. I realise I am lucky. I have never felt picked out in an intellectual sense because I am a woman; these distinctions are not made at Oxford. But I do notice when I come up to London that people under social pressure develop sexual masks, adjust their behaviour at a physical level—giggling and so on. This is something I dislike and which doesn't happen in my world."

6

STEPHEN GLOVER

Iris Murdoch Talks to Stephen Glover

Stephen Glover was founding editor of *The Independent on Sunday* (London) and has since become political columnist with *The Daily Mail* (London). This interview was published in *The New Review* in November 1976.

GLOVER: Why did you write your first novel so relatively late?

MURDOCH: I don't think I did. I started writing when I was nine. I wrote my first complete novel when I was about twenty. I didn't publish anything till late on. I wrote a lot of bad stuff, most of which indeed I didn't even attempt to publish. The war took, of course, seven years out of my life. One was working so hard at other jobs.

GLOVER: Was it that you were thinking very carefully about what kind of first novel you wanted to write? You published your book on Sartre before you published your first novel.*

MURDOCH: I'd written a lot of novels before I wrote the stuff on Sartre. So I'd been reflecting on it. I can't remember a time when I wasn't reflecting on it. I really started very early knowing that I was a writer, or at any rate hoping to become a writer.

GLOVER: Do you think the first impulse was purely instinctive when you were young, or was it because you'd read a lot of literature?

MURDOCH: I think it's hard to distinguish these things. My father was a bookish man. I learnt to read very early, and we discussed books when I was a very small child.

---

* Murdoch, *Sartre* (1953).

GLOVER: The status of the modern English novel since the war seems to be very different from . . . its French counterpart, in that, obviously with some exceptions, it has veered back to a fairly conventional concept of the novel.

MURDOCH: Well, I don't think it has veered back, because apart from a few eccentrics, and some very clever ones too, such as Joyce, it hadn't really gone so far away. I think that the English novel tradition is very strong, a stronger tradition than the French novel, and it has just gone on. I don't think it has veered to and fro very much. . . .

GLOVER: So people like Joyce are in a sense aberrations?

MURDOCH: Joyce is a tremendous aberration.

GLOVER: And can such aberrations be followed up, or easily repeated?

MURDOCH: Well, no. I think you have to be a genius to write well, like Joyce writes. He's a dangerous model, obviously. Beckett is another dangerous model. They can get away with it. One might think of Kafka here too, though he's more of a storyteller than they are. People who copy men like this do so very much at their peril. But I see no reason to leave the English novel tradition unless you have a good reason for doing so. It's a marvellously versatile form; within what looks like—and I suppose is—a conventional novel you can do anything under the sun. You can investigate anything, you can use any mode of thought you like, you can use language almost any way you like. It's a very big house as it were, the novel, within which all sorts of things can happen and a lot of experiment can take place without the reader being necessarily disturbed.

GLOVER: You've said, or written, that you wish you could write novels more like the great nineteenth-century English and Russian novelists.

MURDOCH: I think any novelist would feel that!

GLOVER: But you also said it's more difficult to write such novels now.

MURDOCH: Yes, I don't know quite why. Possibly because we're less talented than our ancestors.

GLOVER: Is it more than a lack of talent? Is it because of the nature of our society, and if so, what particular nature?

MURDOCH: There are mysterious connections between different phases of history, and art forms are very difficult to generalise about, except in a feeble kind of way. Obviously the nineteenth century was a great period of capitalist expansion, social movement, excitement, of liberation of all kinds. At the same time society had got tremendous stability and strength. It was something real, a real network in which people sort of crawled about and changed their positions. But this doesn't really explain anything. I think it's very hard to explain why art forms change; there are so many mysterious interlocking causes.

GLOVER: In your book on Sartre you criticised Sartre for not being sufficiently concerned with "the stuff of human life," which you implied the Victorian novelists were.* You seemed to throw your lot in with them at the beginning of your published novel writing career. Do you think you've fulfilled that commitment, or have you indeed changed your mind?

MURDOCH: I haven't fulfilled it in the sense that I haven't written novels which reached these standards. But I go on trying. I haven't changed my mind on that point.

GLOVER: You seem to distrust Sartre for his revulsion against the bourgeoisie.

MURDOCH: Well, this is a slightly different kind of question. One might make this into a remark about novels or a remark about politics. I don't agree with the extreme leftism that he's now taken up, though he wasn't of course so "left" in the days he was writing the novels. I don't think that Sartre would reject the great bourgeois novel. He would probably have said then what a lot of more liberally minded Marxist critics used to say, that the novel was very good at dealing with the bourgeoisie in that period because it showed the tensions of society. I think this is probably true. Dickens does it enormously, deliberately too of course, showing the different parts of society and how they are at tension with each other. But I think that Sartre's theoretical preoccupations when he's writing the novels do slightly damage the novels. I think perhaps only slightly, because on the other hand if he hadn't

---

* "Sartre has an impatience, which is fatal to a novelist proper, with the *stuff* of human life" (Murdoch, *Sartre: Romantic Rationalist* [London: Chatto and Windus, 1987], 146).

had these preoccupations he might not have wanted to write at all. But I'm slightly bothered in his and Simone de Beauvoir's work by the insistent presence of a theory.

GLOVER: You don't think you impose your own philosophical theories on your novels in a different way?

MURDOCH: I hope not. I think it's a very dangerous thing to do, and I certainly don't want to mix philosophy and fiction—they're totally different disciplines, different methods of thought, different ways of writing, different aims. A little theory may come in just for fun in a sense, and because a particular character may hold a theory, but that won't make the theory into the whole texture or background of the novel.

GLOVER: Do you think many modern novels are needlessly obscure?

MURDOCH: Sometimes one may have to be obscure, but again some people almost aim at obscurity.

GLOVER: Can you think of any modern English writers who do that?

MURDOCH: I am not an expert on contemporary literature. But obviously Robbe-Grillet aims at a certain type of obscurity: he's probably one of the less obscure of the modern obscurantists. Beckett is obscure, but I think that is somehow of the essence of Beckett. I think it's a kind of innocent obscurity. He is a great language user, so the piles and mountains of language go with his particular sort of obscurity. But it's not wilful.

GLOVER: You admire Beckett?

MURDOCH: I don't think I admire and love him as much as I used to, though I still admire him. I like his early work, the stuff written in English, which I think did influence me, or at any rate inspire me, when I was young. I don't terribly like the stuff which was written in French. But I'm not an expert on any novels, though I know a lot about nineteenth-century novels. I don't know a great deal about present-day ones.

GLOVER: Is that simply because you don't think they're as good?

MURDOCH: Well, one has a limited amount of time in which to read and I don't terribly want to read them. I'd rather read nineteenth-century novels. I read novels all the time.

GLOVER: Coming back to this idea of writing novels in a rather open, naturalistic way, as most of the nineteenth-century novelists did, do you think perhaps that in comparison with, say, Dickens, whom you say you admire, you just have a very different outlook on life? Dickens was very critical of society but ultimately he felt he could celebrate life, even if it was very idealistic. But perhaps you may be critical of society or have reservations which go much deeper.

MURDOCH: Oh, I don't think one can go much deeper than Dickens.

GLOVER: No, not deeper in the sense of his criticism of society, but his attitude to life. It seems as if your premise is very different not only from Dickens but from almost all nineteenth-century writers, that it is one of despair, that you believe that human beings are almost irredeemable.

MURDOCH: I wouldn't describe my view this way. I suppose philosophically speaking I hold a rather pessimistic view, but in a work of fiction one isn't necessarily putting forward a deep metaphysical view. Of course we may be doomed and irredeemable, but we have an awful lot of fun on the way—life is so fantastically various and after all one is dealing with its variety. No, I don't think I am a pessimist in the novel.

GLOVER: But isn't there a decline of humour throughout your novels?

MURDOCH: What a terrible thing to say! I'm stunned. I think the later ones are funnier than the earlier ones . . . *An Accidental Man, The Nice and the Good,* I think, are funnier than *Flight from the Enchanter* or *The Sandcastle.* They're much better novels and the funniness is funnier, I think.

GLOVER: What is the funniness?

MURDOCH: I can't say, but there are plenty of funny things in them. All novels contain funniness: it's very difficult to find one that isn't comic.

GLOVER: Isn't someone like Miss Wingfield in *Flight from the Enchanter* roaringly funny in a way not repeated in the later novels?

MURDOCH: I suppose she was a comic character, yes, but I think I do this sort of thing much better later. The early ones may be more superficially funny, but the later ones are more profoundly funny. I may be wrong. It's very hard to judge one's own work. The stuff disappears and recedes into the past with such speed. One tends, I think, to dislike one's early work, instinctively, and also it's terribly far off.

GLOVER: You don't think about it or reread the novels?

MURDOCH: No, I don't think about any of the stuff after it's gone. When it's finished, the sooner it's gone the better, as far as I'm concerned. I'm glad if people read it, and of course I'm always delighted if they like it, but I don't want to think about it.

GLOVER: Is there any particular reason for your relatively large output of novels, almost one a year since your first one? Is it because you're addicted and must keep writing?

MURDOCH: Well, I enjoy it. But I do a hell of a lot of other things besides writing novels, I write philosophy, and I was a full-time teacher for many years.

GLOVER: Do you still do any teaching?

MURDOCH: Yes, I still teach a certain amount. I haven't got any formal teaching now, but I still occasionally give lectures . . . I'm fantastically busy really, and the novels have to fit into a pattern.

GLOVER: Doesn't that make it more strange that you manage to write novels so often?

MURDOCH: Well, I enjoy it. I write when I can. For what it's worth, I don't usually have blockages. I can usually carry on once started. The difficult part, of course, is inventing the story. That's the really important part of the thing, inventing your characters and your plot, which I do—not everybody does and obviously one finds one's own method of writing—but I invent the whole thing in enormous detail before I start writing at all. That can take longer than writing. I always write two drafts, and when I've finished the whole thing I start it off at the beginning again, and write it all through again. But still, the crucial part is the invention.

GLOVER: So in a sense you don't surprise yourself once you've started writing?

MURDOCH: No, one changes minor things, but fundamental things I've usually invented first, and I think—and again I speak of myself— I think it's wise to do this because one's ability to invent changes as soon as one starts to write. As soon as you're engaged in putting down the sentences which may be the final ones of the story, you're involved in a slightly different kind of creation. In the beginning part there are very, very deep creative things involved, and I think it's worth spending a lot of time on that business. After that in a way the novel writes itself, the characters create their dialogue, they even partly invent the plot.

GLOVER: With dialogue how conscious must one be of the different ways in which people talk, even in fairly mundane and everyday situations?

MURDOCH: I think tone of dialogue matters a lot. Some people are very good, very detailed mimics. Dickens and Scott do it, for instance—it can be very funny or moving. I don't think I'm particularly good at that. I wish I was. I can do certain varieties of dialogue. But I think one can give the impression. If one has a cockney character one needn't always be writing down that he dropped his "h's." One can imply speech patterns of a different sort without going into tremendous detail. I think this is a very interesting technical point. I've got in my own life two very different sorts of speech patterns. Some people might have twenty-five. I've got two deep ones—one the kind of Oxford English one, and the other Irish, which is a completely different way of talking. So if I want to portray an alien character, I can make him either implicitly or explicitly Irish, if I want a different sort of rhythm. Also, one can invent what one can invent, and if you've got an interesting character he will often give you an interesting way of speech.

GLOVER: And is it something which one can improve upon, by a sort of scientific, linguistic study, or is it more an instinctive awareness?

MURDOCH: One improves on it by practice and observation. I would keep away from scientific linguistic studies. I think it's looking at life that does it. If you've got a deep feeling for the rhythm of speech, out of this deep place you can invent different modes of speech. And of course the more you listen to people.

GLOVER: Another remarkable thing about your novels is the way in which the same world—the person who read Greats at Oxford and got a first—always reappears.

MURDOCH: Sometimes they get thirds.

GLOVER: They sometimes get thirds. But in a way that is almost a black mark against them. In your new novel, *Henry and Cato,* one feels that you are using the fact that Henry got a second as a sort of question mark against him.

MURDOCH: Well some of the people come out of this world, they don't all by any means. There are oddities, bohemians, drop-outs.

GLOVER: But there is a large number of civil servants, dons, or professional people. . . .

MURDOCH: Yes, well, these are the sort of people I know. I don't write about Oxford. It gets mentioned but I think it's very difficult to write about Oxford or Cambridge, and I keep away from dons if possible, though I expect I may have done one, perhaps two. But one can only write about the world one understands. I would be very pleased if I did know more. I would be very pleased if I'd been a sailor, or a coalminer, or had kept a shop. This is just limitation of experience, really. The more you know, the more different things you can do.

GLOVER: If that sort of equation is true, and if one is interested in the stuff of human life, shouldn't the novelist be more ubiquitous?

MURDOCH: No, I don't think so, not artificially so. If you want to write a travel book, you can go to India and write something. But it's very difficult to write a novel except about what you deeply understand. In fact I've travelled a great deal and I've met an enormous number of different kinds of people. But it's very difficult to write about this because it's not really deep inside.

GLOVER: But your civil servants who got firsts in Greats—they could be businessmen. Businessmen aren't that different. Sometimes you investigate what goes on in the office, but you're really interested in the private life of the civil servant, and the private life of the civil servant is presumably very similar to that of a businessman.

MURDOCH: Yes, but this detail is important and must be convincing and is part of one's feeling for the character. I have portrayed businessmen, it's just there are more, I agree, civil servants. I don't for instance portray doctors. I don't know anything about doctors. What one deeply knows about, at least in my case, is fairly limited. But this is nothing to be pleased about, I wish it were larger. But I wouldn't want to extend my scope by forcing myself outside the area where I feel I understand. I have very shadowily touched America in one or two of the books, and I'd like to write about India and Japan, and Australia—well Australia I do touch slightly too, India and Japan are countries which I am very interested in—

GLOVER: Philosophically?

MURDOCH: Well, everything. I'm interested in Buddhism and Hinduism, but also somehow or other something about the smell of these places makes me very excited and interested. But I couldn't write about them, really. One could bring in little funny details and oddities, bits of background, quirks, little vistas and so on, but I could obviously not set a novel in India or Japan because I don't know. And I think it would be absurd to say well, all right, go and live there for six months. It would just be a bad novel, in my case anyway. One could write a travel book, but there is all the difference in the world between putting a kind of travelogue into one's stuff, and really understanding what it's like to be in the place.

GLOVER: But don't you think there is something too middle-class about the modern English novel?

MURDOCH: This is a familiar cry! Why should one have to write about the working class to write about reality? It's very difficult to do, to jump out of your class.

GLOVER: But if you're like Dickens, and born on the borders of two classes, perhaps it's easier. It seems to me that one of the outstanding things about Dickens and Shakespeare is that they haven't got these class demarcations.

MURDOCH: Yes . . . Dickens has of course got class demarcations. He's very good at the comic servants.

GLOVER: Patronisingly?

MURDOCH: Not exactly, no. He can do people like Little Dorrit, who are déclassé, very well. But really to get inside—I can't think of Dickens getting inside a completely working-class character in the way in which he is obviously inside all sorts of other people. I don't think one should worry about this. I think there is a kind of silly and even slightly dangerous anti-middle-class feeling growing up which goes with saying "we don't want bourgeois culture" which very often means "we don't want culture." There isn't bourgeois culture and working-class culture. There's culture and education, there's learning, there's literature. The middle-classes are an enormous area. In a way the idea of the working class, if one is self-consciously thinking of working-class culture and so on, is a very much smaller area. I think one will find points where one has to make decisions and acts of will about what direction to push a fictional character. Do you, in relation to the other characters, class him in some way; do you make a point? In one of my novels, *A Word Child,* for instance, there is a point about the boy having had this deprived background, and that then comes in very naturally. But I don't think one need force the pace on this because one feels one ought not to be writing "bourgeois novels." In fact this criticism of novels on the basis of class is very silly and very artificial. I write about human nature.

GLOVER: But you do sometimes introduce working-class characters, or at least characters with working-class backgrounds.

MURDOCH: Yes, but they are usually déclassé of course, déraciné people, it's true, who have become intellectuals.

GLOVER: What about Joe in *Henry and Cato?*

MURDOCH: I don't really think he is quite alive enough: there isn't enough to him in a sense. Of course he's young and unformed, and he doesn't himself know what he thinks, and he thinks incompatible things and so on, in quite a genuine way. I didn't quite know what Joe was like. Whereas I knew very well what Henry and Cato were like.

GLOVER: I thought you caught his working-class/young dialogue very well.

MURDOCH: But he's Irish of course, so the particular lilt of Joe's voice is Irish, although I don't think it's stated that he's Irish. But he obviously is Irish—he's got an Irish name, and he's Catholic. I feel if I could have made him a more sympathetic character without being in any way sentimental about him, it might have been a better book, because he is a rather important figure.

GLOVER: It seems to me that one abiding question, which I get from reading many of your novels, is the problem of morality in a godless or post-god age.

MURDOCH: Yes, I'm very interested in religion. As I said at the beginning I'm not a philosophical novelist, and the philosophy really comes in rather incidentally. Of course I suppose one has reflected on moral problems in other contexts in an abstract way, and that may affect certain ways of looking at the novels, but I don't think very much so, really. I am very interested in this subject, in what happens to morality when you chuck religion. And what religion itself is like.

GLOVER: Would it be wrong to say that in the character of Brendan in *Henry and Cato* you become more sympathetic to the idea of religion?

MURDOCH: But I'm exceeding[ly] sympathetic to the idea.

GLOVER: Yes. Not so much the idea. But Brendan says at the end of the novel that God is—I don't know what the expression is—but beyond one's reach and so on. Whereas you say at the beginning of *The Sovereignty of Good* that Bonhoeffer has said a similar thing, that God is there and has forgotten about us.* You say there that this is something of a copout. . . .

MURDOCH: Brendan says that in the context of one who—whatever he believes, which he probably isn't going to tell anybody—is speaking in a Christian context. And although I was brought up as a Christian I'm not a Christian; I don't believe in a personal God. I feel sympathy towards Buddhism, a religion which is thoroughly religious without having the kind of dogma that Christianity has. But I think I've probably become in recent years more sympathetic towards religion, including Christianity, without wanting to adopt a formal belief. I feel very close to the Christian church, both Anglican and Catholic, but I can't believe that Christ was God; and a lot of Catholics and Anglicans now quietly dismantle the thing behind the scenes. They somehow agree with themselves that they don't have to take it too literally.

GLOVER: Is that wrong?

MURDOCH: No, how can we say it's wrong? I think they're in difficulties.

---

* "When Bonhoeffer says that God wants us to live as if there were no God I suspect he is misusing words" (Murdoch, "The Sovereignty of Good," 365).

7

MICHAEL O. BELLAMY

An Interview with Iris Murdoch

Michael O. Bellamy teaches in the English department at the University of Saint Thomas in Saint Paul, Minnesota. He completed his dissertation on Murdoch's fiction in 1975 at the University of Wisconsin—Madison. This interview was published in *Contemporary Literature* Vol. 18, no. 2 (1977).

Note: The interview took place on June 23, 1976, at Ms. Murdoch's flat in London. Ms. Murdoch has seen and approved the text.

BELLAMY: In your previous interviews and essays you have compared the nineteenth with the twentieth century in terms of the fiction that is typical of each. When we talked several weeks ago you referred to this difference in terms of Proust's nineteenth-century sensibility and the crucial importance of D. H. Lawrence as a twentieth-century figure. Could you account for your choice of these two novelists as typical of the distinction you have in mind?

MURDOCH: They are both oddities, both unique, great writers. I feel Proust belongs to a much more universal world, whereas Lawrence has something peevish and propagandist about him that seems to belong rather more to a later period, and he's anxious to persuade us of particular views. Proust, on the other hand, is reflective in a calmer and more general sense.

BELLAMY: Are you saying that nineteenth-century writers had a universal set of norms which they could appeal to—or even assume—

while the twentieth-century artist feels compelled to communicate a more personal, unique statement?

MURDOCH: Of course, if one thinks of Dickens and George Eliot, they are tremendously propagandist in their own way. They were very critical of their society and had very strong, positive views that they wanted to put forward. The difference has to do with the universality of the interest one feels. Perhaps I am being unjust to Lawrence. I think he is a marvelous writer and I admire him immensely, but I do feel that there is something local about him; I feel I am in a smaller, more personal world. Whereas with Dickens, George Eliot, or Proust, I feel I'm in *the* world, where great art belongs.

BELLAMY: How do you account for the falling-off in this century from the universality to which you refer?

MURDOCH: It's a very difficult question. There's a kind of optimism which has gone. I think people in the nineteenth century felt great confidence in a unified civilization; they didn't feel local. In spite of the fact that television is supposed to be "unifying the world," we feel much more provincial than we used to, and we haven't got a confident feeling about society and the future. Even in the 1930s there was a kind of deep optimism, a sort of vital pressure, a general feeling of steadily moving life and significance. Of course, there are many factors here. I think that the development of science deeply affects people's minds in all sorts of roundabout ways, that space travel and modern physics somehow produce a very unsettling background. We have no sense of a big, universal human world or a universal human audience.

BELLAMY: Didn't the religious crisis, brought about by the discoveries of science, coincide with what you consider the great age of the novel?

MURDOCH: Well, yes. The Victorians were always worrying about religion, but they worried, in a sense, within a religious context; there was still a kind of confidence in the solidity of spiritual values.

BELLAMY: How does your nostalgia for what you feel is the era of the "true novel" affect you when you sit down to write your own fiction?

MURDOCH: I don't think about that, really. I just think about my work, and there's a kind of vitality in the work itself which cheers one up. No, this is all theoretical stuff. This is critics' talk and as such may not be very important.

BELLAMY: Do you read the critics who write about your work?

MURDOCH: No, I don't; I have so little time to read anything. I'm not interested in my work once I've finished it. I'm only interested in what I'm doing at the moment. I know what's wrong with my work.

BELLAMY: How do you feel about Sartre? Have you thought about him at all since your early study of his ideas?

MURDOCH: No, I'm not very interested in his later philosophical development. I have read quite a lot of the Marxist stuff. I think he's a marvelous man and his whole career is very interesting and the changes he has undergone have a general significance. He's a heroic figure and perhaps a great writer. I love *Les Chemins* and I immensely admire *La nausée* and *Les mots*. And what a fighter! I'm just not very stirred by the later philosophy.

BELLAMY: My curiosity about Sartre has to do with your similar pre-occupation with the conflict between contingency and necessity, as well as Sartre's pessimistic definition of "love" as a kind of solipsistic struggle for the recognition of the Other. These two themes seem to be at the heart of your fiction.

MURDOCH: I don't think he has had any influence on me as a writer or, indeed, as a philosopher. I'm very anti-existentialist. I can't be sure, of course, but I don't feel any wave of influence there. I don't think philosophy influences my work as a novelist.

BELLAMY: Hilary Burde, the narrator of *A Word Child,* says, among other depressing things, that it is "better not to have been born." It seems to me that this kind of despair is more typical of your more recent dark comedies. Do you agree with this evaluation?

MURDOCH: Obviously, one's work changes as one changes oneself. I think it's partly an increase in confidence. Of course, when one is younger one is more optimistic and cheerful, and I think my early work rather tries to be quaint and funny. I admired Beckett and Queneau, and I was deliberately trying to write something which was sort of funny, sort of absurd and touching. I think this is something many young writers do. Later, one becomes calmer and one's subject matter increases, so that one can deal with sad or awful things more directly. This is what I meant by the increase in confidence. I suppose I am slightly more pessimistic than I was, but I don't have a pessimistic temperament.

BELLAMY: In one of your previous interviews you said the novel is inherently comic. Do you still hold this view?

MURDOCH: Well, almost everything is comic. I think tragedy is a very small form which belongs to poetry and the theater. Of course, some of the greatest works of literature are tragedies but are not, as such, models for the novel. However sad and awful the things it narrates, the novel belongs to an open world, a world of absurdity and loose ends and ignorance. In real life, that which is horrible lacks the significance of art. The novel is intensely aware of this fact. In fact, particular novelists endeavor very often to close the form by various artifices, to make it more like a poem, and this may work; but I think that the nature of the novel is somehow that a sort of wind blows through it and there are holes in it and the meaning of it partly seeps away into life.

BELLAMY: One of your most interesting novels, from a formal point of view, is *The Black Prince.* This work strikes me as far more experimental than any of your others. The framing device of the introductory remarks and the postscripts by the *dramatis personae* is perhaps the most obvious evidence of this experimentation.

MURDOCH: Well, I don't want to experiment in a really large way. In fact, there is a great deal of experimentation in the work, but I don't want it to be too evident. I am happy in the tradition.

BELLAMY: *The Black Prince* is also unusual in that its narrator, Bradley Pearson, seems closer to the author than the narrators of your other novels. In fact, Bradley makes a similar point about *Hamlet,* which he feels is the only Shakespearean play in which the playwright dared to place himself at the center of the drama.

MURDOCH: *The Black Prince* isn't Hamlet, of course, but that's by the way. I'm not a Shakespeare critic, but I do feel the presence of Shakespeare in that play as kind of trembling emotional excitement, something that makes it, in fact, a rather dicey play. It could have all gone wrong in some way, but it hasn't.

BELLAMY: Speaking of narrators, have you ever thought about electing a woman to play this role in one of your novels?

MURDOCH: The books written in the first person all have a male hero, but all the other books have plenty of female narrators; there are always at least as many women talking, I should think, as men.

BELLAMY: Is your choice of men as first-person narrators a way of avoiding the introspective, solipsistic novel you have so frequently criticized? I should think that imagining you were somebody of another sex would ensure the creation of a character different from yourself. This process would involve quite an impressive leap for the imagination.

MURDOCH: I identify with men more than women, I think. I don't think it's a great leap; there's not much of a difference, really. One's just a human being. I think I'm more interested in men than women. I'm not interested in women's problems as such, though I'm a great supporter of women's liberation—particularly education for women—but in aid of getting women to join the human race, not in aid of making any kind of feminine contribution to the world. I think there's a kind of human contribution, but I don't think there's a feminine contribution.

BELLAMY: I was curious about your avoidance of women's rights in your novels—or rather your failure to scrutinize the issues explicitly. You also seem reluctant to consider politics, in the literal sense of the word. Are you wary of the propagandist tendency you have discerned in Sartre's literary studies of politics in the trilogy, *Les Chemins de la liberté*?

MURDOCH: I admire those novels of Sartre's very much indeed. I think they're marvelous; it is very difficult to write well about politics unless one knows a lot about it. I did once try to write a novel about the Trade Union movement and put M.P.'s in it and so on, but I don't know that world. It's no good; I don't understand it and I don't want to write political propaganda in that form. I prefer to write political propaganda in other forms, in the forms of pamphlets or articles. Every artist has to decide what he really understands. In fact, in a quiet way, there is a lot of social criticism in my novels.

BELLAMY: Your two plays *The Three Arrows* and *The Servants and the Snow* are more political than your fiction. Can this be explained by your remark in your study of Sartre that the drama, because of its closed form, is more amenable than the novel to this sort of allegorical statement?*

* Murdoch, *Sartre* (1953).

MURDOCH: Yes, I do slightly think that, though I might do different things if I worked more for the theater. Those two works are "plays of ideas," and they both happen to have political implications. I feel that sort of talk is most at home in the theater. It certainly is for me, anyway.

BELLAMY: Your belief in a conservative personal ethic and a progressive political ideology is especially reminiscent of Simone Weil, the French philosopher and mystic for whom you have expressed so much regard. Do you also feel an affinity for her paradoxical reluctance to be baptized in spite of her tremendous appreciation of Christianity?

MURDOCH: I believe in religion in a sort of Buddhist sense of the word, and in that way I feel very close to Christianity. I used to feel it had all gone out of my life, but I don't feel like that now. It's all present in my life in another form, as a spiritual guide and inspiration, but not as a dogma.

BELLAMY: I am curious, in the light of your interest in Buddhism, about the "Buddhists" who appear in your fiction. Christopher Cather's Buddhism in *A Word Child* is idiotic. Similarly, Monty, the artist in *The Sacred and Profane Love Machine*, meditates without achieving any sort of lasting satisfaction.

MURDOCH: Monty didn't get much out of Buddhism, but Theo did, in a way. Remember Theo in *The Nice and the Good*? He was sort of a runaway Buddhist. No, I think Buddhism is a great religion, and it seems to me to be a very good kind of religion in that it's not dogmatic and it has very much to do with change of consciousness. That's what one wants to find out—how consciousness is changed and how conduct is changed. In Christianity the practice of prayer is so important, and people who don't believe in a personal God and can't, as a consequence, talk to Him lose a very important activity, which can perhaps be regained if one uses a technique of meditation.

BELLAMY: In your interview with Ruth Heyd, you mentioned the conflict between the saint, who manages, presumably, to engage in this "very important activity," and the artist.* Do the virtue of the saint and

* Ruth Heyd, "An Interview with Iris Murdoch," *University of Windsor Review* 1, no. 1 (1965): 138–43.

the artist's love of form relate to Bradley Pearson's remark that art must transcend itself if it is to be a justifiable endeavor?

MURDOCH: There's something which interests me which does appear, to some extent, in the novels in the form of a conflict, usually between two men, one an artist and the other a sort of religious figure—Tallis Browne and Julius King [A *Fairly Honourable Defeat*], for instance, and Ann and Randall Peronett [*An Unofficial Rose*], and Hugo Belfounder and Jake Donaghue [*Under the Net*], and so on. I'm not quite sure how this connects with what I'm going to say next, but I think art's a kind of temptation in a way. I mean, art is a harmless activity, but it represents a sort of temptation, a temptation to impose form where perhaps it isn't always appropriate. That is why, in order to make closed works of art, you have to be a poet in the literary sense; poetry is a stricter mode of speech—its artifice is more refined. Morality has to do with not imposing form, except appropriately and cautiously and carefully and with attention to appropriate detail, and I think that truth is very fundamental here. Art can subtly tamper with truth to a great degree because art is enjoyment. People persist in being artists against every possible discouragement and disappointment, because it's a marvelous activity, a gratification of the ego, and a free, omnipotent imposition of form; unless this is constantly being, as it were, pulled at by the value of truth, the artwork itself may not be as good and the artist may be simply using art as a form of self-indulgence. So I think in art itself there is this conflict between the form-maker and the truthful, formless figure. This happens in art as well as in life.

BELLAMY: Would it be valid to say that *A Fairly Honourable Defeat* is a fable about the failure of the artist (Julius King) to control his artwork without the interference of the saint (Tallis Browne)? Julius King's dramatic demonstration of Rupert Foster's hypocrisy results in Rupert's death; in fact, chaos reigns until the saint steps in and restores order—a chore which Julius, as the artist, was supposed to perform. Is there any connection between this allegory and the relationship between the ethical and the aesthetic ideas which Tallis and Julius seem to represent? Does the book imply that art is properly a function of morality?

MURDOCH: Of course, that book is a theological myth. I think hardly anybody notices this, but it doesn't matter: it's just something in the background. Julius King is, of course, Satan, and Tallis is a Christ figure, and Tallis' father (Leonard Browne) is God the Father, who finds that it's all gone wrong.

BELLAMY: Yes, I was struck by Julius' demonic nature as well as the crucifixion image of Tallis pushing his empty pushcart up the road in Notting Hill.

MURDOCH: And then Morgan (Tallis' estranged wife and Julius' former mistress) is the human soul, for which the two protagonists are battling. When Julius recognizes who Tallis is, he can't help loving him. But obviously the story has to stand up without this kind of structure being too evident.

BELLAMY: Julius is a sort of Old Testament "instrument of justice," as he calls himself, and his real Jewish name is Kahn. Is there any significance to this?

MURDOCH: Yes, this stuff about being an "instrument of justice" is a kind of double-talk, but there's something in it, too.

BELLAMY: Tallis Browne is one of your saint figures, and yet he is also rather grotesque. Some of his eccentricities strike me as reminiscent of Dostoevsky, like the epilepsy and the strange sexual ambience of his religious fervor. Is a good person always that eccentric? Does this, in itself, tell us something about humanity?

MURDOCH: I don't think so. Maybe one had better keep away from Dostoevsky, although I think I'm probably influenced by him in a way. I mean, as far as he's a great and wonderful novelist, one would like to be influenced by him, but I think he's also a dangerous model because these demonic men are difficult characters; one can just have fun with them without really clarifying them or understanding them, and they have a kind of charm which is illegitimate. I think Ann in *An Unofficial Rose* is a good character without being demonic, but then, of course, it may be that she's not interesting enough. There is always this problem.

BELLAMY: What, to change the subject, do you make of structuralism? Do you feel that it has helped, or can help, us to understand literature?

MURDOCH: I doubt if there's such a thing as structuralism. Or, to put it another way, I think we are all structuralists now. This is a fashionable name for a trend of thought which has been going on for a long time. I'm against the intrusion into literary criticism of jargonistic philosophical theories. I don't think it helps. One has to keep a very open mind about literature and just look and respond to the work with one's whole self. Structuralism seems to me like the sort of thing Wittgenstein does when he says he doesn't have a particular philosophical theory, but he does have a way of looking at all philosophical theories. I don't know a great deal about the area in which so-called modern structuralism originated—that is, linguistics—but I'm bothered by the erecting of this particular kind of critical attitude, which in a way is anti-theory, into itself a theory. And I'm certainly hostile to its intrusion into literary criticism and into ethics.

BELLAMY: I sense that you feel this way about the so-called "Wittgensteinians" in your fiction—those anal-retentive, pedantic types who quote his words without understanding the spirit in which he wrote them.

MURDOCH: Yes, I'm a great admirer of Wittgenstein, and I suppose I am myself, in a way, a Wittgensteinian; but if I am a Wittgensteinian, I am one in a proper, as it were, negative sense. It isn't that one has got any body of theory, but one has got a style and a way of looking at philosophical problems. He's a great philosopher.

BELLAMY: One definition of structuralism I have encountered which makes a great deal of sense to me has to do with the Continental tendency to see a dichotomy between the phenomenal world of ordinary experience and the noumenal structures which phenomenal modes of experience tend to disguise. I know you have attacked this sort of dualism in your essays, but I sense a conflict between what I would call ordinary behavior and the way many of your characters behave. This discrepancy reminds me of Lawrence's remark about his interest in the allotropic aspect of the human personality. He was interested, in other words, in modes of consciousness that do not ordinarily become evident in public behavior. Are you Laurentian in this respect, or are you a realist in the sense that you use the term in your consideration of nineteenth-century fiction?

MURDOCH: Oh, I'm attempting to be a realist. I think real people are far more eccentric than anybody portrayed in novels. Real people are terribly odd, but of course they keep this secret. They conceal their fantasies. Obviously people don't tell most of the things that they think to anyone, not even their psychiatrists. Human beings are very odd and very different from each other. The novel is a marvelous form in that it attempts to show this. I think it does explain people to themselves in a way. Of course there aren't that many really great novelists, but the novel aspires towards that sort of explanation, or at least most novels do. I think that people create myths about themselves and are then dominated by the myths. They feel trapped, and they elect other people to play roles in their lives, to be gods or destroyers or something, and I think that this mythology is often very deep and very influential and secretive, and a novelist is revealing secrets of this sort.

BELLAMY: Is it ever possible to escape this mythmaking?

MURDOCH: Well, this is the problem, isn't it? I think it is possible, yes, but difficult. You see, one is talking of something which in ordinary life—this is where the whole problem of truth is so important—which in ordinary life one doesn't necessarily see, which one guesses at. And one may have one's own motives for wanting to think that other people have a certain mythology, and one may be wrong. What is the test of this sort of speculation? After all, what is the test of psychoanalysis? The fact that the man managed to get his job back or something? That doesn't prove that all that stuff that's been going on is true. The test of truth here is very hard, and I think the novelist must be awfully scrupulous about playing this game of explaining people's secret concerns. But, after all, it is the essential game. To come back to your point about eccentricity: Dickens is accused of exaggeration and so on, but I don't think he exaggerates; he just discerns how strange human beings are. This is something which very much belongs to the novel—to emphasize truths which are normally concealed. Because they are concealed, however, it may be difficult to know when one is just romancing for one's own benefit.

BELLAMY: "Romancing" is a particularly suggestive word, for romantic love seems to be the main occasion in your fiction for both constructing and destroying the fantastic myths to which you refer.

MURDOCH: I think romantic love is an occasion for significant change in the way people create these myths. Love is a kind of bombshell that breaks people's lives, really falling in love. It's obviously a dangerous condition, because it's so tremendously self-centered. To really love somebody in an unselfish way is not perhaps thoroughly natural to human beings; certainly in romantic love, in "falling in love" love, one is tremendously selfish. One feels that everything in the world has gone away to the other person, but then this becomes a function of one's own will, too. This is the sort of thing which has been discussed by Hegel and Sartre. It's a great subject for a novel. I mean it should be, because it's a central drama in the lives of so many people.

BELLAMY: Would you call the comedy that typically issues from this drama in your fiction "black comedy"?

MURDOCH: Well, I aim at being an ordinary writer, a realistic writer in the tradition of the English novel, and I wouldn't want, as a writer, to belong to any group which could be named by such special names.

BELLAMY: Do you ever find the impetus for one novel in the process of writing another? There are several instances in which themes and ideas that are peripheral in one work become central in a subsequent novel. I was especially struck by this process in *A Word Child* where a character refers to *Peter Pan* as "a fairly honourable defeat," the puzzling title of one of your previous novels. Even though the process is reversed here, the same "spillover" from one work into another is still evident.

MURDOCH: The "fairly honourable defeat" is the defeat of good by evil. On your general question, I never look outside the novel that I'm writing. Everything that I am or think at that particular moment I try to make bear on the novel I'm writing, and I try not to think about the future at all.

BELLAMY: Do you still try to free your characters in the process of writing your novels?

MURDOCH: The creation of character is a difficult thing. I'm not yet particularly good at it. My plot and the kind of central magic are so strong that they tend to draw the characters too much towards the center.

BELLAMY: Are you working on a novel now?

MURDOCH: No, I'm writing some philosophy at the moment, something about Plato.*

BELLAMY: As a Platonist, do you feel that you're always trying to write the same ideal book, or do you feel yourself significantly evolving? Do you feel changes going on right now?

MURDOCH: Oh, I think I do, yes. Obviously, there are certain common themes, but the novels seem to be very different from each other. I feel change going on.

BELLAMY: Are you writing another pamphlet, or a book?

MURDOCH: It's a short book. It's about Plato's view of art, but it's terribly difficult, much more difficult than writing a novel.

BELLAMY: Do you think you will ever teach philosophy at Oxford again?

MURDOCH: I'd like to in a way—I mean, if I had endless years at my disposal. I enjoy teaching, but, you know the sands are running out. I haven't got a great deal of time left now to do the things I want to do.

---

* Iris Murdoch, *The Fire and the Sun: Why Plato Banished the Artists* (Oxford: Clarendon Press, 1977). The text is reprinted in *Existentialists and Mystics,* 386–463.

8

JACK I. BILES

An Interview with Iris Murdoch

Jack I. Biles (1920–87) was professor of English at Georgia State University until his retirement in 1983. He wrote and edited books on William Golding and other British novelists. This interview was first published in *Contemporary Literature* Vol. 11 (1977), and was reprinted in Biles's *British Novelists Since 1900* (New York: AMS Press, 1987).

The interview took place at Miss Murdoch's home in Oxfordshire.

BILES: I should like to begin by asking a question about Joyce Cary. I have got the impression that at one point you showed the manuscript of *Under the Net* to him. His biographer, Malcolm Foster, refers to this and suggests that Cary was rather negative about the novel. Foster states that you paid no attention to Cary's censures and quotes you as saying "his ways were not my ways." Do you remember that?

MURDOCH: I knew Joyce quite well and I liked him. And I admired him, although I have read only two of his books.

BILES: Which two did you read?

MURDOCH: *The Horse's Mouth* and *Mister Johnson*. Certainly I didn't show him the manuscript of *Under the Net*. He read the book after it was published. Joyce had a rather interesting way of working, in that he wrote a great deal of stuff about the characters which wasn't actually part of the novel as published. He did the whole thing in fits and starts—and worked on the end first; I found this particular technique surprising. I suspect I said "his ways are not my ways" in the context of saying that writers have very different techniques for writing. For example, I plan everything in immense detail before I start; the writing is the very last thing which happens. When I've got the story clear, every single word, at that point, matters. The planning stage is just rough notes.

BILES: At one time, [William] Golding told me that writing *Lord of the Flies* was "easy," that it was very like "tracing words already on the page," because he had planned it to "almost the last flick of an eyelid," as he put it.

MURDOCH: Yes, I know. That is what I feel.

BILES: Let me ask you to recall something else. I read in an old *New Yorker* [1961] an item by an unidentified writer who came up to Oxford and talked to several of you in the Philosophy Department of your college.*

MURDOCH: Ah, that was the blind Indian, Ved Mehta. A nice man.

BILES: I recognize the name. He asserted it was quite clear to him that you are much more an intuitive person than an analytical person. To be sure, he was describing you as a philosopher and not as a novelist; but I wish to ask how far he is right, considering the analytical turn of mind that seems to me implicit in the careful and detailed planning which you do for a novel.

MURDOCH: Well, this is the sort of thing that people like to say—particularly about women. It's just a bit of journalese. I don't know: most writers are both intuitive and analytical. I happen to be trained as a philosopher, and philosophy, too, is a combination of intuition and analysis. And if you're writing anything important either in philosophy or literature, you can't really do without what people vaguely call "intuition," which I'd call "imagination" perhaps, an ability to fuse together things which are highly dissimilar, to see similarities in their connections, and so on.

BILES: Sounds like Wordsworth.

* Ved Mehta, "Onward and Upward with the Arts: A Battle against the Bewitchment of Our Intelligence," *New Yorker,* 9 December 1961, 59–60+; repr. in Ved Mehta, *The Fly and the Fly-Bottle: Encounters with British Intellectuals* (London: Weidenfeld & Nicholson, 1963), 50–53.

MURDOCH: Well, it may be. Yes. I think it's something which both in philosophy and writing I am conscious of. To my mind, philosophy is a completely different game, although the intuitive element enters into it. This is quite unlike writing stories, and I play the game according to the rules. It's a separate operation and one's mind is working very differently in philosophy.

BILES: You admire Dostoevsky, for example, and everyone terms him a philosophical novelist. Now, here you are—a philosopher *and* a novelist—and the matter continually arises: but, do you see yourself as a "philosophical novelist," whatever that means?

MURDOCH: No, I don't. Or, if I am, it's in the same sense in which Dostoevsky is and not in the sense in which Simone de Beauvoir is or Sartre is. I have definite philosophical views, but I don't want to promote them in my novels or to give the novel a kind of metaphysical background. Of course, any seriously-told story may have metaphysical aspects and will certainly have moral aspects. And morality does connect with metaphysics; so, in this sense, any novelist has got a kind of metaphysic. But, I don't want philosophy, as such, to intrude into the novel world at all and I think it doesn't. I find really no difficulty in separating these activities. I mention philosophy sometimes in the novels because I happen to know about it, just as another writer might talk about coal mining; it happens to come in. No, I wouldn't say I'm a philosophical novelist. I wouldn't say Dostoevsky is, either—in the kind of strict sense. Though he is a highly reflective novelist.

BILES: I should like to turn our discussion toward the drama and your own plays. A couple of years ago, in a book about the dramatic in contemporary fiction, a man named Alan Kennedy says near the end that he hasn't talked of your novels because you have a special definition of "dramatic," which is markedly different from the one he uses in his book.* Then, he does speak about you: he quotes from "The Sublime and the Beautiful Revisited" and declares that you clearly equate the word "dramatic" with the word "self-centered." Would you accept such a view? Do you equate "dramatic" and "solipsistic?"

---

* Alan Kennedy, *The Protean Self: Dramatic Action in Contemporary Fiction* (London and Basingstoke: Macmillan, 1974).

MURDOCH: No, I don't think so. It seems a rather odd idea.

BILES: Something to do with Hegel's idea concerning Spirit's struggling with itself in an internal effort to reach a higher state?

MURDOCH: Yes. I think there is a kind of self-centeredness which takes a dramatic form, but I don't think it is the only kind. What I mean is that it is consoling to feel that you are taking part in an inner drama. In a way, psychoanalysis depends upon this idea, doesn't it? The patient is cheered up by the analyst's picturing a drama in which the patient figures. I think this is a very ambiguous idea.

BILES: He had in mind what he identifies as your "central theme," namely, "the necessity to admit the reality of the other person"; that is, how, if you are completely self-centered, you can't see the otherness, the reality, of other people.

MURDOCH: Well, certainly in the books I am concerned about egotism. After all, a story is dramatic; one is dealing with drama the whole time as well as using drama as one's medium—in the novel as well as in the theater. But in a way, plays and novels are very different: in the play, the drama has necessarily got a central and poetic function which in the novel it hasn't, I think. In fact, many novels rightly—this is something I also do—fight against the drama. I mean that ordinary life is not dramatic. I think it was the word "tragedy" that your critic might have been playing with; probably, I have said somewhere that I believe novels are comic and not tragic, that tragedy belongs to the theater. Some sort of drama must belong to the theater, where everything is highly significant and rather poetic and where there is a definite shape.

It seems to me that in the novel very often the novelist quite properly is destroying this shape, because ordinary life doesn't have shape. Ordinary life is comic and absurd. It may be terrible, but it is absurd and shapeless, and the novelist very often attempts to convey the shapelessness by having a dramatic shape, which if he is telling a story, he usually has to have. At the same time, he is fighting against it and blurring it—even destroying it. For me, this is a proper proceeding in the novel, but the theater is a very different matter. The theater is more like poetry.

BILES: When you say "absurd," do you mean ridiculous or do you mean absurd in the Existential sense?

MURDOCH: I mean absurd in the sense of being purposeless and senseless.

BILES: Regarding your plays, I have had the good fortune to see one of them performed. In the mid-1960's I saw the production of *A Severed Head* at the Criterion theater in London and found it altogether brilliant. This play came out of a collaboration between you and J. B. Priestley. Will you tell me about the nature of that collaboration?

MURDOCH: Well, I wrote, as it were, the words. Jack contributed very important things in structure. At that time, I knew really very little about the theater. I don't go to the theater much; I don't actually *like* the theater very much. But I would like to write for it, which is a paradox. I hadn't got much perception of dramatic theater structure, at that time, and Jack helped me a great deal with that. Of course, he is a great craftsman. As far as I remember, the whole operation took about a week. Jack had a bottle of whiskey, and somehow or other it happened!

BILES: I understand that there is a play version of *The Italian Girl*.

MURDOCH: Yes, there is. I am not pleased with that. I was told that nothing would happen until I was satisfied with the version, but in the end I was hustled and it was a botched job.

BILES: Where was it produced?

MURDOCH: It started off in Bristol. It had quite a long run in London. It was successful in a commercial sense, but I didn't like it. It was imperfect.

BILES: The distinction is one I'd expect you to make.

MURDOCH: I'd never collaborate with anybody again.

BILES: How long did *A Severed Head* run?

MURDOCH: About two years. *The Italian Girl* ran for more than a year. I can't remember precisely.

BILES: These other two plays: *The Servants and the Snow* and *The Three Arrows*?

MURDOCH: They were both put on in the provinces and scheduled for limited runs. They haven't, either of them, been put on in America; so if you know anybody who is dying to put something on in New York or Washington, I trust they will get into his hands! *The Three Arrows* was beautifully done here, with Ian McKellen. I think it is a rather good play.

BILES: Are there any others?

MURDOCH: Well, there is another one. Somebody saw it and didn't like it, and I haven't really tried to sell it to anyone else.

BILES: It hasn't been produced?

MURDOCH: Not yet. But in any case I certainly hope to write more for the theater.

BILES: Here is a matter that I find curious and extremely interesting: I can't remember exactly, but you have written perhaps half-a-dozen novels with first-person narrators and in every instance that first-person narrator is a male.

MURDOCH: I'm writing one at the moment, actually.

BILES: I'm sure it is unique in the history of the English novel for any novelist to have written consistently in the opposite sex, when writing first-person narratives. Emily Bronte is an exception of sorts, since she wrote *Wuthering Heights* as a first-person narrative by Mr Lockwood, but only one novel is involved. And, of course, there are men, like Angus Wilson, who can write excellently and convincingly from the female point of view, as in *The Middle Age of Mrs Eliot*, though that is not actually a first-person work. But, no one does what you do. I am curious as to why it was that you chose such a narrator in these instances. Was it something in the particular story which dictated a male narrator or what?

MURDOCH: Well, I don't really see there is much difference between men and women. I think perhaps I identify with men more than with women, because the ordinary human condition still seems to belong more to a man than to a woman. Writing mainly as a woman may become a bit like writing with a character who is black, or something like that. People then say, "It's about the black predicament." Well, then, if one writes "as a woman," something about the female predicament may be supposed to emerge. And I'm not very much interested in the female predicament. I'm passionately in favor of women's lib, in the general, ordinary, proper sense of women's having equal rights. And, most of all, equal education.

BILES: But not in the stridency?

MURDOCH: I'm not interested in the "woman's world" or the assertion of a "female viewpoint." This is often rather an artificial idea and can in fact injure the promotion of equal rights. We want to join the

human race, not invent a new separatism. This self-conscious separation leads to rubbish like "black studies" and "women's studies." Let's
just have studies.

BILES: Your mentioning the difficulties inherent in working with a
black character reminds me of your charming black girl, Pattie, in *The
Time of the Angels*.

MURDOCH: I hope she was successful. Of course, a writer attempts
to inhabit all sorts of consciousnesses. My point was that as a main
explanatory narrating consciousness, especially in the first-person novel,
I find I prefer to be male!

BILES: In "Against Dryness," which I see as absolutely fundamental
to the reading of your novels, you talk about one of the major problems
today being the absence of a commonly-accepted background of views,
attitudes, the Victorian "eternal verities."* And you say that nowadays
all that is fragmented and gone. Will you elaborate a little and indicate
what you suppose caused these changes? The failure of Progress and
Liberal Humanism and such?

MURDOCH: I don't know; there are many causes. The general disappearance of religion from the background of the human mind is one of
the most important things that have happened recently. There are all
sorts of causes to do with science and the scientific method and the
breaking up of capitalism, and the loss of confidence in a single human
world, which came after Hitler. A whole complex of causes.

One is tremendously struck, reading the great Victorian novelists,
with how much religion *was* taken for granted. In some way, even
when people were skeptical, there was a kind of Christian attitude or
morality or something, which was absolutely unshaken. I think all these
things *are* shaken, now. The disappearance of prayer from people's
lives, the disappearance of any sort of practice of religion, is, in any
case, a sad phenomenon.

I am not myself a Christian believer, but I was brought up as a
Christian and I feel close to Christianity. I believe in religion, in some
sort of non-doctrinal sense—in a Buddhist sense. I think people miss
this particular steadying influence, this spiritual home and spiritual
center.

* Murdoch, "Against Dryness."

BILES: I am reminded that, early on in her writing career, Muriel Spark said of her conversion to Roman Catholicism that she denied being specifically a Catholic novelist but that her conversion gave her a framework. This absence of a framework is what you are talking about, a moral framework which religion gives.

MURDOCH: Yes.

BILES: As I understand it, Existentialism tends to be rather against that.

MURDOCH: Yes. Well, I am against Existentialism! I think it is less fashionable now than it used to be: as the assertion of a sort of undirected freedom as being a central human attribute, it is surely wrong. It is psychologically unrealistic, and I think it is morally misleading.

BILES: I want to return to a literary subject we have discussed before. You told me the other day that students should be reading Homer, and last year you said Chaucer and Shakespeare and that they should not be studying contemporary writers. As you know, the novel always has been on its last legs and there always has been a new novel. I am curious as to whether you find no genuinely significant novelists today or how you do see the state of the novel.

MURDOCH: The novel is in rather good shape. A tremendous variety of stuff is coming out in England and America. And in France, too. The thing is that the novel can be practically anything. It is so versatile you can do virtually anything you like with the novel. In the last twenty years, novelists have been realizing this versatility and there is a lot of experiment, which I think is good. Quite honestly, I don't read a great many modern novels, so that I'm not an expert on the subject.

BILES: Apropos of experimentation, the strong influence of James Joyce, Virginia Woolf, and others, seems to have slackened somewhat, though there still has been considerable innovation and experimentation in the novel. Do you take this to be the influence of Joyce and Woolf, or do you see it as a going on *from* that influence?

MURDOCH: I would think something going on from that. I feel that the sort of direct impetus of those two is, in a sense, over. This is just my instinctive feeling. I'm not an expert. I've not read enough modern stuff; but I think there is a new atmosphere and a new world and that novelists feel really liberated from the past. A long time has passed since that particular revolution was going on. And novelists learn from poets and the theater. There has been much experiment with narrative techniques, which has been of different kinds, not just of the Joyce and Woolf types. I think it is a new phase.

BILES: *The Horse's Mouth* and Golding's novels are examples. On this subject, Angus Wilson said to me years ago that, though there is this experimental aspect of the contemporary novel, also there is a kind of leapfrogging which some writers—he mentioned himself and Snow specifically, at that time—do, rather hopping over the modernist people back to the Victorians. Thus, a traditional kind of social novel is still being written.

MURDOCH: Yes, this probably is true. The great models are still there, and, in a way, one is closer to Dickens than one is to Joyce. These great models offer story and reflection and social comment and so on; they are *more live* models. Though in a sense you can't go back. One's consciousness is different; I mean our whole narrative technique is something completely different from that of Dickens. But the model still inspires. I personally feel much closer to Dickens and Dostoevsky than I do to James Joyce and Virginia Woolf.

BILES: In tracing to me his literary forebears, Angus has pointed to George Eliot, to Jane Austen, and, of course, to Samuel Richardson, which seems a very accurate assessment. You have referred to Dickens and Dostoevsky already, but the question remains: which writers do you see as your literary forebears? Besides Henry James.

MURDOCH: Well, Homer and Shakespeare most of all! At least, these are the people I want to be influenced by! As far as novelists go, I suppose Jane Austen, Dickens, Dostoevsky, Tolstoi, James. I think probably not the Turgenev aspect of Russian literature. Not French literature at all, apart from Proust. I like Proust. I can't get on with Stendhal particularly; I don't actually like that aspect of the French genius. Proust I find very congenial and feel very happy with. But, it's mainly Dostoevsky, Dickens, Tolstoi.

BILES: Which is all the more interesting, in the light of Dostoevsky's and Tolstoi's having been influenced more strongly by Dickens.

MURDOCH: Yes.

BILES: Do you mind if I ask some rather impertinent questions?

MURDOCH: No.

BILES: You have published some seventeen novels. Generally, how well content are you with that as a body of work?

MURDOCH: Oh, I am not particularly content. I mean I know what's wrong with the stuff. And one tries to improve it, one does one's best to improve.

BILES: In *The Black Prince,* Arnold tells Bradley Pearson that you can't simply sit and wait forever, trying to make one book perfect, you do the best you can and go on.

MURDOCH: That's right.

BILES: But in overall terms, you feel that you've produced a fairly solid body of work, don't you?

MURDOCH: Well, there it is. Yes, I suppose so. But, all the time, one is terribly conscious of one's limitations as an artist. I think I *have* improved: the later stuff is better than the earlier stuff. However, one's ability to improve is still extraordinarily limited. One's always hoping to do better next time: to create better characters, to break out of certain patterns. One knows one's mind pretty well after writing for some years and there are certain patterns which show up.

BILES: Perhaps this is an absurd question. Nevertheless, the early novels tend to be short and the later ones have come to be quite long. Is there any connection to your trying to work out some of the problems, so that more space simply was required?

MURDOCH: Well, in a way, I have become more relaxed and, in a sense, more confident. There is more reflection in the later novels than in the early ones. I think it is true of many writers and, indeed, of many other artists, because there is a parallel in painting, for instance: that the young person is anxious and afraid to ramble round. Then, later on, you don't care if you ramble round. You know what you can do and what you can't do, and you're not frightened of destroying your form by blurring it.

BILES: You wouldn't want to say which of your novels you like best and which least, would you?

MURDOCH: I don't really know. It's not the sort of question I answer for myself. I suppose—just in general—that I like the later ones better than the others, but I haven't any favorite.

BILES: I don't know how far you'll wish to pursue this topic, but I do want to raise the question. In my study of the contemporary British novel and my contacts with novelists, I have been surprised at how some of them assert flatly that they didn't consciously put in certain metaphoric or symbolic elements which are clearly present in the books. Graham Greene is a prime example. If you know *Carving a Statue,* you may recall that Greene wrote a somewhat petulant brief preface for the version of the play published after it had been produced at the Haymarket. He says he was "accused" of encumbering the play with symbols, but "I can detect no symbols in this play." Despite his protests, the fact remains that one can choose many—possibly all— of Greene's fictions and show highly-detailed and apparently carefully-worked-out patterns of metaphor—not to say symbol.

In your novels, there occurs a great deal of interlinked and very important detail. For example, in *A Severed Head* Martin Lynch-Gibbon is called a "violent man" throughout and Martin means "war-like"; and the first part of his surname is that of the man who originated the extra-legal practice of lynching. Martin is a military historian and you apparently name him after Edward Gibbon; Gibbon had a number of things wrong in his view of history, and seeing things mistakenly is Martin's stock-in-trade. One can go on and on, and the things seem demonstrably in *A Severed Head.* One could make equally obvious statements to Greene about a book of his and he'd say "No." What do *you* say?

MURDOCH: I am sure that people can go too far in playing these games, for sometimes this can be actually misleading, because somebody can see a pattern which *really* isn't there. I think out matters of symbolism and I'm very careful about names and so on; thus, the chances are, if there is something fairly telling in the book, then, that is something I intended. I feel there is a *small* area of conscious activity of this kind. By the way, there's nothing in that Lynch-Gibbon idea!

BILES: And some of it is unconscious?

MURDOCH: This is possible. I should be surprised, in fact, if anybody pointed out anything of this sort in my work which I wasn't conscious of, but I wouldn't rule out the possibility of there being an area of this kind. It isn't very profitable to look at.

BILES: The reason I bring up conscious symbolism is the enormous amount of planning you do. Examples: one of Martin's secretaries is named Seelhaft, which means "soulful"; now, that's not an accident. I had a student at one time who investigated the names of the wines mentioned specifically in *A Severed Head* and they all are meaningful; unfortunately, I can't recall at the moment the identifications he made.

MURDOCH: They are all roses. The names of old-fashioned roses.

BILES: I am fascinated by the usefulness of this device, but you are quite right that preoccupation with it can be overdone.

MURDOCH: Henry James is a fruitful subject of this kind of exploration. He was very deliberate; one can find an awful lot of things of this sort in James, things which were put there by James, things which are not necessarily obvious. I think this is part of the charm of the novels—as an area of subliminal effects, if you see what I mean.

BILES: As I said, I am much struck by the utilization of this indirect means of communication, but some novelists deny making use of it. I don't understand whether it is from some distorted concept of modesty or what. [William] Golding is the only novelist, except you, who has ever acknowledged to me so employing metaphor or symbol; in a discussion comparable to this, he once said to me, "Things just present themselves that way," namely, with a literal meaning and some other kind of meaning.

MURDOCH: Yes, this is true. When you are imagining the whole thing, much of this happens absolutely instinctively. Sometimes, one notices later on things one has done, things which were done instinctively at the time. The total situation is thoroughly set up and you are thoroughly imagining it; then, many of these effects happen automatically.

BILES: Another question—a specific perhaps not directly relevant to our discussion. When I was reading *The Black Prince* the long disquisition on *Hamlet*, when Bradley has the girl Julian studying the play, it seemed to me that there were some distortions in *his* arguments about *Hamlet*.

MURDOCH: Oh, yes!

BILES: I took it that you did this deliberately to show us the element of unreliability in Bradley himself. The *Hamlet* incident is most stimulating, for some of Bradley's declarations about the play are self-evidently correct and others are mighty peculiar.

MURDOCH: Yes, yes. Part of this is, in a manner of speaking, the writer entertaining himself. Some of Bradley's observations, I think, are quite acute; others are dotty.

BILES: Exactly the impression! Speaking of the unconscious or the instinctive—and for reasons which I cannot give you, except perhaps the quality of destructiveness on his part—the character's name, Bradley, continually calls to mind Bradley Headstone of *Our Mutual Friend*.

MURDOCH: Yes. Oddly enough, here is another of these things. I love *Our Mutual Friend*, and Bradley Headstone is a marvellous character. There is a connection, although obviously the characters are totally different. Bradley is a good name.

BILES: Bradley seems definitely appropriate.

MURDOCH: The surname Pearson has got a private origin. I once wrote a philosophical piece—I don't type, so I send all my material in longhand to a typist—and in this piece I constantly used the word "Reason," with a capital R. Talking about Kant, I believe. The typist misread this on each occasion as "Pearson"! With extremely comical results as you can imagine!

BILES: The Alan Kennedy I was referring to earlier offers an ingenious interpretation of the name Pearson. He praises this novel, although he confesses to having had no great sympathy for your novels. He finds that you do go dramatic, according to his definition, in *The Black Prince,* and (what you continually wish for) that your characters do get free of authorial manipulation and control. At any rate, Bradley does.

MURDOCH: Yes.

BILES: Then, Kennedy singles out the name Pearson and proclaims it an "obvious anagram" for persona.

MURDOCH: I think he's going too far, there!

BILES: He also talks about how you are the omniscient narrator directing everything; yet, at the same time, Bradley has got completely away. Bradley is both authorial persona and an independent person.

In my opinion, *The Black Prince* is an excellent book. And a difficult one. A genuine masterstroke is those appendices, in which the other people tell their individual screwy versions of what happened. And there is no way in the world to know what really did happen. Which is what you were aiming for.

MURDOCH: Yes, yes. I should say just one thing about this matter of symbolism: that I certainly don't aim at any kind of, as it were, allegorical method of telling the story. That is, I think the symbols must be very carefully controlled and, very often, the symbolism in a novel is invented by the characters themselves, as happens in real life. We're all constantly inventing symbolic images to express our situation.

BILES: I'm afraid I have about run you out of time; so, we'll just break off in mid-career. Thank you so much.

9

JEAN-LOUIS CHEVALIER, EDITOR

Closing Debate, *Rencontres avec Iris Murdoch*

This symposium took place in January 1978 at the University of Caen in France, and the proceedings were published by the university's Centre de Recherches de Littérature et Linguistique des Pays de Langue Anglaise in 1978. Papers presented at the meeting were "L'Art est l'imitation de la Nature," by Iris Murdoch; "*A Word Child;* ou l'Héautontimorouménos," by Fiona MacPhail and Jean-Louis Chevalier; "*A Fairly Honourable Defeat:* Jeux formels," by Valerie Burling; "Le Symbolisme dans les romans d'Iris Murdoch," by Aline Henry; "Passion et salut dans l'oeuvre d'Iris Murdoch," by Michele Morin; and "Roman et philosophie chez Iris Murdoch," by Bernard Le Gros.

MURDOCH: I want to say again how extraordinarily nice it is to be here and how touched I am that people should have thought so much about this "stuff"—it's a great feast of egoism for me to listen to your thoughts, too, though I can't help feeling that you would have got on better if I hadn't been here because then you could have said all sorts of rude things about me which you felt you couldn't say because of my presence! I thought that we'd organise this part of the scene if it is O.K. by everybody, by my talking first of all quite briefly about various points which I noticed in the "communications" which I'd like to pick up and perhaps slightly elaborate upon, and then we could go on to questions, and I will do the best I can. [. . .]

First of all, about the illuminating discussion, or rather "communication," we had this morning about *A Word Child* which I found so good and so touchingly detailed and clear. When one hears one's works discussed, of course, in this sort of detail, one sees very clearly what's wrong with them, and I think one of the things which I feel is wrong with that novel, and which did come out somewhat in the discussion of it, is (well, whether it is something wrong or not I'm not sure but one might reflect on this) that I haven't actually made Hilary's telling of the story itself into part of the story. Now, this is something which a modern novelist often tends to do—if he's writing in the first person he will situate the first person narrative within some kind of hint of how it has been written, or when it has been written, or why it has been written, or what the writing of it is going to do, and this I've done myself in other novels, in *The Black Prince* for instance. I haven't done it in this one, that is, I've stuck to an older convention and actually, now I come to say it, I don't see why one shouldn't use that convention; but it leaves, of course, unanswered the question of what Hilary would have done next and whether the telling of the story would have helped him, and anyway, who's he telling it to, and why, and what is one to think of the end of the story? I felt myself that the end was meant to be unresolved: whether Hilary would find any sort of salvation, either by himself or with Tommy, or whether he wouldn't fall back into some hopeless kind of neurotic obsessional repetition of what had happened, so that the next twenty years of his life might resemble the twenty years which are described in the book. Another mistake that I saw in the book when I listened to this very clear "exposé" was—I'm not sure how important these mistakes are—that I tied up too many loose ends. I think this is always a temptation that a novelist has (particularly a novelist like myself who is interested in plots and patterns), that he must relate everybody to everybody, and I related Crystal to Gunnar through that rather odd incident. I don't mind the incident itself because this is the sort of odd thing that seems to me not impossible to tell in such a context—how Gunnar seduces Crystal on the night that Anne dies—but this very close connection of Crystal with Gunnar was perhaps a mistake.

It might have been better if I'd left that completely open. Then a more minor matter: making Christopher marry Biscuit. I think that was a mistake too and that it would have been better to leave these things mysterious and unclear. Novelists must resist the temptation to tie up all the loose ends. And perhaps that's the context in which I should say that I do regard myself as a realist novelist—that what I'm trying to do is imitate nature and hold the mirror up to the world and do those things which are in fact so frightfully difficult to do, to create characters who are like real people. This doesn't mean that fantastic things can't happen—fantastic things happen all the time in ordinary life and people are very, very odd—but there's some kind of air of open plausibility and open connection with life which I would want my novels to have and which perhaps it's difficult for them to have because of the conflict which I always feel between character and plot. This I think was also mentioned, that the *"situation"* and the *"personnages"* can get in each other's way.

[. . .] Another thing to say perhaps about *A Word Child:* Kitty I think is a very silly woman, and this is something that should emerge in the novel, that she's a touching figure, and she means very well, but she's very silly. It was a rational and a good idea that she should try to get rid of Gunnar's obsession by involving Hilary, but it was an idea she couldn't possibly carry out without involving herself in all kinds of folly. On the other hand, Gunnar really behaves with great rationality and the exorcism does work for him—simply to see Hilary and talk to him briefly makes the whole thing vanish and that could have been the happy ending which of course doesn't come about chiefly because of Kitty's folly and also of course because Hilary can't resist this particular situation. I think it is important in this novel, and perhaps in all my novels, that the story is to a very large extent a funny story. The novel is a comic form. Tragedy appears only in a kind of remote sense in the novel. Terribly, terribly sad things happen in novels but I don't think they're tragic things because of the form. Tragedy belongs to the theatre, it doesn't belong in real life, as somebody observed (perhaps me)—and it doesn't belong in the novel either, which in this sense is like real life and not like the theatre; so that what happens to Hilary, although it is terrible, isn't tragic in that sense. It isn't given a final significance. M. Chevalier talked very well about Hilary's use of language and repartee and quips and escapes into superficial witticism and so on, and this was a very good image of what he was suggesting about Hilary's relation to language which I think I hadn't seen fully myself until I heard it explained, but which I think is there—though one might also say that Hilary is an exponent of what in English we call "trench humour," or "humour noir," the jokes of somebody who's in a pretty awful state but is always making jokes, and it is fortunate for the human race that we can do this. It is, I think, a real release, a real consolation—a minor one perhaps—that one can always make jokes. And I was very pleased that, whether it was in the "communication" or in the questions, somebody picked up the reference to *King Lear* where Hilary says "Crystal and I won't be able to be like birds in a cage"—the reference to Lear, what Lear thinks that he and Cordelia are going to do, but of course he's wrong. This is a very moving thing in *King Lear.* Lear thinks that somehow or other it will end in a kind of solemn, tragic peace and they'll be alone together at the end, but they aren't, and it ends in a much more terrible way. This is the sort of peace which Hilary thought perhaps would be his final consolation; and that little picking-up of that quotation I was very grateful for.

To move on to the discussion of *A Fairly Honourable Defeat,* perhaps I should say something in general about that novel, which has annoyed various people because they couldn't see what it was doing, or else because they thought it was anti-semitic because Julius King was Jewish—which stunned me because I'm pro-semitic and the idea of being accused of anti-semitism is so alien to me that I couldn't imagine how anyone could see it in this way, but I think perhaps some people were indeed offended by the fact that this character was Jewish. I should say that Jews, in my novels, always appear as spiritual figures and tend to gather the spirit of the novel towards themselves and this is usually a case of good spiritual people; in this case it was a bad spiritual person. I should perhaps say in general, about the novel (which I hope won't seem too tiresome) that it is, in a concealed way (I mean so concealed that it doesn't in a sense matter) a theological allegory. Tallis is the Christ figure or the "high incarnation" to use a sort of Eastern term—Julius is of course the Prince of Darkness, King of this World—Morgan is the human soul over whom they are disputing— that explains the title incidentally, that Tallis is of course defeated but it is a "fairly honourable defeat." Leonard is God the Father—a very gloomy figure—that's Tallis's father who realises the whole thing went wrong from the start, and if you like to go that far Tallis's dead sister is the Holy Spirit. This is an unnecessary allegory in a sense, I mean it was necessary through being connected with the construction of the work, but it doesn't emerge *in* the work in any very clear way. Tallis, I should say, is one of my attempts at portraying a good man. I think it is very difficult to portray a good man in fiction for reasons explained by Plato and I noticed in the discussion of the book, practically nobody mentioned Tallis, and he is rather an invisible figure, but, of course, an important one. Another in a sense accidental thing in the book was that I wanted to portray a happy homosexual relationship, which I succeeded in doing, I hope, with Simon and Axel.

I was very interested, in this discussion, about the idea of theatre in the book and I think this is revealing and good, I mean, the notion of *"arène"* in which human beings can be seen as the puppets of their own emotions, and Julius, of course, manipulating them in a completely careless way. Tallis and Julius, incidentally, recognize each other in a significant scene where Tallis sees the concentration-camp mark on Julius' arm. I don't know whether this is theologically sound or not, but perhaps the Devil suffers all the time too, just through being the Devil, and perhaps he does homage to Christ, even loves him. As for manipulating people, people are manipulated in real life, and I think the notion about power which was being hinted at in the discussion is real too, that people are not only manipulated by others but want to be so. This is a subject that interests me very much. People very often elect a god in their lives, they elect somebody whose puppet they want to be, and a group of people can elect somebody in this sense as their leader, or their angel, or their god or whatever it might be, and then perhaps, almost subconsciously, are ready to receive suggestions from this person. And again here, I was touched and pleased that the background in Shakespeare was seen. Much more obvious here, of course, are the references to *A Midsummer Night's Dream* and *The Tempest.* So the end, with Julius going off to Paris and feeling happy, is important—he's all right, he's going to go and make some more mischief somewhere else. And another thing about Tallis, à propos of modes of speech which you have been at different times interested in discussing: Tallis has got no particular mode of speech, he hasn't got any voice really, he hasn't got any kind of ringing voice which one hears in the book, it's all a kind of jumble and muddle and this is important too.

Mlle Henry's piece about symbols I also liked very much. (*Under the Net,* of course.) The titles are important, the titles are all the *names* of the books, the title is what the book is about in every case, so they are important. *Under the Net* is an immature, childish work, it was much influenced by Samuel Beckett and Raymond Queneau, though I don't think it particularly resembles anything by either of them, but that wasn't my fault, I was copying them as hard as I could!

The "net," of course, under which one cannot get, is the net of language. It's interesting that the discussions which were in my head, at that time, in the 1950's, are very much the discussions that we're hearing now about silence, about language moving towards silence, and the difficulty of relating concepts to anything which lies behind them, or under them. The unicorn again is an obvious symbol, of a Christ figure, a highly ambiguous one. This is a subject which interests me very much, the ambiguity of spirituality, that the spiritual person is suffering particularly strong temptations, and that what looks like giving up the world may in fact be an exercise of power in another sense; and I think that Mlle Henry picked this up when she spoke of enchanters. There are powerful figures in many of the novels who attract other people, such as Misha and Calvin (who are the same person divided into conscious and unconscious)—and there are enchanters like Hannah who are unconsciously so, even in a sense innocently so, who attract others because of a kind of discharge of confused spirituality. The point about twins, perhaps I should say something about twins, and siblings, which is important perhaps just in a minor sense. I am an only child, and this may affect my interest in brothers and sisters; and I notice that Sartre, in *Les mots,* says the same thing. He says that he, as an only child, has also had this great fascination with twins—the lost, other person whom one is looking for. I was also pleased—a tiny point—to have the sound of the bird singing on the telephone picked up—I mean these are the kind of things which please novelists—they put in these little, tiny decorations, and then they hope that somebody will notice them, and it's very gratifying when they are actually noticed.

A general point about symbolism perhaps, I think critics can make too much of symbolism. I mean, as I say, I am a realistic novelist, and try to be, and I think that symbols are just an ordinary part of life—one doesn't have to go very far in life before falling over a symbol—we all make symbols the whole time, we make symbols in family life, in love relationships, in all sorts of power relationships and in work. We use certain things as symbols, this is a natural activity, and the invention of interesting, amusing symbols is a part of our ordinary, literary activity as human beings (though I agree that in some of my books there are what one might call "external" symbols). We might distinguish between internal symbols, which are invented by the characters themselves as part of their ordinary existence, and external symbols which the author has put upon them in some way.

[. . .] To proceed to Mme Morin, this question, this complicated question of morality and art. Here, I'm not sure what to say because I don't know that I have any very definite view, or in so far [sic] as I have views, these views have been changing quite a good deal. Perhaps I should say here that of course I owe a great debt to Simone Weil, who is a marvellous thinker, and who opened my eyes to a great many things and set me onto various paths which I've followed since. I'm not a Christian; I was brought up as a Protestant; in so far [sic] as I have close relations with Ireland, I have family both North and South of the border (Protestants), I have a Puritan background. I don't feel that religion departed from my life when God the Father departed. I used to think that when God the Father went it was the end of religion for me, but I have learnt better. I feel now that I don't have to have this image or to believe in a personal God in order to have religion—after all Buddhists don't believe in a personal figure like this. Buddha is an image of spirituality, a teacher, and a centre of spiritual power, and I would want to regard Christ in this sort of light, the Buddha of the West, and I'm rather pleased to see that theology itself, at any rate Protestant theology, is changing in this direction, so that a number of people who thought they were outside the Church wake up one morning and find that really they're inside after all and they didn't know.

To relate all this to *The Black Prince:* again, perhaps I should say something explanatory about this book. The "Black Prince," of course, is Apollo—most critics who reviewed the book in England didn't appear to realise this, even though there was a picture of Apollo on the front! I got a dear friend of mine to do a picture of the head of the great statue of Apollo at Olympia and I thought really this is going too far in telling them what to think, but they didn't seem to know who this was a picture of or to interpret the name Loxias, after all perhaps rather obscure, which is in fact a name of Apollo. Apollo is the god of art, and is also identified by me with the black Eros, destructive and violent: Apollo, a murderer, a rapist, as is said in the novel when they're discussing who Mr Loxias is, who killed a fellow musician in a horrible way, a great power figure, but not necessarily a good figure. So that there is—talking of mystification which M. Le Gros mentioned—a profound mystification in the book in relation to Bradley, and in Bradley's relation to the Black Prince, and indeed Bradley's relation to Arnold. As Mr Le Gros said, there is a caricature of a one-book-a-year man who gabbles and writes, as Bradley judges, bad novels; but then are we to believe Bradley here? Bradley is presented in the book as a man full of prejudices and self-deceptions and delusions. We certainly can't, I think, altogether believe Julian in her postscript, and can we even believe all that Mr Loxias himself says, although I think that Mr Loxias, in saying that art is very much greater than all these definitions which have been offered of it, is right. There is a sort of background of conflict, intentionally put there, in that novel, which may or may not be justified aesthetically. I was glad that Mr Le Gros spoke of absurdity and funniness in the books because this is important in the way that I create, that the medium is, is supposed to be at any rate, funny. Awful things happen and very serious things are said, but people should laugh at the books too. And I followed with interest and agreement the remarks which Mr Le Gros made about the different kinds of background symbolism—the references to the weather and so on—and also what he said briefly about fetishism and the references to Sartre which I found very interesting. One might notice that Sartre is also a Puritan, and this is a bond which I feel with him. At the time that I wrote the book about Sartre I was not entirely in agreement with him, and I feel now very far away from him, but I do continue to admire his novels.*

* Murdoch, *Sartre* (1953).

People have sometimes gone too far in saying that he was not a good novelist. I think he is a good novelist, I think he's really a very good novelist. Perhaps as a philosopher I'm particularly fond of *La nausée*, but I think that *Les chemins de la liberté*—these are good stories, they're about something, they're full of memorable characters, and I think being memorable is a test of poetry, and it's a test also of the novel. Perhaps I should just say in conclusion—this relates both to Mr Le Gros and Mme Morin—that I'm not sure in what sense I am a philosopher. I am a teacher of philosophy and I am trained as a philosopher and I "do" philosophy and I teach philosophy, but philosophy is fantastically difficult and I think those who attempt to write it would probably agree that there are very few moments when they rise to the level of real philosophy. One is writing about philosophy, one is *"philosophant"* if this word can be used. One is not actually doing the real thing, and I don't think that I have done it in more than a few pages in all the stuff that I have written about philosophy. Certainly in the Plato book I have used my reflections on Plato to say something of my own. I did try very hard in that book to give a general account of Plato's thought, which actually is a very difficult thing to do, and I don't know whether I succeeded, but it isn't exactly real philosophy, it's thoughts about Plato. Anyway, I'll stop at this point if anyone would like to ask questions.

C. MACDONOGH: You were speaking about the difficulty of writing philosophy—what about someone who knows absolutely nothing about philosophy. Apart from writing it, to try to think a little bit—what would you advise them to do—to read—or how to begin an approach to a philosophical way of thinking about things?

MURDOCH: [. . .] Well I think the first thing to say is that it's not necessary to enter it at all—it's an extremely obscure, and in many ways, unrewarding subject, and curiously baffling, because one can read quite a lot of philosophy and not feel that one is getting into the centre of the subject. On the other hand, there are such wonderful things written by philosophers. I would think, try oneself out on fairly short texts. I mean if one was reading philosophy in a university with a teacher, then one might adopt some other method; but thinking of somebody who wants to read and reflect and see if this is something for them or not, I would advise them to read a number of different short books. They might read the *Symposium* of Plato, that's not actually a very good introduction to philosophy because it's so erratic and extraordinary and in many ways generalized and unclear, but one must read that anyway whatever one is thinking about or going to do. One might read John Stuart Mill's little book called *Utilitarianism* which is a good piece of philosophical argument about what justifies moral judgements, and this after all is a point where people would do well to try to start philosophy—at a point where they have a lot of their own experience which they can bring to bear on what's being discussed, and where the issue is important. What justifies my moral judgements?—how do I make moral judgements in difficult situations?—the sort of thing much discussed by existentialists. I think Mill's attempt to connect this with the idea of happiness is a very interesting one—I don't think he is right—but then very few philosophers are absolutely right. The thing is to start thinking in some way. And Kant's book *The Fundamental Principles of the Metaphysic of Morals* is a very good, short, extraordinarily illuminating and exciting book about morality, putting another completely different point of view. So, if you read Kant and Mill, and made them fight each other, as it were, you might then, in your own reflection, be getting somewhere. Sartre's little book called *Existentialisme et humanisme* is worth looking at. It's very difficult to say about the great names in philosophy, because of finding something which one can readily get out of them. I think one might read some Berkeley, to puzzle oneself about sense perception and material objects. Or of course Descartes: *cogito ergo sum.* That's a great moment in philosophy and something one can reflect upon. The thing is to find a starting-point. Morality is a good starting-point, or worrying about problems of perception. One might read something by Merleau-Ponty after that. David Hume, again, the beginning of Hume's treatise about problems which also concern Kant—his discussion of the concept of cause. And it would be a pity not to read something by Hegel, but it's very difficult to say what. One might read the stuff in *Phenomenology* about the master and slave—the famous part which Sartre is so interested in. That's terribly exciting and might make one want to read the whole of the rest of the book. One could go on for a long time on this. Thank you for asking!

S. LEBERT: In your novels, does the mystery in the plot correspond to the mystery inherent in human beings and their lives?

MURDOCH: [. . .] Well, yes and no. I think that any artist goes in for mystification, to use the word which was used before, and mystification and mystery I suppose are different things, but they can be connected. The artist doesn't want to be too simple. This is something very important about art, that it's a game of tricks, the artist de-simplifies what he's doing, in a way, deliberately, in order to present it perhaps with a certain air of reality, or possibly to conceal things. There is an element of mystification in a great deal of art. I think the word "mystery" though is important here, and I would say yes to your question, separating it perhaps from the idea of mystifying. I think somebody quoted something which was out of me, that the person cannot be known [. . .] I think it's important that the human person—and in this sense one could use the work of art as a kind of analogue of the human person—isn't knowable in the end. I think this is something that's dawned on me more and more as I've grown older, that one knows frightfully little. One knows very little about anything, and one knows awfully little about the other people and awfully little about oneself. There's a kind of enormous jumble on the top, and what exactly is underneath is very obscure so that I would feel that a novelist especially, who has a responsibility because he's presenting people, should, unless there's an aesthetic reason otherwise,—I'll explain that point in a minute—present his people as being not totally explicable. This of course could be an excuse for not working hard, one would have to see what it looked like; but I think that great characters in great novels have got this inexhaustible quality. This is why they're so interesting, you want to discuss them; people argue endlessly about characters in Henry James, characters in Tolstoy, characters in Proust, characters in Shakespeare. There's something profoundly and interestingly unclear about them. But there can be aesthetic reasons in a novel why you don't do this. One might take Robbe-Grillet as an example. There is a great deal of mystery and mystification in Robbe-Grillet, but I don't think it bears on real ambiguity of people treated as real people. I'm not certain about this, but I think it comes out of a different aesthetic motive, and one might say something the same about people in Kafka. There can be aesthetic reasons for by-passing this aspect of the problem.

M. MORIN: I'd like to ask you a couple of slightly related questions. Firstly, do you think there's any basic difference between the three novels that are written in the first person and the others? and secondly, is there any particular reason why in the three novels that are written in the first person, the narrator should be a man?

MURDOCH: Yes . . . I think there are more than three of them. . . . I can't remember.

M. MORIN: *Under the Net. The Black Prince. A Word Child.*

MURDOCH: And *The Italian Girl.* That's also written in the first person.* I've just actually finished one which is also in the first person [*The Sea, The Sea*]. Well, I think this is a very important decision that the novelist makes. When I make that decision I'm always anxious about it, for I know that things will come out quite differently if it's written in the first person. The advantages of writing in the first person are obvious. In a way, they are enormous because you can then ramble around endlessly, you can address your reader, and you can produce a tremendous amount of verbiage which has got a sense in relation to the speaker. Also, I think, there's often a bigger emotional charge. . . . There probably is a more direct emotional punch if the thing is written in the first person. On the other hand, the danger of this is that it's harder then to create other characters who can stand up to the narrator, because they're being seen through his eyes. And I think my ideal novel—I mean the novel which I would like to write and haven't yet written—would not be written in the first person, because I'd rather write a novel which is more scattered, with many different centres. I've often thought that the best way to write a novel would be to invent the story, and then to remove the hero and the heroine and write about the peripheral people—because one wants to extend one's sympathy and divide one's interests. This is what I want to do at any rate as a realistic novelist writing in the English tradition and the Russian tradition and the tradition of Proust. The advantages of writing not in the first person are that it's easier to spread your interests, and you get a more balanced story, and you have the added pleasure of animating all sorts of different characters.

---

* *A Severed Head* (1961) is also written in the first person.

The ability to animate all sorts of odd characters is very valuable. I mean, as Tolstoy describes the feelings of Levin's dog—suddenly he becomes a dog! This is very pleasing, and something that a novelist likes to do, and I think it pleases the reader as well, and it provides a method of relieving tension and taking the weight off and going off somewhere else, as it were, towards the side, which is good. About writing as a man, this is instinctive. I mean I think I identify more with my male characters than my female characters. I write through the consciousness of women in the stories which have different narrators, so I write as women also in those stories as well as men; but I suppose it's a kind of comment on the unliberated position of women. If I were black, I'd feel I ought perhaps to bear witness by writing as a black person, and not writing as a white person. On the other hand, if you write as a black person, you're introducing all sorts of compulsory problems which you may not want to deal with at the moment. There are very important problems about being black, but you mightn't as a black person always feel primarily interested in these problems. You might want to write about different things, when it did not matter whether you were black or white; and I think I want to write about things on the whole where it doesn't matter whether you're male or female, in which case you'd better be male, because a male represents ordinary human beings, unfortunately, as things stand at the moment, whereas a woman is always a woman! In fact of course I'm very interested in problems about the liberation of women, particularly, for instance, in so far [*sic*] as these concern education. I'm interested in them both as a citizen and a writer, so they do come in to some extent.

J. BAYLEY: It's interesting that women writers often feel it necessary to appear "in the right light."

MURDOCH: I think it is true that, in a way, one would feel that one was letting something down if one's main female characters were very bad whereas it doesn't matter what you do with the male characters! It's a freer world that you are in as a man than a woman. It's an interesting question and I don't think I've probably given the whole of the answer, but that's a part of the answer. A woman is much more self-conscious than a man, just as a black person is more self-conscious than a white person.

M. BARIOU: Could you give an estimation of approximately why there seem to be more great women writers in Britain than perhaps in any other country of the world?

MURDOCH: [. . .] I don't know. There are a lot of good women writers in France and in America. I wouldn't be sure without counting up. But there are certainly a lot of good women writers in Britain, yes. Perhaps I can't offer any answer which isn't chauvinistic! I think that, in some very general sense, women are more liberated in England than they are in France or in America. I think that an aspect of this is that they are better educated; although I would add that I think English education is deteriorating, and French education is good and much more disciplined. But I think there has been a great liberation of women in England. This is something important to say when people moan about how everything is getting worse. Many many things have got very much better, and this is an important thing that has got better, that women are more liberated, they are more *ordinary*. The point of liberation is not, and this is to differ with certain views of women's lib, to say we're better, or we're special, or we're wonderful, but just to be equal, to be ordinary, to join the human race, to be people, just people like everybody else. I think that over quite an area of British society women have come out into the open, in this sense, possibly more than they have in France. I'm not certain—perhaps somebody would like to say something about this? And I think that women in America, in becoming liberated have tended to produce a kind of cult of consciousness which is damaging to them as novelists, in that they think they've got to write as women in a rather aggressive manner, and I don't think English women feel this so much. I disapprove of "separatism" as a mode of liberation: women's studies, black studies, and nonsense of that sort. The point is to join the great main stream of thought and art from which we have been excluded.

CHEVALIER: Do you think the sex of a novelist is important at all? I wouldn't mind Dickens being a woman or George Eliot a man.

MURDOCH: I don't think at a high level of work there's a significant difference. I think it is possible that the soppy romance is, at a low level, more natural to women, and the rather brutal thriller more natural to the men, and this is to allow a kind of sex differentiation which

I'm reluctant to mention, because I so much want to say that there isn't any difference between us! But at a higher level—a more spiritual level—I think the difference vanishes. I don't see any difference between the man and woman good novelists. If someone says "Look at George Eliot, how soppy she is about Will Ladislaw"—well, Conrad's soppy too. Soppiness can exist in the great writers of either sex!

C. CHARPENTIER: Three questions. Number one is about power and truth in connection with what you said yesterday about mimesis. Number two is about the way your novels are generated. And number three is about the use of the word "Gothic" in some reviews of your books.

At the beginning of *The Black Prince,* on page 11, in Bradley Pearson's foreword, you make Bradley Pearson say—I suppose *you* make him say that "all art deals with the absurd and aims at the simple." Could you please comment a little on that, although you have already partly answered. [. . .]

MURDOCH: This is what Bradley Pearson says. I'm not certain that I go along with it absolutely. I think it's an interesting remark. Think for a moment of Tolstoy or someone who wants to say that good art is not obscurantist, but has got some kind of lucidity about it. Here one would be opposing the simple to some kind of "bogusity." I mean the word "bogus" in English. What's French for "bogus"? "Bogus" is a very good term. It means false, pretentiously false. A lot of art is pretentiously false and one might use the word "simple" or "lucid" to mean the opposite of that. And "dealing with the absurd" means not by-passing the kind of contingent, messy, rubbly aspect of ordinary life. You have to see ordinary life as it is. It's not tragic, it's not clear. It's not even knowable. It's a sort of mess. I think one might try to think of Shakespeare here. Well, Shakespeare very often seems remarkably simple. Of course, it's a kind of illusory simplicity because it conceals a very great depth of thought. But if you think of marvellous things in Shakespeare, for instance when background characters are relating to each other in some natural way, there's a kind of pure sense of simplicity and lucidity and clarity, and at the same time justice is done to the oddity and randomness of ordinary life. Of course, the fact that Shakespeare writes poetry is rather important! Poets can express much more than novelists: this concentrated sense of something which is simple and lucid and true and non-bogus and at the same time oddly accidental. I think this sums up something about poetry really perhaps rather than about the novel because in the novel it's not so concentrated, so one doesn't see it so much. I don't know whether this is at all clear, but this is, perhaps, what Bradley meant anyway.

CHARPENTIER: Question number two. When I asked you a few questions a couple of years ago, if I may allude to this, about *The Unicorn*, you very kindly explained a lot of things about the way your novels are generated, if I may use the word, and you said that generally when you begin you can see the whole, that is, you have a pattern in front of you, a relation between the various characters, and you see the plot. May I ask you if that is still true now. I mean, would it apply to the recent works, particularly to *A Word Child*?

MURDOCH: What novelists say about how they invent their novels is often very uninteresting because the whole process is complicated, and different novelists write in very different ways. I think I wouldn't say that I see the whole thing, like Mozart's seeing a symphony or something like that. It's a different process. I usually start with a little nucleus of two or three characters and some kind of general idea of a conflict; but of course one's head is full of stuff. I mean when one's writing a novel, there's an awful lot of stuff which is collecting, which one's got in a sense to ignore and which is there longing to rush about. I attach great importance to plot, and I usually start with the nucleus of the plot given in the relationship of the characters. For instance, take a family of five brothers, one brother's gone to Canada, and then suddenly, after twenty years, he comes back: I mean, anything will do as a starting point for a plot where there's a tension in a relationship. At least this is how my plots usually begin. Then, very gradually, the story unwinds itself, and when one has got the thing really going, the story invents itself, and the characters invent the story, and they invent their dialogue, and they invent all kinds of things about their childhood and so forth; but the beginning is that sort of nucleus.

CHARPENTIER: In many of the reviews, the word "Gothic" has been used. I often feel it isn't justified at all. How do you react to this yourself? I often feel it's just an easy word which is used. There are some Gothic elements but I don't know what the elements are. We don't quite know. Do you accept this? It's often used to describe some of your novels, particularly *The Unicorn*, and it's been used recently again for *A Word Child*.

MURDOCH: Well, it was used earlier today to describe my London, the Gothic London? That's O.K. by me. I don't mind the idea of Gothic London, the sort of Piranesi London; though in so far [*sic*] as London is a sort of main character in the books it appears differently in different contexts. That's O.K. and conjures up something which I think I'd accept. I don't like it as a general word about the novels because, as you say, it's an etiquette, it gives you a certain way of looking at the stuff which I think is rather limiting. It's an easy description. And as a would-be realist, and somebody who I hope is writing novels that have a lot of different characteristics and different atmospheres, I would not like to be labelled as a Gothic novelist. I would regard this as limiting in a slightly derogatory sense.

CHEVALIER: Even when it links you with Ivy Compton-Burnett, as in a paper by A. L. Rowse which calls either Miss Compton-Burnett or yourself "the Mrs Radcliffe *de nos jours*" and speaks of your "Gothic fantasies and unreal horrors"? This was written in October 1977.

MURDOCH: I'm sorry to hear that this is still going on. I think I would object very much. I do admire Ivy Compton-Burnett, but she is totally unlike me, and I don't know what these "unreal horrors" are that he's speaking of. It is ordinary life that I'm talking about which after all is full of horrors.

CHEVALIER: It was used to describe somebody else's work as well.

MURDOCH: This is a different point about Ivy Compton-Burnett. I don't think I bear any resemblance to her. And I don't think there's a kind of "Castle-of-Udolpho" atmosphere about my books. *The Unicorn* is about a castle and in *The Time of the Angels* people wander in the fog, but I don't think this sort of thing is a particularly important or general aspect of the work!

M. DEBELLE: You have said that Art imitates Nature several times. I think you said this. Don't you think that for aesthetic reasons, you might come to terms with the opposite statement made by Oscar Wilde that Nature imitates Art?

MURDOCH: Art imitates Nature. Nature imitates Art. Yes, of course. I mean this would be to make the obvious countercharge to somebody who wants to take a mimetic view of Art, to say that of course we are "making" Nature. Art is acting upon our view of Nature and making Nature look like Art. And I think that Nature imitates Art both in the sense that we are bestowing meaning upon Nature which we then rediscover in Nature, perhaps with surprise; and also that people can, consciously or unconsciously, be influenced by aesthetic images. I mean aesthetic images of themselves. I dare say Oscar Wilde was. I mean that one has an idea of oneself which may be taken from Stendhal or something. Professor A. J. Ayer in Oxford admits that he identifies with the hero of *Le rouge et le noir,* and one constantly takes prototypes from literature who may actually influence one's conduct. But although it's true that Nature imitates Art, Nature is very much larger than Art and is going to have the last word. In the fight of Art against Nature, Nature is bound to win and Art had better realise this. That is, the artist must always be readjusting what he says, the good artist is learning the whole time by looking at the world. One can see this in the work of a painter.

Yesterday, when we were in the Louvre, we saw two self-portraits by Rembrandt, one when he was very young, one when he was rather old, and somehow one could see what an extraordinary amount he'd learnt by looking at Nature. So the artist had better watch out and always be humble, he mustn't get a kind of luciferian pride in thinking that he can make Nature what he pleases, because Nature will get some kind of revenge on him. And he'd better go on readjusting what he does. I think every serious artist does constantly, says to himself, "Well, what I've just done isn't really the right thing. What I'm going to do next will be the right thing."

F. MACPHAIL: When we were studying *A Word Child,* we were struck by the number of references to that rather sinister personage Peter Pan. We wondered why this importance in relation to Hilary and perhaps to you?

MURDOCH: Yes, Peter Pan means a great deal to me. I expect everybody knows about Peter Pan. Is Peter Pan a popular figure in France? My first introduction to Peter Pan was in Kensington Gardens when I was about four or something, and I went to see that famous statue of Peter Pan which is so weird and sinister, yes, as you say, sinister, although that did not occur to me when I was four, but rather later on.

The play of *Peter Pan* has an extraordinary story, if you reflect on it. For instance, the very interesting oddity of the same character being both Mr Darling and Captain Hook. And the retreat of Mr Darling to the dog kennel, and the division of Wendy's life between Peter and the real world. And the crocodile. It's full of strange symbolisms. John very kindly introduced me to a remarkable book, which I didn't know existed, which is the novel of *Peter Pan,* in which the figure of Hook comes out, I think, much more.

BAYLEY: The novel is full of fun.

MURDOCH: Yes, it's a funny book. Hook turns out to be an old Etonian. It's more witty and light-hearted than the play. The play, it's a famous play for children after all, does not appear to be sinister when you see it. I think it contains for me one of the greatest of all moments of theatre which is the first appearance of Peter which always I find very exciting and very moving. In the silence of the nursery, this sinister figure appears at the window. It's frightening, and it's moving too. These ambiguous symbols about paternity are of course most interesting, and the division of the world between the real life of the Darlings and the never never land, land of lost boys is somehow ambiguous and very powerful. It's a play about the subconscious mind and one's relationship to it. In *A Word Child* I play with the idea, and different people give different interpretations of it. Of course, it's liable to a number of interpretations. I connected it in some kind of very general way with Hilary as a lost boy.

F. MACPHAIL: Peter, I think, ends the play by saying, "To die would be an awfully big adventure" . . . and also of course possibly to live would be an awfully big adventure?

MURDOCH: Yes . . . and the division of Wendy's life and Hilary as a lost boy and as a fatherless boy and as a boy who can't establish a relation with a woman. Wendy is a mother-figure. There's everything in that play. One could work this out I suppose with Hilary, but it just somehow happened. I mean Hilary happened to be living near Kensington Gardens, so Peter Pan got into the story somehow.

S. LEBERT: What do you think about the psychoanalyst and psychoanalysis?

MURDOCH: Yes, I've got very mixed feelings about psychoanalysis. I would very much dislike to be psychoanalysed, and I don't know how much good this does people. I think it's a rescue operation. As a rescue operation, as an emergency therapeutic operation, it's something which may be justified in many cases. But the analyst has too much power, and the idea of transference I find very alarming indeed, and I think this can disturb somebody's life profoundly. Also it produces this tremendous concentration upon oneself which is not necessarily therapeutic in a spiritual sense at all, maybe indeed the opposite.

This endless reflection on one's childhood and so on, and this dependence on the analyst and seeing him so often, I don't know, there's something—it's taking people away from ordinary life, and I think people should live in ordinary life and get on there, and try to enjoy themselves there, and notice the claims and troubles of other people. On the other hand, I find Freud very interesting. One can't blame Freud for everything that analysts do. I find him, as a thinker, enormously exciting, he's full of insights. He wrote very interesting things about art, both what he actually says about works of art and also in general. It's the application to human beings in a therapeutic situation which raises the problem, but the general speculations are wonderfully rich. And I find this view of the human soul very sympathetic and realistic. Freud was influenced by the "tripartite soul" of Plato. The soul is divided into three parts. Freud also divides the soul into three parts, but he mistrusts the top part, I mean the super ego. He thinks that one must live in the ego and I wouldn't accept this, I would regard the ego as continuing into the super ego and in a Platonic sense I think this is very good human psychology, though not necessarily good as therapy.

J.-C. CASTANGT: Is not novel writing a way of purifying philosophies, of putting them to the test of facts whether heard of or invented by the novelist, because philosophies may be patterns, and patterns in many of your novels, I think, prove of no avail, crash, and you have a deep sense of the uniqueness of people and situations?

MURDOCH: I think that philosophers increasingly realise that it's quite useful to pay attention to novelists. A philosopher might now ask his pupils to read a novel and might find it valuable to discuss it with them. I agree with you that philosophers can be pedantic and can be shut up in the world of theory. This was noticeable in English philosophy, not so much now, but twenty or thirty years ago or before the war when there was a logical positivist moral philosophy of a highly over-simplified sort, which had got a very clear theory so that it fascinated people. It fascinated the philosophers themselves and their students and produced a kind of special language. This is a difficulty about philosophy. It's the difficulty about any sort of very strong theory that it produces its own jargon. I think that structuralism isn't without difficulties of this sort. As soon as you have a very strong specialized technical vocabulary, it becomes impossible to *state* certain problems. In moral philosophy the technical vocabulary was so strong that if you tried to object to what was being said, you were reduced to some kind of very simple language which did not sound like philosophy at all. And this is where, I think, the resort to the novel is good because then one sees the moral problem in a real context. One's got to have both philosophers and novelists.

I think that the role of ordinary language in philosophy is very important. I know this is something which belongs to *"les pays anglo-saxons"* rather more than perhaps to here or Germany. Not all philosophers now in England or America would agree, but I do think that philosophy ought to be written in ordinary language, that the invention of technical terms is a dangerous occupation. It may seem a shortcut to a clarification, but it may produce its own problems because then it carries a value judgement of some sort with it usually, perhaps sometimes an invisible sort built into the language; so that the outsider, the critic of the philosopher, must always be trying to persuade the philosopher to explain in ordinary terms. This is like the presence of the jury in the law court. There are arguments about whether there should be juries because juries are stupid people who don't understand the law. There seems to me to be a conclusive answer to this. Juries make the lawyers explain. It's not just lawyers talking to lawyers. It's lawyers talking in the presence of people who don't have a technical vocabulary. And I think that philosophers should endeavour to use ordinary language which is also incidentally very good for ordinary language in that if you attempt to use the language for such purposes of clarification you are strengthening it.

J. BAYLEY: Are you against any kind of formalist vocabulary—critical vocabulary, then?

MURDOCH: I feel diffident here, because although I know a certain amount about formalist criticism I'm not an expert on it. But I feel a little alarmed. Young people, students, or people who don't know very much pick up a bit of jargon and use it in argument, and it would be very much better if they tried to produce the explanation without the jargon. I certainly think this in moral philosophy. It's very difficult to clarify things philosophically but it is always rewarding to attempt to clarify in ordinary terms.

x: This is not a very important question. It is about your novels being more centred on ordinary life than before. Are you more concerned with ordinary things than with extraordinary ones?

MURDOCH: I'm glad you think this. Young writers are often afraid of writing about ordinary things because they think that this would be rather dull and of course they are anxious to startle their friends by writing something rather odd, and also they imagine that it's more original to write about something rather odd. I think the artist that has worked for a long time in his craft is less concerned with any desire to shock or any desire to search for oddities. He can find plenty of oddities without looking for them. I've been endeavouring for a long time to write about ordinary life and ordinary problems. Of course, one is the prisoner of one's own mind. Any novelist who has been writing for a long time has in a sense psychoanalysed himself. He can see what he's up to. He can see all sorts of things which he's not going to tell anybody else about himself and which he'll conceal from his reader, and all sorts of obsessional things and so on. And one tries to get out of these cages and one obvious way of getting out is, as we were saying just now, just to look at the world and try to identify with what's different and far away.

R. DALIGAULT: You seem to stress that your principal characters are tragic. Tragedy doesn't belong to the genre of the novel. Yet, would you say the world you create is a world of despair?

MURDOCH: I don't think so, no. Of course a lot of the characters are people in despair, like Clifford in *A Word Child,* a picture of a man in despair. Incidentally, thinking again of Clifford and Hilary; it's possible that Hilary could have rescued Clifford if he'd attended to him a bit more, and not been frightened to feel affection for him and show affection for him. There's a certain pessimism in the books. I feel pessimistic about human personality in an obvious sense. This is just part of a realistic attitude to it. I think that people are pretty bad on the whole, not bad in the sense of wicked, but selfish and so on, selfishness is absolutely ingrained in human beings. And terribly few people ever climb out of this, and very often the people who do climb out are people who appear very simple or even dull to the outsider. I tried to portray another good person in *An Unofficial Rose* with the figure of Ann. No, I would not say despair, I think there's quite a lot of hope. The reader has got to put his own bit of hope into my bit of hope as it were. I mean, like at the end of *A Word Child,* there's a hint of hope in that it happens to be Christmas Day, and there's Tommy still there, and so on . . . but who knows what will happen next? And funniness is never far away. I think in all the books there are plenty of indirect hints or indications of hope, and these are very important.

M. MORIN: I'd like to ask you a question about something you said earlier on. You said that you don't think you have any philosophy and don't you think that in the novel you're bound to express a coherent vision of life even if you wouldn't call this philosophy?

MURDOCH: [. . .] I would not use the word philosophy, but this is a verbal point. People often talk of somebody's philosophy of life, meaning their general outlook. The novel itself of course, the whole world of the novel, is the expression of a world outlook. And one can't avoid doing this. Any novelist produces a moral world and there's a kind of world outlook which can be deduced from each of the novels. And of course I have my own philosophy in a very general sense, a kind of moral psychology one might call it rather than philosophy. I have views about human nature, about good and evil, about repentance, about spirituality, about religion, about what religion is for people without God, and so on. And these views may add up to a world outlook, which comes to be expressed, directly or indirectly, in the novels. Also of course in the strict sense I have a philosophical position. I am a kind of Platonist, though I'm also a linguistic philosopher. I was trained as a linguistic philosopher and in many ways I remain one, but for purposes of moral philosophy I'm a sort of Platonist. I might describe myself as a Wittgensteinian neo-Platonist! If I were shut up in prison for ten years and told to write my philosophy I could have a shot at explaining this, but it would take a long time!

MACDONOGH: Do you write poetry?

MURDOCH: Do I write poetry? Well you ask a very delicate question.

MACDONOGH: Somebody told me you did write some.

MURDOCH: I try to write poetry. I would much rather be a poet than a novelist, and I would imagine that no poet would ever want to be a novelist, only Philip Larkin says he would like to be a novelist.

BAYLEY: He wrote several novels which he never published. He wanted to become a novelist, but he's fortunately a poet.

MURDOCH: Well, I think he has a happy destiny being a poet. I'm not sure that it's not happier to be a painter, but I think to be a poet or a painter must be the nicest thing of all. Novelist comes third. I would very much like to be a poet, and I write a lot of verse. I think poetry is terribly difficult. It's as difficult as philosophy. It's much harder than writing a novel. I go on trying. I have published a small amount of verse, but I think I'm probably not a natural poet. I can strive and produce something that looks like poetry and may deceive some people but it isn't really poetry and this mysterious gift which your Papa [Donagh MacDonagh] had is barred from me.

BAYLEY: Did your father ever try to write a novel?

MACDONOGH: Yes, he tried, and he lasted until about the seventh page, I think. He didn't manage very well, so he just gave up.

MURDOCH: He was very sensible. If one can write poetry, why bother with writing novels, except that you earn more money writing novels of course. Poets don't earn money.

MACDONOGH: I think you're very fond of people and situations, and this one cannot express in poetry in the same way, one cannot convey one's moral philosophy and describe characters as one can do in the novels.

MURDOCH: Yes. This is very true.

B. LE GROS: Could you say something about the Englishness of the novels, or wherever the Englishness of the novels lies?

MURDOCH: Well, I was using the word "English" here in the sense of the English novel tradition. I use the word "English" partly because our island is falling to pieces as you probably know. The Scots have become power-mad since they've found some oil and they've got all that whisky. And the Welsh have always been power-mad, and my poor native land has its troubles, and the English have become conscious of themselves as separate. Of course, I'm not English, I'm Irish. But I live in England and I identify with the English novel tradition although I suppose some people in that tradition are also Irish. I'm using the word "English" really to mean Jane Austen, Dickens, Emily Bronte, George Eliot, Henry James, as far as the English tradition spreads. I didn't mean anything very specially separate. I'm of course very conscious of myself as Irish, and as I say I'm a Protestant and I come from both sides of the border, and the unhappiness of Ireland is something which I think about all the time. Some Irish ass wrote to the newspapers in England a couple of weeks ago, writing from the Republic, saying "What are these Irish troubles? We have no troubles." And this of course is such a grim, cynical thing to say, if one thinks what Belfast is like and what Londonderry is like, and how awful the situation there is. How much people are suffering. How much children are suffering, which is one of the awful aspects of that hideous business. I mean their being demoralized and frightened and filled with hate and fear and so on. This is a part of being Irish and something that I carry with me. *The Red and the Green* which got mentioned a few times: I would regard that as an historical novel. It certainly, I think, is a good textbook for understanding Ireland, if anybody wants, quite apart from reading a novel, to get a glimpse of what Ireland's like, and what the conflicts in Ireland are like.

That book is quite a good introduction and it represents actually a lot of historical research. For that particular week (the week of the 1916 rebellion which the novel is about) I tried to get everything right—what day a particular article was published on, what day and how they changed the plan for the insurrection, and what the English were doing, what everybody was doing during that week. Of course there is also an invented story which distracts attention from the historical background, but it's certainly a novel about Ireland and about the awful tensions involved in being Irish.

BAYLEY: We learn something from reading a novel that isn't in any sense English or nationalistic. I mean this is a thing that all good novelists do, don't you?

MURDOCH: Yes.

BAYLEY: You could attach it to someone like Balzac who I think is a marvellous person to actually tell you the way people work.

MURDOCH: Yes. I'm sorry. I should perhaps have made that clearer, that I was speaking about *"le roman"* in relation to my own personal ancestry which includes of course the Russians and Proust. I don't feel so connected with Flaubert and Stendhal although I admire them, but for me the French novelist who is closest to me is Proust. And he is very much one of my ancestors, so that I come out of a mixed tradition.

J.-C. CASTANGT: Would you attribute the sense of marvel and sometimes even fantastic trend which I think I find in your novels to the Celtic heritage which Mr Bayley pointed out yesterday, to which you would add English realism?

MURDOCH: Yes. Of course I'm not a Celt (selt) or Celt (kelt) or however you pronounce that word. My ancestors on my mother's side are pure Anglo-Irish, English people settled in Ireland as landed gentry. My father's ancestors are lowland Scots I assume from my name, although I don't know much about the history of my father's family except that they were farmers in County Down for a very long period. So that my Irishness is Anglo-Irishness in a very strict sense. I think this is a very special way of being Irish. People sometimes say to me rudely, "Oh! You're not Irish at all!" But of course I'm Irish. I'm profoundly Irish and I've been conscious of this all my life, and in a mode of being Irish which has produced a lot of very distinguished thinkers and writers. It is a particular tradition in Ireland. It's one which has been connected with sad things of course, because the Anglo-Irish are identified in some people's minds with intruders and exploitation.

MACDONOGH: What about the Puritanism of the Irish? What do you think about that?

MURDOCH: Well, about Puritanism. I don't know what makes people Puritans. Some people are and some aren't, and I *am,* and I don't think that I got it from my Ulster ancestors, although they certainly are Puritans. Sorry, this is going to be probably terribly boring, but my father fled from that world of black Protestantism. He ran just as soon as he could, immediately after the war. He grabbed my mother, and I was just coming into existence, and off we went to England, and this tension has always remained in my life between this ancestry, the removal from it, the removal from Ireland, the fact that my parents were exiles in England, that Ireland was for me, as a child, a very romantic land, a land I always wanted to get to and find and discover. So I don't think that I acquired this Puritanism in any direct way. Nevertheless, there's something there which must perhaps have come out of Ireland, I don't know. I think there's a lot of Puritanism in Ireland, both among Protestants and among Catholics. *Ulysses* can tell us a good deal about that.

10

CHRISTOPHER BIGSBY

Interview with Iris Murdoch

Christopher Bigsby is professor of American studies at the University of East Anglia in Norwich, England. He has written more than twenty-five books on aspects of English and American culture. This interview was conducted in London on 5 December 1979 and was published in *The Radical Imagination and the Liberal Tradition: Interviews with English and American Novelists*, edited by Heide Ziegler and Christopher Bigsby (London: Junction books, 1982).

[Introductory matter omitted.]

BIGSBY: I want to start by asking about your philosophical position. You were once strongly influenced by existentialism—I think you said once that that was what drew you into a concern with philosophy—and also, to some extent, by Marxism. Why do you find those unsatisfactory now?

MURDOCH: Well, they are very different cases. My Marxist phase, when I was an undergraduate, was really just part of a general political attitude. I didn't really regard Marxism as a philosophy and indeed it scarcely is one. And now, of course, my political position is quite different, and I am critical of Marxism in many fairly straightforward ways. If you regard it as a philosophy it is a very jumbled one, not at all without interest, and of course, not without importance. But that wasn't part of my philosophical life at all, really. I didn't originally intend to be a philosopher. It was the war that brought this about in my life because

I wanted to go on studying at Oxford and I wanted to become an art historian or archaeologist; that was my ambition. But of course one was conscripted and one wasn't able to pursue one's studies. When I began to think, I didn't know what I was going to do, except that I wanted to be a writer. I was always quite clear about that. At the end of the war it was a very, very exciting time and existentialism was part of that time. I always loved France. I was very interested in France and getting back to contact with France for me was very much existentialism. I met Sartre actually in 1945 and I got hold of a copy of *L'être et le néant* when hardly anybody else had managed to get one and things like this. So that was part of that excitement and then I'd studied philosophy at Oxford and then somehow I began to see myself as a philosopher. So it had that influence in that sense, but I don't think I ever was an existentialist. I think that my objections to existentialism went right back to my first meeting with it.

BIGSBY: How would you characterize your philosophical position at the moment?

MURDOCH: Well, it has developed a great deal I think. I mean it sounds rather grandiose to talk about one's philosophical position, and it is very difficult to have a philosophical position.

BIGSBY: Not if you are a philosopher.

MURDOCH: Well it is, even for a philosopher it is difficult. But granted that this may sound over-important or not too clear or something, it is not easy to do this briefly, I think probably the major influence on me, philosophically speaking, when I was younger, was Wittgenstein. I was a graduate student in Cambridge—unfortunately I just missed being taught by Wittgenstein—but I met him and I lived, in terms of philosophy, in the aura of his work and I knew a great many of his disciples and this, I think, is a continuing influence. I am still within that world and I think the work of Wittgenstein has still got many things even to be discovered about it and I think that he was a great philosopher. So that travels with me, that particular sort of—I think it is misleading to call it linguistic philosophy because that has come to mean an awful lot of other different things since—that particular sort of philosophical attitude travels with me. Also, I think very slowly over the years I have become much more interested in religion.

I have become interested in Buddhism, and I've once more become interested in Christianity, not in a dogmatic sense. I hold no dogmatic religious belief at all, but I feel now close to certain religious attitudes which are most easily expressed in Buddhist terms for me, though I am not a Buddhist. It is very difficult for Western people to be Buddhists, perhaps. But at any rate I wouldn't think of myself in those terms but it is expressed by Buddhism in a non-dogmatic, non-supernatural sense of spiritual life. That is something which is different from morality if one thinks of morality as excluding this sort of dimension, and of course many philosophers have spent a lot of time trying to define morality in terms which do exclude this dimension. I mean these are difficult questions but I think that Plato has meant a great deal to me, but I didn't understand Plato when I was an undergraduate and even when I started to teach Plato at Oxford—I taught Plato and Aristotle for quite a period—I didn't understand him. To pretend to understand him now, is, of course, ridiculous because a great philosopher is never understood in that sense. He is always beyond one in a way. But I feel very close to certain aspects of his thought now and I did write a very short little book about him a while ago.* I think that something to do with the aspiring and religious aspect of Plato's moral philosophy is very congenial to me.

BIGSBY: Is this a sense of reaching for some transcendent reality, reintroducing transcendence?

MURDOCH: Yes, it is to do, if you like, with reintroducing the concept of transcendence, and let me add here, if you don't mind me talking still about this, just to complete the picture, the other philosopher who has travelled with me, certainly since I was an undergraduate, is Kant. I feel again so extremely close to Kant's thoughts and Kant and Plato, of course, are in many ways contradictory to each other, or incompatible with each other. So that this is the sort of philosophical picture as far as I am concerned. My main interest is in moral philosophy and in explaining morality in a philosophical sense which I feel can't be done without the reintroduction of certain concepts which in the recent past have been regarded as metaphysical in some sense which made them impossible.

* See note 3, chap. 7.

BIGSBY: Does that mean that the character of James in *The Sea, The Sea* contains a position or represents a position that in a sense you would endorse?

MURDOCH: Oh no, no. I mean James is a lost soul really and is too mystical. . . .

BIGSBY: Too mystical?

MURDOCH: . . . in a precise sense, that he is pictured as a Buddhist and interested in the magical tradition. I mean he represents—this is a theme that I treat elsewhere in the books—somebody who has in a way sold out to magic. I think he is a spiritual being and as such, of course, he is incomprehensible to his cousin. Nobody understands James in the book, but he lives in a demonic world, he is a demonic figure, and he has got the spirituality of somebody who can do good, but can also do harm.

BIGSBY: So is that the distinction you make elsewhere between fantasy and imagination; he is a fantasist in some way?

MURDOCH: Yes, one could say that. He is a complicated fantasist because he is a religious one. I mean he is not just fantasizing in an ordinary self-centred way, he is somebody who is really hooked on the absolute; he has got a religious passion but he is also in love with the magical aspect of religion which of course is anti-religious. This is one of the paradoxes of religion that it is partly magical, but that in a way magic is the greatest enemy of religion.

BIGSBY: And yet in a sense in that book it is presented very ambiguously, that is the protagonist himself half believes in the magic, in fact half believes that he saw something that was indeed magical.

MURDOCH: Oh, I think that something paranormal happens in the book, but I see no difficulty about that. I think that paranormal things do probably happen, particularly in Tibet. I think that this is just a fact that certain kinds of concentration can produce paranormal powers. The reader has to lend credulity to the writer I think in a quite harmless sense, about pulling him out of that pool and so forth. I mean whether any Tibetan could really do anything like that I really don't know, but I think one should think of it as having actually happened, that is that Charles is not mistaken in thinking that James hauled him out, and James did haul him out.

BIGSBY: By standing on the water?

MURDOCH: Yes, or something, yes.

BIGSBY: You've urged the novel itself as a place where freedom can be exercised, a house for free characters to live in. But isn't the novel in some ways an image of determinism, more even than the play, in that the play is available for some kind of modification which may be quite radical?

MURDOCH: Well, I think that the good artist builds indeterminism into his determinism. Of course in some sense any work of art is a closed object.

BIGSBY: Some are more closed than others.

MURDOCH: Some are more closed than others but if there isn't a closed object there isn't a work of art present, I mean there is a happening or some other kind of emotional disturbance. A work of art has got to have a form, it has got to have notation, it has got to have something which is fixed and authoritative, it must have authority over its victim, or client or whatever you can call the person who is meeting it. This of course is a principle which is now very much disputed and even attacked but in this sense I am an authoritarian. I want the work of art to stand and have authority and be able to endure. Again the notion that it should endure is criticized by many now, and a character in my first novel [Under the Net] raised this question long before it was raised elsewhere. I mean Hugo thought that one should make fireworks because they didn't endure. This was long before Barthes and Co. had ever appeared on the scene. But I don't hold this view; I think the work of art should have a very strong internal structure. This is a problem for every artist to decide how he does this but I think it is a problem he has got to solve artistically. On the other hand, the novel, particularly, is such that within this closed structure you can picture free beings. Look at Shakespeare, Shakespeare is the king of this whole business, I mean he is the king of the novel, he is the greatest writer that ever wrote and if one thinks how those plays combine an extraordinarily strong form with the cohabitation of these characters who are so independent that they were strolling around in real life as it were, they are strolling around in our minds as independent people.

BIGSBY: But where does that freedom come from?

MURDOCH: Well if you are raising the general question of whether any human action is ever free that is [a] different kind of question, isn't it?

BIGSBY: Yes, the reason I raise it is because you talked about free characters and I wondered in what sense they were free and where that freedom derived from.

MURDOCH: Well I am pointing out a distinction with which I think, if you see what I mean, you are bound to agree—I say confidently— that is between people that we think of as great novelists in the nineteenth century—and let's leave aside rubbishy, structuralist criticism of Dickens and so on, I mean I have heard such nonsense talked by structuralists. I'd better not say who this is, but one distinguished person said to me, "I hope to make it impossible for my pupils to read Dickens." Leaving aside nonsense of that sort and thinking in an open-minded way of the great writers of the past, say the nineteenth-century novelists, Shakespeare, one of the things that strikes one is the ability of these writers—say Tolstoy, Dickens, Shakespeare—to create characters who have got such inner strengths that they seem to be self-determined, they don't seem to be determined by the author. Contrast say Lawrence: Lawrence is a great writer and a genius but many of Lawrence's characters are not self-determined people, they are Lawrence-determined people and for this reason I think this is a fair criticism of Lawrence. I mean if you think of *Lady Chatterley's Lover,* for instance, where Mellors is Lawrence and Chatterley is wickedly treated by his author and made to look a figure of fun and so on all for the benefit of Mr Mellors. I think these are faults, these are aesthetic faults in the work. This is not a house of free characters; I mean this is not a novel where these people have any kind of self-determination. Whereas in *War and Peace,* for instance, or in a play by Shakespeare, or in the better plays by Shakespeare, because he didn't always write at his best, the characters are so substantial, they are so imaginatively created, this seems to me to be where the word imagination comes in. This is the work of imagination, to create things which are not just part of one's mind in a narrow sense; they are as if they were separate from one's mind, they are different, they are not projections of me, they are entities on their own and they relate to each other in a free way. Now

Clifford Chatterley is not related to Mellors in a free way; he is related in a way which is entirely determined by Lawrence's cruel and ferocious prejudices.

BIGSBY: But even with Shakespeare they may be the embodiment of abstractions, say of evil, for example, with Iago.

MURDOCH: Well, Iago is an interesting case. If Iago was just an embodiment of evil I think we wouldn't be so interested. But Iago's psychology can be very much argued about. I have heard people in Oxford arguing quite passionately about how one should see Iago. I mean he is so wicked. If you make somebody very wicked I think you do raise difficulties for yourself because I think it is hard to see what might seem to be wanton wickedness as personal. Iago's wickedness is not altogether wanton; I think there is a lot of psychology in it. If you really look at that play, if you really look at all the lines, if you really look at all the things that happen you can make quite an interesting argument about Iago's psychology.

BIGSBY: But you could argue that the characters are trapped within a cosmology.

MURDOCH: You mean the speculations about Shakespeare's religious beliefs and that kind of thing? It is remarkably hard to speculate about actually, isn't it? That is what is so great about Shakespeare. The same is true of Tolstoy at his best; it is very difficult to see exactly what the author is thinking. Shakespeare's plays are extraordinary in that they present a very strong moral world. This has been denied of course by, for instance, eighteenth-century writers who didn't see Shakespeare in this light. But they were wrong. There was a tremendous moral charge in these things. It is morality at its most refined, and at the same time it is not dogmatic, it has got an element of extraordinary openness in it. It gives this amazing atmosphere both of moral judgement and of poetic freedom.

BIGSBY: You talked of yourself just now as an authoritarian but isn't *The Black Prince,* for example, an attempt to work against those authoritarian principles within a work?

MURDOCH: The thing is *The Black Prince* has got its own inbuilt mode of explanation. It is made pretty clear in that book how you should interpret the wanderings and maunderings of a narrator and

where you should believe him and where you should not believe him.
I think this is true. The epilogue is just play. I mean it adds, pretty
clearly, further comments on the characters of the people who were in
the story but I think it is quite clear what you are supposed to think. In
that sense the authority is there. But any novel contains this sort of
mystification where the reader has to move with the author from perhaps a straightforward portrayal of character to a more indirect mode
of narration where the character is giving himself away. I mean obviously any novel contains this device where the character is saying
something which the reader is supposed not to believe.

BIGSBY: So that you have a model of reality which is not problematic? There is a manifest reality which the reader will penetrate?

MURDOCH: Yes, I think so. An author may leave certain things puzzling deliberately. These things are play, just play. Take an example
from a novel I have just finished (this is terribly minor, it is not of the
slightest importance), it just occurs to me as an example, there is a
character who appears at intervals and it is never clear what the sex of
this character is.* If this was a main character this would be important,
but it is a minor character so this is just a joke. Now if somebody said
what sex was the character I can reasonably reply I don't know, in fact
I have an idea what sex this character is but it doesn't matter. As far as
the novel is concerned the character is of indeterminate sex. Jokes like
this are one thing but deliberate and total mystification, a willingness
to hand over the interpretation to the reader, is another thing and
I don't want to do the latter.

BIGSBY: You have written for the theatre as well as writing novels. Do
you find that a play is a less authoritarian form in that it is available for
mediation by directors, actors?

MURDOCH: Yes, I don't want to let them do much. I want to have
authority over them too. Well, I think I am better at writing novels,

---

* It is not clear exactly what Murdoch means here. The last novel to be written before
this interview is *Nuns and Soldiers*, published in 1980, and the first draft of the following novel, *The Philosopher's Pupil*, was not begun until June 1980 (see John Fletcher and
Cheryl Bove, *Iris Murdoch: A Primary and Secondary Annotated Bibliography* [London
and New York: Garland, 1994; new edition forthcoming]). However, no androgynous
character appears in either of these novels.

I know how to write novels now. It took me a long time to learn but in some sense I think I know how to write a novel. I don't know how to write a play and therefore of course it interests me because I like to learn. I think the reasons why people can't write plays are probably quite various. The thing is, in an abstract sense, it would seem that I ought to be able to write a play because I can invent plots and I can write dialogue. Now there is something else of course which a play has which isn't covered by these two headings and that is the thing which I can't get right, and I am not quite sure what it is. I think it is something to do with the structure of the play, though that would come into the question of plot but not altogether, it isn't quite plot, it is something about dramatic structure which I can't do. But the thing challenges me really because it is more like poetry. Now I am a poet manqué. I have been writing verse all my life and I think I have probably written about eight poems, I mean I constantly beaver away writing poetry and trying to get that right. But that is another question, that has nothing to do with the play thing except it is an analogy, that the charm of writing plays is like the charm of writing a poem for me.

BIGSBY: Because you have to condense?

MURDOCH: Yes, because it is a tremendously condensed object, it is a magical object. I mean a novel is a magical object, too, but a play is much more obviously a magical object . . . It is an enchantment, it has got to be a magical object or people aren't going to sit in a theatre three hours. There has got to be some immediate spellbinding quality which is more, in my mind, like writing a poem.

BIGSBY: The theatre seems important to you as an image, as well. I notice that in a number of your novels your characters have a theatrical background which perhaps is offered as a clue to the role-playing that is constantly going on. It is there in *Under the Net* and to some extent *The Black Prince*, and there in *The Sea, The Sea*.

MURDOCH: Yes, but I think it is different in these cases. I think in *Under the Net* it is a play really, it is part of the playful aspect of the book. In *The Sea* it is perhaps more important because that is about *The Tempest* in a way, it is about Prospero and theatre is a great magical thing which you then have to give up and it is about giving up magic. And you see James and Charles are parallel cases of magic.

I mean Charles has spent his life in magic in the theatre; James has spent his life in magic, in religion. They never, of course, understand each other and in a way James's problem can be seen as the same as Charles's. Charles's is an attempt to give up magic, to give up power and of course he doesn't succeed, he just gets himself into a complete mess because he is not a spiritual person. He is not even a particularly good person. He can't get things right. James, I think, has apprehended his own problem about giving up magic, that is that he wants to die, to die well, he wants to release himself from the wheel. But I think that he is deeply afraid that he has enmeshed himself too deeply in the magical side of religion. And then of course he has to do this thing for Charles which involves summoning all his magical power at a moment when he wanted to get rid of it. On the other hand, and this I think is a deep thing in the book, which no critic will ever see, but I will tell it to you, in a way I think James could be thought of as having saved himself because he goes on in the book, he says things to Charles, about how in order to be liberated you mustn't have any emotional attachments. Now the deep thing of course is that James has always been in love with Charles and this he more or less says at one point (and again nobody notices this kind of work in a book) and this is what is worrying James. This is why he comes to see Charles and say goodbye in a friendly way, as it were. Then this thing happens where he has to save him and James—this isn't displayed I think in the book—he may have thought I really am done for because I have enmeshed myself again in this affection. But I think that the action itself sets James free, that having done this thing—remember he is very exhausted afterwards— I think he realizes that somehow or other the magic itself has broken its own spell or that he is going to be let off. This isn't a particularly Buddhist idea but one could imagine. . . .

BIGSBY: It sounds more Christian.

MURDOCH: It sounds more Christian in a way but I think that at any rate one should picture James as having escaped from the spells, that when he is sitting there dead and smiling he actually has escaped, and that he won't be in *bardo* being tormented by the demon.* I think this

* *Bardo* is a reference to states of being intermediary between this world and Nirvana, as described in the *Tibetan Book of the Dead*.

is a terrible image of the nemesis of living a life of tormented anxiety and demonic imagining that this would go on. *Hamlet* picks up this idea: "in this sleep of death what dreams may come, when we have shuffled off this mortal coil." This could be one's fate but I think that James escapes from that. And I think, incidentally, while we are talking about this book, one or two people wrote to me saying well of course James wasn't really dead was he? He really was in Tibet or something. No, I don't think one should think that. Now what were we talking about before I started off on this particular line? Oh, yes, roles, the theatre and role-playing. I don't believe I do think that people are constantly playing roles like that.

BIGSBY: But they are trapped in fictions. Charles is trapped in his own fictions.

MURDOCH: Oh yes, people are trapped in fictions. I think I would rather talk of this in terms of art rather than of theatre because theatre is just one kind of art and for me the role idea doesn't do very much. That is, as far as theatre comes into the novel it plays a different role in different books. Again you ask a philosophical question, you asked one earlier about the freedom of the will and now you ask one about the basis of morals.

BIGSBY: You seem to equate moral sense with common sense. Is there a natural morality, which is instinctively perceived?

MURDOCH: Well this is where this Kant-Plato contrast comes out. I don't think anybody knows the answer to this question really. Kant's moral philosophy rests on the idea of recognition of duty and the notion that this is a rational thing, that it is something which everybody can do, and that the unconditional nature of duty is something which is self-evident to every rational being, in fact to every human being if they are not mad or something. I am inclined to think this. This, of course, is a very unpopular view now; all kinds of ethical relativism are popular. So this would be a kind of common-sense idea and I think in a non-philosophical way some of the people in my books want to say this, that it is perfectly obvious what you want to do and if you fudge around and say well it is all very complicated and so on you are evading something. And, of course, the desire to evade what is obviously one's duty is a very deep human thing, I mean one is always being caught by this desire to evade something which in a way you also think is obvious because even the mind is so divided against itself. And this would be another Kantian image of the mind, absolutely divided against itself. This would be one way of looking at morality and one which would involve a metaphysical assumption, in a sense. I mean Kant's moral philosophy is metaphysical in that particular sense, it is one way of being metaphysical. You see another image which attracts me and which is rather different is a sort of platonic image, the notion that the good is very, very far away and that, this would be more of a religious picture, one's task is to transform oneself, to discard selfishness and to undergo a very long process of conversion.

BIGSBY: That is the process of any of your books in fact isn't it, discarding?

MURDOCH: Yes, though nobody in my books ever gets anywhere really, or gets very far with the process. It is extremely difficult, there aren't any saintly people—there is only one, to speak of another book—there is only one real saint as it were, or symbolic good religious figure in the books and that is Tallis, in *A Fairly Honourable Defeat*. This would be an image which isn't common sense but rather a religious image, that one has got to change oneself very fundamentally. It is an original sin kind of image, too, the notion that one is almost irredeemably selfish and must try to do something about it. Philosophically speaking these may be incompatible views, but I don't think really they are in ordinary life, and this is how we live. We live by these conceptions we have and in moral arguments you do come to these points where something is self-evident to one person and not to another. And it is very difficult to produce reasons. If you think about this ghastly business of the hostages and so on, I mean there are things which seem to us self-evident, such as that you can't treat people like this, it is contrary to some natural law to do so. . . .*

BIGSBY: But doesn't that acknowledge that in some way values are culturally derived?

MURDOCH: Well of course they are culturally derived. You see one has to say all these things in a context. It is rather like the argument of

---

* This is a reference to the holding of American diplomats in the U.S. embassy in Iran from 1979–1981.

freedom of the will in that one has to admit that, for instance, now a great many things which people do are excused because we know the psychological background to them which makes us regard them no longer as responsible actions. All the time one is balancing what one can find out about history and the human mind and all these things, these factual things, one is balancing these against these other factors which are to do with things which seem self-evident, with natural law, with a conception of human nature, with certain religious ideas, and so on. This is the human condition, there isn't any alternative to this as far as I can see. One is always fiddling around with these different elements both in philosophy, of course, and also in real life, which is much more important than philosophy.

BIGSBY: Doesn't this approach presuppose a continuous self, a self which is not subject to discontinuities, disjunctions?

MURDOCH: Don't we assume this?

BIGSBY: Well, I am asking you if you assume that to be so?

MURDOCH: Yes, I do. Again, problems arise about responsibility. "I wasn't myself when I did it" could be something you said in a law court and somebody would let you off because you showed what you meant by this, that you were under the influence of drugs, or that you were tremendously under the influence of another person and so on. I mean these are things that we fiddle around with. In making a moral judgement you have to take into consideration a lot of things. A particular case is so particular. This is why novels are interesting objects; they explain particular cases in very great detail.

BIGSBY: But your sense of an absolute responsibility of the individual suggests that you haven't drifted very far away from existentialism.

MURDOCH: Oh, no. There are different kinds of existentialism but Sartrean existentialism, which is the kind I know most about, separates the individual so much from his context and from any sort of moral framework which is independent of his will that it either makes his responsibility absolute or it abolishes it. One could look at it either way. I never thought that it was a satisfactory notion to say each person invents his own values. There is some sense in the idea in some contexts but we enter a world where there are things which we discover and these things are discovered, not invented. It may be very hard to say what one means by the word discover, and this is where all these problems about transcendence and so on come in. This is very deep water, but I think the Sartrean picture is so simple and in so many ways seems to be so unrealistic and I think, morally wrong. You see one is also making moral judgements on philosophy. One rejects a philosophy because it seems to advocate things which one's own moral sense will not accept. I think that existentialism does advocate a sort of irresponsible self-centred kind of luciferian attitude to the world. It can also of course be useful as corrective against what Sartre called *mauvaise foi.* I mean Sartre is so—the same is true of Roland Barthes, incidentally— Sartre is so anxious to abolish bourgeois sanctimonious taking for grantedness of certain values and so on that he wants to suggest that everybody has always simply invented values. You see the word bourgeois crops up again in Barthes and I think it would be best to abolish the word bourgeois from this argument because it raises other problems—and to talk about people who just accept certain conventions which suit them and never criticize them. Such persons should be stirred up and made to realize that they don't have to believe these things; they choose to believe them, they ought to criticize what they are doing instinctively. But I don't think that this suggests the only possible philosophical image, that of somebody who is simply inventing his values, because discovery about the world is very closely connected with the evolution of the moral person and I think the word discovery is very much in place here. One is just not inventing it out of oneself, one is finding it out for instance by observing other people, and from art and from all sorts of sources.

BIGSBY: In "Against Dryness" you rejected a particular model of liberalism but urged the creation of another kind which was a post-Kantean, unromantic liberalism with different images of freedom.* Isn't that actually in a sense a description of your own work? Would you accept the label liberal?

MURDOCH: Yes, I mean "yes" very roughly answers the question. I am not sure now, I can't remember that essay very much, it was a long time ago and I am not so sure that I'd put it like that now. I think it is

---

* Murdoch, "Against Dryness."

very important that politics has got a complicated relationship to personal morality; they are not absolutely hand in glove, these systems as such. Most obviously, of course, it depends how you see personal morality, but looking at personal morality as I would look at it, I don't think this is far from what people actually believe anyway; there is nothing very eccentric about it. There is some very absolute demand which is made upon one in personal morality, that one has to think this thing out in one's own heart and there is a moral demand which won't go away, which is always there. This is what Kant would say, what Plato would say, and, I think, what the chap in the street would say, actually, if he hadn't been corrupted by some pseudo-philosophy.

BIGSBY: But not what one of the writers whom you admire would say: Samuel Beckett?

MURDOCH: I admire Beckett less than I used to, I confess, perhaps we will come to that in a minute. But politics has got to be a different game because governments are fighting for their own people and if a head of state gave up fighting for his own people and said I am going to fight for mankind so I don't care what happens to our fisheries policy, or whatever it might be, then he would be rightly told to go away. I think politics has got a built-in ruthlessness, an individualism, which is unavoidable and which does clash with certain moral views and this is one of these paradoxes. This is why liberalism is always in a fix because liberalism wants to combine the most high-minded sort of morality with a political ideal and this is absolutely OK in certain areas of thought; for instance, I would think, in everything to do with freedom and human rights. This is the glory of liberalism in that it puts this thing absolutely in the centre and makes it one of the compulsory aspects of any political policy. But also there are all these problems about what it is possible to achieve and whether you should cooperate with a state which has a wicked policy. It is all very well to say that Americans should never have cooperated with the Shah (the Shah incidentally was at least amenable to influence and change and so on—the regime improved, it was better about women for instance). Countries do have to support sometimes a wicked regime out of reasons of self-interest, and out of the kind of complicated reasoning that goes into politics. So that liberalism is a complicated creed in this sense and this thing that I said, about inventing a post-Kantean unromantic liberalism, I don't know how I thought this could be done. But to talk about literature for a moment, I think that I felt at the time that probably we had had enough of the romantic hero in the existentialist sense. I think part of this was directed against the existentialist romantic hero, the kind of rather dreary chap who is against society, who is a rebel and who is a solitary chap inventing his values every day and so on. He is rather idolized by certain kinds of literature and I think I was fed up with that hero and I don't like that hero, and I don't want him in my books. He might be said to be in the first novel and not in the next, I am not sure. But at any rate if that is a literary comment then it is about the existentialist hero.

BIGSBY: Does this mean that you see literature as having primarily a moral function?

MURDOCH: No, its function is art, forget about morality, its function is to be good art. This will of course involve morality absolutely one hundred per cent. If you are writing novels, you can't avoid morality. But if you are making a pot or something I can't see how morality comes into that.

BIGSBY: So a novel excluding a moral world is an impossibility?

MURDOCH: Well I think people have tried to write such novels, but I think the artist has got to decide this. I think his first duty is to his art and I think it probably is possible to write novels which exclude a moral world but this, in an odd way, can't help having a moral dimension, what you exclude. What are you thinking of for instance here, have you got any examples in mind, Beckett for instance?

BIGSBY: Or Robbe-Grillet.

MURDOCH: I don't think Robbe-Grillet excludes a moral world. I don't know, the only one that I have read lately, well I have only read two of his novels, I read *La jalousie,* which I admired, and I read *Les gommes* which I thought was a stunningly good novel. I mean somebody who wanted to make an exercise in literary criticism could try comparing it with *Edwin Drood.* It is totally different and yet not utterly different. *Edwin Drood,* of course, has a tremendous moral thing and evil and so on; the Robbe-Grillet thing has got morality in it actually but I can't think of an image here. It is like a picture where the things are made by very, very fine lines which you could hardly see; it looks as if the lines are doing something else, they are delineating something else when in fact they are actually delineating this thing so that morality is there in this book. He couldn't do it you see if there wasn't a moral background; the detective story wouldn't exist. I mean it is about the failure of the detective and then there is the suggestion, I don't know whether this is poor mystification, I couldn't understand this, or whether if one worked hard enough at it one would see what it meant, there was an implication of a connection of the detective with the story which isn't manifest. Somebody who is murdered is connected with him in a way which doesn't appear. This is a frightfully good novel but the thing is it's the background of conventional morality which gives it its force. I mean it is absolutely electric with power, that book, but if you thought that the whole world was totally non-moral it wouldn't be interesting. You wouldn't be interested if somebody had been murdered for instance. Morality arises in the judgement of the reader on this work. . . .

BIGSBY: So it is moral because the reader exists in a moral world?

MURDOCH: Well it is moral because the writer exists in a moral world. If he uses his artistic ingenuity to deny this then the denial is of interest but it is of moral interest. I mean he can't escape from morality. It is a big thing to say that he can't escape from morality, but I don't think that is the mode of escape. There are people who recognize non-moral demands. You may say that Camus tried to do this but the force of Camus's book is that his hero of course is living in a world where people's moral responses are ordinary. All right you may say well let's have no ordinary people, let's just have these persons who are portrayed in terms of momentary figments, with no sense of continuity. Well I would think this would seem to be a morally eccentric person that is being portrayed, perhaps a morally wicked person or at any rate a morally unrealistic person, and the interest of this would be the moral judgement and I don't think that this would be just the reader's reaction. This would be something which the writer couldn't avoid delineating even negatively by what he writes. That is, what is he denying? Is it that he wants to deny something which other people want to assert? I think there could be a kind of poetic stuff, and I think Beckett sometimes comes close to this, which is sort of hygienically demoralized as it were, and if it is poetic enough . . . I think that *Watt* might be thought of in this way. I don't like Beckett's later stuff, I have read some of the French stuff and I don't think this is very good.

BIGSBY: Are you talking about his prose or his drama?

MURDOCH: Prose. Drama is different, drama has got to be magic anyway and I have only seen *Waiting for Godot* and I think that works very well as theatre. The French stuff seemed to me to be rambling and just not good enough, just not bloody good enough, to do what he was trying to do, it wasn't poetic enough. I thought, and I think he should have gone on writing in English. I think he pays a penalty there. But if one takes *Murphy,* that is really an ordinary novel, an ordinary romantic novel written by some sort of very remarkable writer and very funny writer. The interest of it is partly the touchingness of the girl, the touchingness of the old man, the kite flying. Murphy's own character has got a sort of charm about it and one feels a kind of mixture of pity and exasperation in relation to him. And then, of course, the funniness which is frightfully important. *Watt* I think is an odd case; I haven't read *Watt* lately but if you are looking for an example of a novel which has really given up the ordinary world and yet still tells a story, I think it is possible there, partly because of a kind of metaphysical philosophical game which he plays in the book. I wouldn't deny that it is possible to do something like this. I don't think it is necessarily worth doing. I think it is frightfully difficult but I think certain curious geniuses would be drawn to it and I think that Beckett can write frightfully well. I don't think this is anything to do with what literature is about or anything of that sort.

BIGSBY: Why is story important to you?

MURDOCH: Well it is important to everybody. I am just an ordinary human being. I like stories, we all like stories. It would need a lot of explanation to suggest why there shouldn't be a story. I happen to like plots and also I think a novelist ought to have a plot. If he weakens his plot he has got to have something else. That is just an aesthetic judgement. I think plot is a very important part of novels and if one produces a lot of marvellous characters and a very shadowy plot, then OK jolly good luck. I think the average novel needs both plot and character, plot and character help each other along.

BIGSBY: A number of your protagonists are themselves plotters, that is to say they create coercive fictions, and that is true of *The Sea, The Sea,* which has a man who has an image of the world and then forces other people actually to inhabit those fictions and play them out.

MURDOCH: Yes, I think that is something which human beings do. This is an aspect of power which interests me. People force rules on other people and the other people like it. This is the important aspect of it very often that people want to admire somebody, people elect somebody to be their king and a group of people—I mean I have seen this happen quite a number of times—that somebody gets a kind of inflated reputation, they are given the role which they then play. For instance everybody is afraid of so and so or so and so is dictatorial and he suddenly says "Look you have got to come and see me tomorrow" and you come however inconvenient it is. And people like this, they like to be bullied by some kind of quasi-fiction which they set going in their own environment.

BIGSBY: Do you see any connection between the coercive plotters in the novel and yourself as a coercive plotter, a writer of fictions?

MURDOCH: No, because it is quite different. I mean what the people in the novel are doing is working out their fantasy life in terms of some sort of pattern which suits them and I very much hope that I am not doing that. Of course any writer is tempted to—art comes out of the unconscious mind and there are bound to be personal obsessions and images which are around the place. If there isn't any force from the unconscious you haven't got a work of art so that the force is something you must thank the Gods for if it is there. The rational intellect is also involved. I have got no shortage of the stuff from the unconscious; it is rather a matter of sorting it out and preventing it from following patterns which it wants to follow. So the intellect comes in very much to prevent it, say, from being too coercive, to prevent the plot from being coerced by unconscious forces.

BIGSBY: On the other hand, if it makes sense to talk like this, there is an element of coercion over the characters. You were talking earlier about Lawrence as, in effect, a coercer of his own characters. That presumably is a risk.

MURDOCH: Yes, I think every novelist runs this risk and one hopes not to do it. I think some of my earlier novels do this. I hope I have improved; one likes to think this. Lots of people sometimes madden me by saying I thought *Under the Net* was quite your best novel, and of course it is not good news to a novelist. I hope I don't do this. I think perhaps I was unfair to Nan in *The Sandcastle*. I coerced Nan. And this is perfectly clear, it would have been a far better novel if I had spent more imaginative time detaching Nan from the story and not letting her just play the part of this rather tiresome wife but making her somebody with quite extraordinary ideas of her own, playing some quite different game perhaps, having some dream life of her own which is quite different from that of the other characters. This would have been an obvious way to mend this novel and make it better. I think that one has just got to watch out and not to do this, not to belittle characters for instance.

BIGSBY: But you could, quite apart from characters, say that there is a kind of totalitarian element in art in that it commands the imagination and the attention of others. Without doing that it couldn't exist.

MURDOCH: Yes, it couldn't. If it didn't attract attention and maintain attention people wouldn't enjoy art. One terrible speculation about the future is that people will stop enjoying art, partly because they will be sitting looking at television all the time, partly because artists will destroy themselves. They are destroying themselves in front of our eyes, painters are destroying themselves, writers are destroying themselves.

BIGSBY: In what sense?

MURDOCH: Well they are stopping making authoritative objects; their desire to do it is weakening. I have noticed this with young people.

BIGSBY: That was the point in a sense I was getting at, that they are afraid of that totalitarian element in art because they are afraid of it in society.

MURDOCH: Well yes, totalitarianism is a nasty word, of course. Authoritarian is now a rather nasty word too but the old-fashioned art object, as it now perhaps begins to look from some points of view, is a creation of a strong mental impression of some sort, something that has got form and this form is art. Without some kind of strong form there isn't an art object present. If the reader or observer can do anything he likes with the thing then one result, of course, is that he becomes bored, he doesn't want to have it there. This is why in the Tate Gallery you have had these pictures which are just bland pieces of paint which for some reason are revered and people have paid money for. This is a degradation of art and it is a contemptible sort of thing which people support and respect and daren't say anything against.

BIGSBY: I suspect that one of the reasons why people claim the significance of *Under the Net* is that it anticipated a number of things that subsequently became fashionable, that are fashionable now, post-modern doubts about the status of language, for example.

MURDOCH: Oh, yes, all the stuff that Barthes and Co. think they invented. I knew all about that in the 1930s.

BIGSBY: However, I am interested in that because Hugo says language is a machine for making falsehoods and it seems to me that elsewhere in your work there is a kind of suspicion of articulateness, that is your articulate characters are often the most egotistical characters.

MURDOCH: Yes, well the anti-art artist occurs here and there because he is an interesting figure. Bledyard is an anti-art artist in *The Sandcastle*. But this in my world is complicated by the emergence of religion as the competing factor, not anything social, not anything personal, but something religious. For, sometimes, for some people the religious claim runs counter to the artistic claim and counter to the claim of artistic form—like Charles giving up the theatre, giving up the world. Religious form is different from artistic form, and a certain sacrifice is involved. The idea of being a great artist I think is a great moral idea but it needn't present itself so to everybody. The anti-art artist is an interesting figure to me because he becomes in the later novels a religious figure. I mean Tallis is a religious figure. Tallis of course is nothing to do with art, that is a religious allegory incidentally, *A Fairly Honourable Defeat*, and Julius King is the devil in person. Tallis is a high incarnation. It doesn't matter if nobody sees this but it is there, it is very much there in the dialogue actually if you look at it carefully. Julius doesn't at first see that Tallis is a high spiritual figure, he just sees him as a fool, then he suddenly recognizes that he is up against his own adversary here. Whereas Tallis recognizes Julius at once and this conflict then happens and even a sympathy between them because they are both spiritual beings in the middle of a non-spiritual world. Here in the figure of Tallis there is the religious thing which is nothing to do with art at all. Julius is an artist, he is a mathematician and he is interested in art, and he is an aesthetic figure, whereas Tallis is an absolutely non-aesthetic figure. This conflict just brings in this business about the status of art.

BIGSBY: But there is, is there, that suspicion in your work of articulateness? I mean at another stage you say, or one of your characters in *The Black Prince* says, that being is acting, what redeems us is that speech is divine. So that on one hand speech is falsehood; on the other hand speech is a kind of redemptive force.

MURDOCH: Yes, what interesting remarks I sometimes make. OK I suppose that means that speech is falsehood and art is falsehood and yet there is a religious way, as it were, to the divine which rests in these things. And one might ask the question is there any other way? I think there is another way in the sort of Tallis sense, in the sense that people who are simple, who are outside this refined business, are in the game of helping other human beings. But for people who have got mixed up in art very deeply, I think that this can be a kind of temptation to them, a moral difficulty.

BIGSBY: You commented on the tendency of art to console, in a sense a dangerous tendency, but isn't that exactly the function of your own novels, don't they move towards a kind of conciliatory resolution, a sense of balance at the end?

MURDOCH: Oh, I think art consoles, I don't see why not. The thing is to console without telling lies. One tries to be truthful—I think the word truth is very important here—art must be connected with truth in some sense a truthful picture. Of course it is art, it is complicated, it is full of mystifications and it's funny, which I think is very important about the novel, it should never be forgotten. A novel is a comic form. A novel which isn't at all comic is a great danger, aesthetically speaking that is. It is very difficult to do this without losing something absolutely essential. If one thinks of the great novels, you may remember the tragic parts but my God how comic, for instance, Dostoevsky is, frightfully funny, how funny Tolstoy is too. But of course one is creating a work of art here and that has got its dangers. You have got to keep some sense of truth in the centre of the thing. Then you are also creating something which people will really like in some way. I am very pleased if people read my books and think what a good story, I want to know what is going to happen without bothering about any of the intellectual refinements which might be there, or the other things which might be there. I think to be consoled by art is absolutely OK. In a way it is the highest consolation, good art is the highest consolation—well it is not the highest, I think things to do with human love are the highest consolations—but it can be so high, that good consolation. It is not like watching television, it is different, it is high consolation, and that's all right.

11

RUTH PITCHFORD

Iris Murdoch—Set to Music

This interview was first published in *Western Mail* on 12 September 1980.

Iris Murdoch [. . .] has written her first libretto—for the Welsh National Opera's latest production, The Servants, *to be premiered on Monday. She has been watching rehearsals at the New Theatre, Cardiff, and Ruth Pitchford went to meet her there.*

It cannot have looked or sounded too bad in rehearsal. Iris Murdoch is already talking of writing another opera with Welsh composer William Mathias; and she had a little smile every time the voices of the chorus penetrated the floorboards of the upstairs office at the New Theatre, Cardiff, from the stage beneath.

She is clearly excited about *The Servants,* a first opera for both her and Professor Mathias. She always fancied the idea of turning her original stage play, *The Servants and the Snow,* into an opera, and even wrote to Benjamin Britten, suggesting a collaboration. He gave a polite refusal and she gave up—until Professor Mathias heard the play on radio and wrote asking if he might set it to music. "I accepted by return of post. I was absolutely thrilled," she said. Benjamin Britten's reply did not offend her at all: she realised that, for the composer, choosing a suitable libretto was a personal matter. "Opera is a very intense art, very obsessive," she said.

William Mathias saw musical possibilities for her story at once, and she is confident that what he has added more than makes up for the fact that she has had to cut her play by half. She confessed that when Professor Mathias presented her with a pile of opera libretti, she was disconcerted to discover that her three-hour favourites were based on slim texts. But the cuts she had to make came easily enough—a subplot went, and one of the characters—Mickey, the servant boy who had a speaking part in the play, has been rendered mute in the opera; and the whole text was condensed. In return came music, to heighten the story's dramatic intensity, and—to her delight—WNO's chorus.

Her play is set c. 1900 in a Central European mansion where the abuses of a corrupted feudal system live on in the relationships between master and servants. It is crucial to make the audience aware of the powerful and potentially menacing force of the army of servants—"yet the servants hardly had anything to say in the play," she explained. "I'd have liked to have a chorus then, but you're lucky if you can have six or seven people in theatre, because of the cost. It was one of the difficulties of the stage play, because you didn't really believe there were 100 servants in the house. Now you have only to hear the chorus singing, and you immediately have a sense of drama. William Mathias has a dramatist's sense of theatre. If he weren't a composer, I'm sure he could be a playwright."

In this case, he had some highly dramatic material to work with—murder, marriage, sex, seduction, religion and superstition. But the play is also an allegory with strong political implications. The old master was a tyrant, the new master is a liberal. Can he free his servants—from old guilts, as well as from semi-slavery—without sparking a revolution that can lead only to renewed tyranny?

"It's about why a lot of people will follow an individual leader; about the difficulties of having a free society, about the difficulties of liberating a society. [. . .] It's about the preciousness of democracy—how you have to accept an imperfect society if you want to be free."

What about the snow, which may have disappeared from the title of the 'Thirties condensed libretto, but which still rates some evidently symbolic references in the text?

"It's a symbol of historical necessity," she said. The servants and master are trapped by the snow as they are by the past. "In the same way you can't change your nationality—at least, individuals can, but a nation can't. It's not so much trapped as contained by history."

Abstract notions of sovereignty are common currency for a professional philosopher, who still writes papers for the appropriate journals and lectures occasionally. But she insists that she is concerned with the practical politics and is not just playing with ideas. "I'm deeply concerned about political freedom and how it's going to survive—about Russia and Chile. In Britain we live in a little oasis of political freedom." Her own party affiliations put her somewhere on Labour's right wing—"I was a member, when I was a student, of the Communist Party, but I gave that up pretty quickly." She now contributes to *Index,* a periodical published by an international pressure group of artists and writers in support of dissident intellectuals, though she says she is no activist.

[. . .] Her life has not all been sheltered and academic. She finished her degree—Oxford, first-class honours—in 1942 and was allowed 10 days grace before starting war work in London. "I wanted to be a scholar. I wanted to go on learning," she said. "About eight years of my life went into war work, during which I had no time to write." Between work five-and-a-half days a week and bombing raids at night, "one was tired all the time. I didn't have time to read or reflect. One lived in the middle of death and destruction for a very long time. A lot of people I loved disappeared."

[. . .] She gives her *Who's Who* recreation as "learning languages," but these days admits only to good French, Latin and Greek, which she studied for her first degree, some German and Italian, and "moderate" Spanish and Russian. "I love grammar. I like reading grammar books," she said.

[. . .] Now aged 61, there is no sign of her running out of ideas, just the problem of fitting everything in. "I would like to run quite a few lives in parallel. I'd like to do more philosophy, but I can't stop writing novels." Anyway, it is as a novelist that she wants to be remembered. "Art is wonderful—philosophy is a strange business. Sometimes I wonder if I can do it at all," she said. She is equally modest about her abilities as a playwright, and has written more drama than she has had published or performed. "I can make a dramatic story, or write a dramatic dialogue, but that doesn't mean I can write a play," she said.

Even so, she intends to persevere with theatre. She would like to try her hand at a musical next. As for more opera, "I'd love to. Just bring me the composers."

12

JOHN HAFFENDEN

John Haffenden Talks to Iris Murdoch

John Haffenden is professor of English literature at the University of Sheffield and Fellow of the Royal Society of Literature and the English Association. This interview was published in the *Literary Review* in April 1983 and in *Novelists in Interview*, edited by John Haffenden (London and New York: Methuen, 1985).

John Haffenden interviewed [Iris Murdoch] in London, and began by asking about her latest novel—her twenty-first—*The Philosopher's Pupil*, which is published by Chatto and Windus this month.

HAFFENDEN: *The Philosopher's Pupil* is a powerful story of a dark obsession and love, riveting reading. It's the first novel in which you've placed a philosopher at the centre, almost as if you are outfacing critics who have labelled you a philosophical novelist.

MURDOCH: This novel really has more to do with a pupil-teacher relationship, which I've been involved in all my life—in both roles. I think it's interesting and moving, and I made the character a philosopher because it came along with the package, as it were. I am writing philosophy at the moment, but of course in *The Philosopher's Pupil* the character talks philosophy *en passant* rather than as part of the story.

HAFFENDEN: And yet the character, John Robert Rozanov, has covered something of the same ground as your own work in philosophy, including Platonism. . . .

MURDOCH: In a very rough way, yes, but that's not particularly significant.

HAFFENDEN: You didn't intend the novel to be an indictment of a certain kind of philosophy?

MURDOCH: Yes, but I think philosophy is a subject which does lead some people to despair, it's much too difficult for the human mind. If you are an ancient historian or a linguist there is always something you can be doing which is part of your job, but if you're not doing philosophy pretty well you're not doing it at all.

HAFFENDEN: Do you mean that philosophy requires a rigorously disciplined mind, a mind which can live with the knowledge that the ultimate quest of moral philosophy—for the good, that is—can never be completed?

MURDOCH: It is impossible to do moral philosophy without asserting values of your own, and—as you say—virtue is unattainable. It's a very deep subject and can't help being a metaphysical subject, and that's what interests me most.

HAFFENDEN: There's one passage in the novel which may be very difficult for the reader who hasn't followed your earlier work, and that's when the philosopher has his first long and crucial conversation with Father Bernard, who suffers his own doubts.

MURDOCH: Yes, I think that conversation is important. It's about real issues, but of course it is very inconclusive. It's important in relation to the characters, or else I wouldn't have it as part of the story.

HAFFENDEN: John Robert can be seen as a kind of Prospero figure who attempts to dominate and to decide the destiny of other characters—particular[ly] of Hattie and Tom, who are hopeful innocents—while the flailing and angry George, his former pupil, takes the part of Caliban. I wonder to what extent you deliberately assumed *The Tempest* as the myth of the novel?

MURDOCH: I've always got *The Tempest* in my head, just as I had in *The Sea, The Sea:* the idea of giving up magic, the relation between religion and power, and so on. John Robert is a power figure, he can't help exercising power. I don't think too much weight should be put on the notion that the book is about the nature of philosophy: it's about the nature of power in human relations. The teacher is a powerful and potentially destructive person. Of course Rozanov acts wrongly towards George. He should let George off, be nice to him, and become a bit less absolute; but a certain kind of philosophical mind is very absolute in relation to philosophy. This could spill over into real life, as it were, the feeling that you must have perfect truth and never fudge things. John Robert hates messy and emotional situations. George behaves in exactly the way to enrage him, which is what George partly wants: he wants the emotional drama which will make a bond between them.

HAFFENDEN: George is looking for salvation from the mess of his own life, and so he constructs for himself the myth that John Robert should be his redeemer.

MURDOCH: He's been obsessed and dominated by this man: it's a love relationship of a special kind.

HAFFENDEN: The question of whether or not George did actually try to kill his wife, Stella, is never actually answered, is it?

MURDOCH: It's an extreme fit of rage (and he's had plenty of such fits before), and it comes up when Stella mentions John Robert. It happens again later, as the narrator points out, when George thinks he's about to go off with his mistress, Diane, and he asks Stella what she is going to do. She says that she might go and see John Robert, and that remark sets off another frenzy.

HAFFENDEN: I know that you write at least two drafts of each novel. Can you explain how you set about writing this novel?

MURDOCH: The drafts come after I've finished the novel. The invention is what's difficult; everything is over, as it were, when I've finished inventing it, because I invent it in such enormous detail. So that the drafts come at a fairly late stage of the proceeding.

HAFFENDEN: Before you actually start writing you have set out for yourself every character and incident?

MURDOCH: Yes. It's all very strongly related, they all come into being with a kind of necessity in relation to each other.

HAFFENDEN: There seems to be a slight structural problem with the role of Stella, George's wife, who has to be removed from much of the action in order that George himself should become the focus of attention. His private and public turbulence requires him to be set apart from his wife, and the reader may be rather sceptically surprised to discover that Stella has in fact been harboured by N.

MURDOCH: Yes, I think Stella is not a very successful character. I never solved the problem of Stella. She had to be put off the stage for a while, and it occurred to me later on that she was with N.

HAFFENDEN: Did you have a real spa in mind in creating the town of Ennistone?

MURDOCH: No, it's entirely fictional, and inventing it gave me great pleasure.

HAFFENDEN: But the Baths do reflect your own passion for water.

MURDOCH: Yes, there is water in all the books. Thinking of the background of the drowning of John Robert, one image printed on my mind is from a film I saw a hundred years ago, *Les enfants du paradis,* where there is a murder in a swimming bath (though the character in the film is not drowned but shot, I think). When I was in China I visited a bath establishment, which also struck my imagination, and in Iceland I have been in warm pools where it is a great joy to swim on a cold day. I do love swimming. I used to be absolutely fearless in the sea, but I nearly drowned once, and I'm now much more cautious. I used to think the sea and I were great friends, but one must fear the sea.

HAFFENDEN: I know you have felt the strain between determining the form of a novel and allowing the characters to have an open and contingent life of their own.

MURDOCH: The determined form I'm frightened of is certainly not anybody else's form. It has nothing to do with being dominated by Shakespeare or anyone else; it has to do with being dominated by myself and by my own mythology, which is very strong. The book is very scattered, and has a lot of people in it, and that's good. I think there are a great number of points of serious interest, and I hope the characters exist in their own right.

HAFFENDEN: The question of self-expression is relevant here, I think, in the sense that the novelist may have an absorbing interest in other human beings or use the novel as a forum for his own personal concerns and obsessions.

MURDOCH: It begins from an interest in human beings, but any writer is inevitably going to work with his own anxieties and desires. If the book is any good it has got to have in it the fire of a personal unconscious mind.

HAFFENDEN: Which of your anxieties and desires came into this book, do you think? Is it to do with the tension between philosophy and art?

MURDOCH: No, I don't feel any such tension. The only tension involved there is that both pursuits take up time. This book has much more to do with power—being isolated by power, and John Robert's misuse of power—together with the despair of the philosophy. The anguish of the philosopher comes about because philosophy touches impossibility. I think it's something all philosophers feel. I'm sure Plato and Kant felt it, that you can't get it right. It's impossible for the human mind to dominate the things which haunt it. There's the impossibility of being good, and the way in which the human being is doomed to be bad and even evil, and the impossibility of stating the basis of everything. Kant and Plato, my personal gods, come near to doing this: their god-like minds make these patterns, but that isn't quite right either, since one can't really do it.

HAFFENDEN: Is the philosopher seeking power?

MURDOCH: Yes, you want to be god, you want to see the whole thing.

HAFFENDEN: Is there a sense in which writing novels is therefore a relaxation for you?

MURDOCH: No, writing novels is my job, and it's a serious undertaking. I always wanted to be a novelist, but there was a time when I thought I wanted to be an archaeologist and art historian, when I was at Oxford. I couldn't go on with the art history because I was conscripted as soon as I left Oxford; I was working in a Government office, the Treasury, just ten days after I took Schools. My path took me away from the academic world, but then I was taken over by the desire to be a philosopher by the end of the War. I would very much like to have been a Renaissance art historian, and at one time I wanted to be a painter. I think I would have been a moderate painter if I had given my life to it, but that is an absolute hypothesis, without any basis to it! I do sometimes try to paint, but I haven't got any training. So this is just a dream life. I envy painters, I think they are happy people. The painter lives with his craft the whole time: the visual world, which I adore, is always present, and the artist can always be thinking about his work, being inspired by light and so on. Painters can have a nice time.

HAFFENDEN: Do you have a nice time writing novels?

MURDOCH: Yes, I very much enjoy writing novels, but the beginning of a novel is a time of awful torment, when you're dealing with a lot of dead pieces and you have to wait and wait for some kind of animation.

HAFFENDEN: Writing is also terribly solitary, and prevents you from observing and being with other people.

MURDOCH: That's what sometimes makes me want to write for the theatre: you can have company! I very much enjoyed being a teacher, and I enjoyed college life. But I don't cooperate with anybody in writing novels.

HAFFENDEN: You mean you don't discuss your work in progress with anybody, not even with your husband?

MURDOCH: No, he reads the novels only when they're absolutely finished.

HAFFENDEN: Do you think you've been influenced by his work as a critic?

MURDOCH: I don't think I've been influenced as a novelist by him, but obviously if you live with someone for many years your mind and his mind become very closely connected. But he doesn't do any sort of critical job on the novels.

HAFFENDEN: How did you get on with your parents?

MURDOCH: Perfectly. I'm an only child, and I lived in a perfect trinity of love. It made me expect that, in a way, everything is going to be like that, since it was a very deep harmony.

My darling mother, who is still alive, had a marvellous soprano voice—Dublin, as you know, is a great singing city—but she got married when she was eighteen, which was silly of her from the point of view of a possible career! She had a professional teacher in Dublin, and then again when we moved to London.

My father was an extremely good and clever man, and we used to discuss books when I was very young, the *Alice* books and so on. He comes from County Down and grew up in a sheep-farming family. His family were admirable people, but Protestants of a very strict kind, and I think he wanted to get away. He joined a territorial unit just before the war, and went through the entire First World War in the cavalry, which saved his life. Although the cavalry did many dangerous things they weren't in that awful holocaust of the trenches. When he wasn't in France his unit was stationed at the Curragh, and one day in Dublin when he was going to Church on a tram he met this beautiful girl who was going to the same church. She was singing in the choir. So that was that; they got married and he removed her to London where he joined the civil service. My father was a very good civil servant; he started at a low level and rose to the top. We settled down in London— where we knew nobody—and I grew up as a Londoner, and it's only lately that I've imagined how strange that was. I never had any family apart from this perfect trinity, and I scarcely know my Irish relations. I feel as I grow older that we were wanderers, and I've only recently realised that I'm a kind of exile, a displaced person. I identify with exiles.

HAFFENDEN: Your work in the United Nations Relief and Rehabilitation Administration at the end of the war must have been quite harrowing?

MURDOCH: Yes, it was extraordinary. It was concerned with displaced persons, lots of Yugoslavs and Poles, every sort of person who had to be identified and looked after. A number of them, particularly Yugoslavs, didn't want to go back to their homeland. It was absolutely front-line stuff, and much of the time one was simply preoccupied with feeding people.

HAFFENDEN: What impressions are you left with from that time? Is it mostly a sense of hassle and anxiety?

MURDOCH: Yes, chaos, and the sadness of the old people. I did help some younger people to come to England. But in general the problem was so enormous that one couldn't do much, other than feeding them and being nice to them. There was an utter breakdown of society. At least it was instructive to witness that.

HAFFENDEN: One of the interesting aspects of your novels is that you often depict characters—such as Hilary Burde in *A Word Child*, and Charles Arrowby in *The Sea, The Sea*, who are repressed or in some way fixated by their past lives, by certain events or situations they cannot escape.

MURDOCH: It's a salient thing in human life, one of the most general features of human beings, that they may be dominated by remorse or by some plan of their lives which may have gone wrong. I think it's one of the things that prevents people from being good. Why are people not good, and why, without being evil or even having bad intentions, do they do bad things? Schopenhauer, whom I admire, is good on this topic of tragedy. Some people who are not bad find themselves so situated that they are unable to stop themselves from doing the greatest possible harm they can to others. It's an evident feature of human psychology that people have secret dream lives. The secrecy of people is very interesting, and the novelist is overcoming the secrecy and attempting to understand. Readers sometimes say to me that I portray odd characters; but the secret thoughts and obsessions and fantasies of others would amaze one, only people don't tell them, partly because they're ashamed and partly because secrecy is very natural and proper.

HAFFENDEN: I think you've remarked elsewhere on the inadequacies of psychoanalysis.

MURDOCH: Yes, but not in any theoretical way. It's not as if I've studied Freud and found him wanting, though I have read a lot of Freud. I love reading Freud, because one gets all sorts of ideas from him, and he's a great and interesting thinker. But one effect of psychoanalysis is to make you concentrate enormously on yourself, to think too much about yourself, whereas the best cure for misery is to help somebody else. I think analysis can help people as a sort of first-aid. The analyst is in a sense a blunt instrument, and he can work as somebody who cares, and I think a good analyst makes the patient feel that he has value. People can easily feel that their value is lost or blackened, and the analyst can fulfil a priestly role in making them feel there is hope. I don't think the theoretical stuff quite explains what the analyst is doing, but a good analyst knows that the theory is something suggestive and perhaps helpful to him. What is really happening is a very private and emotional thing, a relationship between two individuals of a secret kind.

HAFFENDEN: Do you have any qualms about the fact that as a novelist you are revealing secrets?

MURDOCH: I reveal other people's secrets, not mine, except in the sense that any artist reveals himself to some extent in his work. But it's the secrets of my fictional characters that I'm giving away.

HAFFENDEN: Do you think you reveal your theoretical if not your personal preoccupations?

MURDOCH: My theoretical preoccupations don't come in much. They sometimes come in through the characters, who might want to discuss certain things in a theoretical way. Putting in too much theorising is an obvious danger, but it's not a temptation I especially feel. One could paralyse a book by putting in a lot of theoretical stuff. But knowing things is vital for a novelist. Cleverness and thought and understanding a lot of things are a great benefit.

HAFFENDEN: What areas of Freud's work do you think valuable?

MURDOCH: Well, there's a bit of deep truth in certain things like the notion of the *superego* and the *id*. What I agree with in Freud is what he frankly says he's pinched from Plato. The doctrine of *anamnesis* is a doctrine of the unconscious mind, and the idea of *eros* as fundamental energy, a drive which includes sex and which can be good and can be bad: that's all in Plato.

HAFFENDEN: I wonder what you think of Freud's explanations of dreams? After all, Freud himself writes packaged stories, solved and shaped. . . .

MURDOCH: I think dreams have a great many sorts of explanation. Once the Freud virus has, as it were, got into you, you keep on looking at things in that way. But surely there's a lot of pure accident in dreams. One has kinds of obsessions and fears that can't be given a sexual meaning. I think the inventiveness and details of dreams are amazing.

HAFFENDEN: Do you ever record your own dreams?

MURDOCH: I sometimes do. One invents amazing things in dreams which one couldn't invent in real life. One cure for insomnia is to make yourself dream. I usually sleep extremely well, but if ever I find myself waking I invent a dream, which starts off consciously and goes on unconsciously.

HAFFENDEN: Can you give me an example?

MURDOCH: I don't think I will.

HAFFENDEN: You have written that it's always a good question to ask a philosopher what he's afraid of, and I would like to ask that question of you.*

---

* "It is always a significant question to ask about any philosopher: what is he afraid of?"(Iris Murdoch, "On 'God' and 'Good,'" in *Existentialists and Mystics*, 359).

MURDOCH: I think I'm afraid of somehow finding out that it doesn't really matter how you behave, that morality is just a superficial phenomenon. I don't think one could find this out, it's just a bogey; the impossibility of finding it out is very deep in moral philosophy. I don't believe in God, but I think morality is fundamental to human life.

HAFFENDEN: In *The Philosopher's Pupil,* of course, John Robert determines on the possibility of passing beyond good and evil.

MURDOCH: Yes, he's interested in this question, and George tags on to it.

HAFFENDEN: What do you say to critics who think you take a dismal view of marital love and of fulfilment?

MURDOCH: Well, of course, a novel is a drama, and dramas happen when there is trouble. A completely harmonious life might not produce the drama. But the books are full of happiness; I feel they are shining with happiness. In spite of the fact that people have a bad time—this is true of the novel in a general way—the novel is a comic form.

HAFFENDEN: But comedy can be a consequence of form, which might be illustrating the risible divisions between people's self-images and what they find themselves doing.

MURDOCH: I'm not mocking my characters. The comedy is very deep in the form. The vitality and energy of art make you happy whatever its subject matter. In *The Philosopher's Pupil* Hattie and Tom are radiant and happy people: they have the sort of energy that destines them for happiness, and I think that's true of Emma too. But one tends to be impressed by the people who are demonic.

HAFFENDEN: Yes, you've said elsewhere that demonic characters have a sort of "illegitimate charm."

MURDOCH: That's true in life as well. To dramatise your life and to feel that you have a destiny represents a very general human temptation. It's a magical element in life which is so dangerous, and which is the enemy of religion and the enemy of goodness. I think one identifies with the demonic characters in books, since it's a deep notion to feel that the devil tempts you and gives you power in return for giving up goodness, which is after all often dull.

HAFFENDEN: I imagine you feel dubious about imposing form on the novel for both artistic and ethical reasons, in that form might become a libel on real life?

MURDOCH: A strong form tends to narrow the characters. I felt it particularly about *A Severed Head,* which was the end of a certain road, because a strong mythology can issue in a mechanical and unsurprising sort of writing. Good writing is full of surprises and novelties, moving in a direction you don't expect. The idea of the myth and the form have got to be present, but one has brutally to stop the form determining the emotion of the book by working in the opposite direction, by making something happen which doesn't belong to the world of the magic.

HAFFENDEN: But when you first map your characters and plot you may in a sense be pre-empting the contingent openness of it.

MURDOCH: No, because that has to be invented too, the way in which one destroys or blocks the myth. I am very conscious of this tension at the start, and I play it to and fro.

HAFFENDEN: You have written that Art is the "great *clue* to morals."* I assume you feel that there must be some educational or even didactic thrust to the novel, whereas some theorists believe that the novel can be no more than conjectural play.

MURDOCH: Yes, there is a sort of pedagogue in my novels. I think a novelist should be truthful. Bad novels project various personal daydreams—the daydream of power, for example, or of being fearfully sexually attractive and so on—and this can be horrid. But the contingent nature of life and what human failings are like, and also what it's like for somebody to be good: all this is very difficult, and it's where truthfulness comes in, to stop yourself from telling something which is a lie.

HAFFENDEN: And yet it might seem presumptuous for a novelist to aspire to truth-telling, when there are so many ingredients and variables in a novel, including characterisation, pattern of events, myth, as well as ethics.

MURDOCH: All these are mixed up. A bad painter is lying because he hasn't really *looked*—in the way that Rembrandt has looked. Truth and justice are involved here, because the artist has to have a just judgement. I think it's not presumptuous; it's a humble occupation if it's

---

* Murdoch, "On 'God' and 'Good,'" 352–54.

pursued properly. But then, you see, one is also carried away by the *eros* of the thing. Truth and happiness are ideally frolicking together, so that it is a happy destiny when it's working well. Works of art make you happy. Even *King Lear* makes you happy, and yet it comes near to the edge of the impossible—that you could be made happy by a work of art which is about something terrible.

HAFFENDEN: Your good characters—Tallis in *A Fairly Honourable Defeat,* or those who aspire to good behaviour like the Count and Anne in *Nuns and Soldiers*—can turn out to be ineffectual people, moral touchstones which verge on the symbolic. A virtuous character acts in a disinterested way and therefore, as you suggested earlier, can become uninteresting.

MURDOCH: Yes, that's the paradox. But Tallis is allegorical, he is suppose[d] to be a sort of Christ figure and is recognised as such by his arch-enemy, Julius. Tallis is a symbolic character; it's his job, as it were, to be good. You tend to think that a good character is not strong, but Tallis is strong. The Count, on the other hand, is an innocent and noble character; he's not exactly a good character in any strict sense, but then good characters in a strict sense are not met with in ordinary life.

HAFFENDEN: I want to ask you about your evidently deep response to Simone Weil. . . .

MURDOCH: Yes, I love her.

HAFFENDEN: . . . mainly because it might be thought that her prescription for a kind of hopeless waiting (which is involved in the concept of *amor fati*) could be regarded as life-denying.

MURDOCH: Not at all. It requires the most enormous spiritual energy to decreate yourself in this sort of way. Ordinary life is a kind of dreamy drifting, defending yourself all the time, pushing other people out of the way. I think things like meditation and prayer help you to grasp the unreality of ordinary states of mind. I don't like the idea of *amor fati,* which seems to be the opposite of what I think. Simone Weil does sometimes use the term *amor fati*—which I connect with stoicism, a doctrine I don't at all embrace—but I think her notion of obedience is rather to be understood as breaking the current of the ordinary egotistical life and feeling as if you might as well be anything. I am very much against Jung, who is the enemy here. I think you realise your contingency when you break this current, and not that you have a great sense of destiny—because you don't *know* the myth, you don't know what's happening. It's rather that you relate yourself to your surroundings in a different way, and you relate yourself to other people in a selfless way. It's an exercise in self-denial.

HAFFENDEN: Does this connect with your interest in Buddhism, which has the idea that at death you should feel both fulfilled and mortified?

MURDOCH: It seems to me that some kind of Christian Buddhism would make a satisfactory religion because of course I can't get away from Christ, who travels with me; I was a Christian as a child. But I don't believe in the supernatural aspects of Christianity. Buddhism is a good picture of the thing—not, of course, its mythical ideas about reincarnation, but that the aim is to destroy the ego. Schopenhauer plays with this idea, that one's task in life is to be aware of the world without the ego. It's not at all an other-worldly religion, it's absolutely this-worldly, here and now: this is where it's all happening and there isn't anywhere else. But to deny the ego is the most difficult thing of all. It would be a condition of goodness when you then respond to your surroundings in an appropriate way because you are not blind. Painting is an image of the spiritual life; the painter really sees, and the veil is taken away. You see the world in a much more clarified way, which would be at its most important where one is thinking about other people, because they are the most difficult and complicated things you ever come across. I think people who are good—it sounds romantic, but I think I've met one or two—make a sort of space around them, and you feel you are safe with them. And there are certainly people who are menacing, who breathe up all the air so that you can't breathe, and who diminish you. This is why a good analyst would have to have this quality of making a large space—someone who is reassuring without bolstering up in an illegitimate way, because the good person also comes to one as a judge. Buddhism has very much to do with understanding these things about human life, together with the notion that it is absolutely important. I want there to be religion on this planet.

HAFFENDEN: But what is worrying is Buddhism's radical ruling that all existence is ultimately evil, and should perhaps be annihilated.

MURDOCH: It depends on how you understand this. I think Nirvana should be taken as a mythical idea; there couldn't be such a thing as entering nothingness. Nirvana means that the selfish world is as nothing to the spiritual, and vice versa. Sophisticated Buddhism is very conscious of conceptual limitations, that these myths are saying something which has to be understood in another way. The total obliteration of your present being would mean that the world would exist and not you. This is an idea that Simone Weil expresses—that you want the world and God to be alone together and to remove yourself—and it makes sense to me. I think that in this sense death is happening all the time, and not that one soldiers on through life and then there's something terribly special at the end, which seems to me to be an old-fashioned religious mythical idea.

HAFFENDEN: Some critics have felt that you have a very limited view of the human capacity for improvement.

MURDOCH: I think anybody would have it if they looked around. Perhaps one can improve a little bit, but egoism is so fearfully strong and so natural. One is demanding something which goes contrary to nature if one thinks of attaining goodness, or even of improving oneself markedly. Do you know anyone who has improved themselves much?

HAFFENDEN: Yet it does seem that there is a sort of sub-text in some of your novels, positing an impersonal love which is impossible—quite beyond human happiness, niceness, decency, sexual love. . . .

MURDOCH: Yes, I think one is haunted by this idea. How far it can change one's life is another matter, but I think it's worth having it there. That's why I feel much closer to Christianity now than when I was younger. If you are fortunate to have Christ in your life, it's something you should hold on to.

HAFFENDEN: What do you think is the true function of art? Is it consolation, education, pure pleasure?

MURDOCH: The phrase you've used—pure pleasure—is good, I think. One should live with good art and not get addicted to bad art, which is demoralising and disappointing. Good art is a pleasure which is uncontaminated, it's happiness. One also learns a lot from art: how to look at the world and to understand it; it makes everything far more interesting. It's a mode of reflection, and this is why it's a terrible crime for totalitarian states to interfere with artists. Artists must be left alone, the critics must leave them alone too. I think artists are often in the situation of being bullied by critics, which is monstrous. Artists are essentially free individuals. Art is a great hall of reflection, and that's why it's important from a political point of view that there would be a free art, because art is a place where all sorts of free reflection goes on. It's a mode of thought, a mode of knowledge. Good art can't help teaching you things, but it mustn't aim at teaching. The artist's task is to make good works of art. A novel is a mode of explanation; you can't help explaining characters and scrutinising their motives. The novelist is the judge of these people—that can't help emerging—and it is more difficult for the novelist to be a just judge. In the traditional novel, which is what I'm talking about, the novelist is *ipso facto* revealing his own morality, and he should be doing so.

13

WILLIAM SLAYMAKER

An Interview with Iris Murdoch

William Slaymaker is professor of English at Wayne State College, Nebraska. This interview was first published in *Papers on Language and Literature* 21, no. 4 (1985).

The following interview took place at Iris Murdoch's home in Steeple Aston, Oxford, England, on 18 July 1983. The questions put to her center on the concepts of freedom she has developed in her essays and fiction. Prior to the interview, Murdoch had read my article on the aesthetics of freedom in her fiction published in Papers on Language and Literature *18 (1982): 166–180. The occasion for the interview was our mutual attempt to clarify my interpretation of her views of freedom. In the interview, Murdoch emphasized the more positive aspects of and prospects for human freedom and argued that good people, regardless of their political or social disposition, could attain freedom in some measure. Subsequent to the interview recorded on 18 July, Murdoch read and emended the transcript. The interview below includes (silently) her additions and emendations made in the spring of 1984. [. . .]—W. S.*

SLAYMAKER: Would you still agree with the statement I made in the article I sent you that by the 1970s your growing skepticism had developed into a belief in the severe limitations of human freedom?

MURDOCH: You suggest that I am more of a skeptic than I was, which is in itself an ambiguous idea. I am more interested in religion than

I used to be, and more concerned about religious belief, and this might suggest a move away from skepticism. I am skeptical about "freedom" in general, but this isn't only recently. I was never an existentialist.

SLAYMAKER: You never were an existentialist?

MURDOCH: I was interested in existentialism, but I never held those extreme beliefs about human freedom. I think that my view of human freedom has changed, but it isn't that I think it is narrower exactly. I would interpret it differently, that is, I would connect freedom with knowledge and with the ability to discipline emotion and to love and to live in some more disciplined and better way; I would think this was freedom. And given that this is difficult, then freedom is difficult.

SLAYMAKER: It certainly is. Along with this idea of existentialism, it is interesting that you said what you just did, because in your interview with W. K. Rose in 1968 [q.v.] you said that freedom was once your main subject, but now love is. You kind of amplified that. It was a move from an existentialist to a platonist point of view. Would you not agree this move has made your view of human behavior more deterministic, that is, conditioned by love and searches for it and usually in vain?

MURDOCH: Well, not deterministic, no. I never was a follower of Sartre or of any other existentialist in any kind of dogmatic detail. Certainly, I wouldn't picture the matter in terms of determinism as a theory versus freedom as a theory. I don't think there is such a thing as a deterministic theory. It's an idea that people have, that you can extend scientific ideas of causality throughout the whole area of human thought and conduct. I think this is just a shadowy notion. It is fundamentally unclear. It's something people want to believe in; they want to believe that determinism is a threat to freedom as if there were a contest between total freedom and total determinism. This is a wrong picture; freedom is often identified with casting off of bonds, with emotional unrestraint, with various kinds of unbridled conduct which I would regard as a wrong view. Freedom is rather concerned with self-control, with just understanding, with the liberation of the person from irresponsible motives. This is a very complicated operation, so that determinism appears as a rather shadowy way of describing a whole area of human conduct where we either cannot explain or do not approve of the way in which people behave.

SLAYMAKER: Is that what you mean when you use the words "they want," "people want"? You talked about emotions that are some kind of inward emotional compulsion to want freedom to be this kind of rebellion.

MURDOCH: Yes, I think so. Young people often like to have an image of total freedom as if there were some kind of ideal limit, that you toss off this bond and that bond and then there is a series which leads you on to total freedom. This is an illusion.

SLAYMAKER: Where does this urge come from? I mean, you say young people. Anybody has this urge; isn't this natural?

MURDOCH: There are many causes for such urges, just as there are many kinds of captivity. This problem about freedom and unfreedom is, of course, confused by problems about political freedom as opposed to or as contrasted with intellectual, emotional or spiritual freedom. Of course, if the law prevents you from publishing your book, you are unfree, and if you can get the law changed, then you are free. There's an important political concept of the image of freedom as a barrier which you overthrow; but I imagine we are now speaking about the human soul, and about what conception of freedom one would want to hold in the context of people wanting to live better lives or to be able to control their own destiny in a rational or good way, as opposed to being slaves of immediate impulses or selfish desires. I am not a Freudian. I don't hold any "scientific" view about the structure of the soul. But there are certain obvious ways in which human beings do lose their freedom through neurosis or obsession; and it seems to me to be part of a good life that you become more free through self-knowledge and through being able to get out of yourself and really see things which are outside you.

SLAYMAKER: Speaking of things outside yourself, do you conceive then that freedom is mainly a consolation of aesthetics that is an attention to details in life and art worthy of contemplation? Is freedom mainly a consolation of an aesthetic enterprise, paying attention to life as an artist, paying attention to art as an artist, and contemplating it? Is that the best kind of freedom?

MURDOCH: Well no, I mean if you say "mainly," no. This is one aspect of freedom. I think that art is good for people. Good art is good for people because it takes them away from themselves, and enables them to see many aspects of human life in detail, and all kinds of particular things, instead of being trapped inside their own fantasy, which is one of the opposites of freedom. But all sorts of people who have never heard of art can be free. I mean there are all kinds of routes to liberation, and in this sense I would connect it with goodness through loving people and through doing a good job in a family, or in any sort of context where you have to become just. One introduces all sorts of other concepts here, like being just and reasonable and seeing that the world doesn't consist of one's own wishes and one's narrow ideas. It's an enlarging and purifying of one's ideas. Art is one route, I think, but it's only one.

SLAYMAKER: Now is this one route equal to others? For example, are the levels of freedom whether you are a worker in a factory and trying to be just to your family or you're a genius trying to do something genial, are these equal as two different levels or paths to freedom?

MURDOCH: Well, I wouldn't like to say. I think just that some individuals succeed better than other individuals and they are better than others.

SLAYMAKER: The reason I am asking these questions is because it seemed to me the gist of many of the things that you said and what you show in your novels is that those who strive for liberation through contemplation of art, though they rarely are successful, are at least doing, are committing themselves to a liberating act which a person working in a factory or in everyday life probably cannot do and probably does not do either through art or other means. Now is that unfair?

MURDOCH: Yes, I think it is. We can picture liberation through art. We can also understand why Plato was suspicious of art, because art is a great place of illusion and magic as well as a place of liberation. I think people are liberated in many ways, for instance through human relation, or all kinds of work or through religious beliefs, if they hold any.

SLAYMAKER: How do we get liberated through religious beliefs? Liberated from what?

MURDOCH: Liberation from selfish passion and neurosis and cruelty and egoism and so on. I don't believe in God. I believe in religion in some other sense, but that's not what I'm concerned with here. People who, for instance, are like the people you were speaking of earlier on who have the image of Christ before them, or anybody who has a religious aspiration of any clear kind, or who prays, has got a method, as it were, of curtailing their immediate resentment or envy or jealousy or desire for revenge, all these things which arise up naturally in the human soul, these bad things. They have got some way of saying "stop." I think that religion is very important in this way, that it gives people another picture of the world which isn't materialistic, which isn't to do with advancement and which negates envy and anger. I think that the Poles are very lucky to have Roman Catholicism in their midst which gives them a completely different world view from that of Communism.

SLAYMAKER: Would you not then agree more strongly today with your contention in 1956 in the *Proceedings of the Aristotelian Society* that freedom is a mode of reflection, rather than a power for decisive choices, since you are talking about religion, and it is a method of contemplation, a mode of reflection. Freedom is more that than really the power to decisively choose.*

MURDOCH: Yes, I would agree.

SLAYMAKER: Isn't it true, as you state in 1961 in your article "Against Dryness," that the idea of freedom deforms our moral faculties such that we fantasize a freedom which does not exist when we see freedom as a kind of power, more than just a mode of reflection, when we see it as a kind of fantasy that lets us decisively do an act?

MURDOCH: Yes, but I'm not sure where the quotation ends!

SLAYMAKER: Let me rephrase this. Simply what I mean is that I was trying to link these two, and it seems that you are saying that freedom can be very delusive, or it can be a fantasy of decisive choices, but really what you are saying you want it to be is a more quiet, contemplative type of exercise of self-introspection.

MURDOCH: I think intelligent, just reflection is more important than the notion that in any given situation you can impose your will on the scene. Freedom is always mixed up with work, with study, with deeper understanding, with purification, with knowledge, as when you decide

---

* Iris Murdoch, "Vision and Choice in Morality," in *Existentialists and Mystics,* 76–98.

to study a subject seriously instead of trying to get by without doing any serious thinking. That kind of contrast. Freedom is to do with understanding and work, whatever the work may be. It's to do with how you work, in any situation, doing housework for instance. Freedom is something that acts deeply in the mode in which you live in your hour to hour consciousness. An ideal freedom is connected with goodness and virtue, and this is something which is a function of every minute of your life; how you work it, how you live it. The contrast roughly would be with somebody who is always obsessed, always thinking "Why did that have to happen?," always filled with vain remorse or resentment. There is a place for guilt and remorse, but there is an awful lot of vain remorse and a sort of stupid guilt which people feel when they think, "I've been unjustly treated," and so on. It's all right to think that sometimes, but not to go on and on thinking it and dreaming of revenge. This is what I mean is the opposite of freedom; instead of trying to work well, to do something constructive, to undo what is wrong, or to learn something, or to enjoy something good or to be friendly and to help people. That's freedom.

SLAYMAKER: Earlier I asked the question whether freedom is really a natural urge and you thought it was. This last question had to do with the word fantasy. Now what is the essence—we can't define it, I know—but when we try to put a finger on the essence of freedom, is it a true natural psychical urge, or is it a fantasy that we have that deludes us?

MURDOCH: This is a kind of distinction I wouldn't want to pick up. Freedom as a natural urge is a very ambiguous idea. I mean, here again, the difference between political freedom and spiritual freedom comes in. It is a natural urge to want to do what you want, to want not to be controlled, not to be subject to laws and so on, and this has been much discussed by political philosophers. In the liberal tradition they generally feel that in a political situation, on the whole, a people should be allowed to do what they want unless it interferes with other people; and there are various other "unlesses"—unless the interests of the state, justly considered, mean they ought not to be allowed to do what they want. This, then, would picture freedom in a political contest as a simple urge, that of "I want to do what I want to do" without going into whether it's right or just "in itself." Spiritual freedom, I think one would have to regard as rather more complex because the original urges are very often bad ones. I mean one has an original urge to get revenge.

SLAYMAKER: I don't know what that has to do with freedom.

MURDOCH: Well, I think it has very much to do with freedom. I would regard somebody whose whole life is given over to a desire for revenge as being unfree. The idea of being a slave to one's passions is a fairly familiar one. I think that in a spiritual sense freedom is liberation from certain urges and desires; it's a discipline of the desires; it's a direction of desire toward better things. This is a moralistic definition of freedom. But I think it is important to distinguish between a political definition of freedom which isn't to do with having good desires, and a spiritual definition which is to do with having good desires.

SLAYMAKER: Mainly, I'm not interested in the political. I am most interested in a definition of freedom that deals with the metaphysical rather than the physical that we have to deal with every day, the political situation.

MURDOCH: Part of one's thought about it is, though this is difficult in a way, that the free man is happier—which of course Plato and other philosophers have urged upon us—than the person who is the slave of mean desires. I mean, people torment themselves—this is obvious, one needs merely to look around to see this happening—by unworthy or irrational desires: envy, jealousy, and so on, frustrated ambition. I would think of "true freedom" as being liberated from these desires, and having desires that are higher, like desires to help people or desires connected with great art or love of nature or one's work, trying to see one's work as something really creative, whatever it might be. This of course is a metaphysical view of freedom, but it is also familiar in ordinary usage.

SLAYMAKER: Do you not make a negative statement about the possibility of freedom in your art when you use so frequently mythical, mystical and magical forces as artistic explanations of human inability to choose and act? For example, Greek explanatory models of human behavior like Ate, Nemesis, the Furies, frenzy, blindness, revelations and epiphanies of Christian spiritual sorts, or natural forces that deal

with love or powers of delusion or confusion cast by others or ourselves. So, it is a complex question. Essentially, don't these mythical,
mystical and magical forces indicate a lack of power of the human
being to exercise his or her freedom?

MURDOCH: One would have to look at the particular novels and the
particular ways in which these things come in, which are pretty various
as far as I can remember. But in general I would think that the fundamental picture in my novels is of a battle between magic and freedom
or between magic and goodness. This may be put as the contrast
between the artist and the saint; the way in which the artist uses magic
and the saint has given up magic is a continuous theme.

SLAYMAKER: So you are saying to give up magic is freedom.

MURDOCH: Well, yes, but you see you're asking for some very general statement! In fact, the way in which magic comes into the novels
is a function of context. Sometimes it is something taken seriously by a
person; sometimes it's a joke; sometimes it's an image, a way of life like
being in the theater, as contrasted with something else. One would
have to look at the particular context. Just speaking generally, I would
regard magic as a lower condition; one has to beware of magic. Religion has always been dogged by magic and been degraded by magic.

SLAYMAKER: In a Freudian model, then, it seems that the power of
the ego is the most important part of the uncontrollable machinery of
the human psyche. Is it not true that most of your characters have
undisciplined or undisciplinable egos? Are not all your fictional characters at the mercy of egotistical fantasies?

MURDOCH: Yes, but they ought not to be, ought they? They are rep-
resentations of persons who are imperfect. I certainly don't hold the
Freudian view that the object of life is to have a satisfactory arrangement settled upon the ego. I think that Freud was a great and wonderful discoverer; though, as he himself said, Plato made the discovery
first, in his picture of anamnesis, the unconscious mind, the deep, dark
part of the soul which on Freud's view can be good and can be bad,
from which ambiguous powers emerge. But the notion that the aim of
life is to keep the superego and the unconscious under control and
center things in the ego seems to me to be wrong; it is a wrong image.
The strife between the unconscious and the magical forces and the

higher forces is much more complicated, and ordinary mediocre egoism is just one of the things to be overcome.

SLAYMAKER: The title of such a book as *Under the Net*—I wonder whether that means Aeschylean nets. One critic, Elizabeth Dipple, suggests Wittgensteinian language nets.

MURDOCH: It's an obvious image for the understanding of particulars. There was a paper of mine that appeared in the *Aristotelian Society* which talked about how one constantly desires to get "under the net" of language toward the thing itself, the difficulty or perhaps impossibility or problematic nature of this idea.*

SLAYMAKER: Other novels like *The Sacred and Profane Love Machine* which suggest some kind of mechanism of erotic behavior; *The Flight from the Enchanter* which suggests some kind of supernatural or uncontrollable powers; *Accidental Man,* something like the wheel of fortune in chance; or *The Black Prince,* demonic power of love and fascination; all these titles suggest that man is beset with powers that he cannot control or can only partially control. Would you agree with this? It's a kind of final question that freedom is an ideal that we all search for, but we just cannot possibly realize it because of all these various different kinds of forces that the titles of your novels suggest.

MURDOCH: Yes, I think freedom is extremely difficult. I would connect it with ideas like sanctity or moral perfection, things which you cannot get, but which are ideal goals which are very important in human life.

SLAYMAKER: So, it's kind of like the platonic city. You try to behold it. Whether it actually exists or not, no matter. You believe in it, and it will exist for the believer.

* Iris Murdoch, "Nostalgia for the Particular," in *Existentialists and Mystics,* 43–58 (first published in *The Proceedings of the Aristotelian Society* 52 [1952]: 243–60).

14

SIMON PRICE

Iris Murdoch: An Interview with Simon Price

Simon Price is a lecturer on ancient history at Oxford University. This interview was first published in *Omnibus* in March 1984.

Iris Murdoch once experienced a miracle at Delphi, the eerie home of Apollo. One evening in the hotel, which is right over the ravine, a huge winged beetle kept crashing around inside the dining room, to the consternation of some of the guests. The waiters flapped their napkins at it, attempting to kill it. "So I willed it to come to *me* and it came and it landed on me just *here* (on her chest), and I took it outside and released it." But did she really will it, or was she, like the Pythia, Apollo's priestess, possessed by the power of Apollo? Is Apollo benign or malevolent? That this anecdote could seriously prompt such questions in my mind is a sign of Iris Murdoch's captivating personal manner. It also indicates the power which the ancient world has for a leading modern novelist. Wanting to avoid obvious questions about her novels, I tried to structure our conversation around her study and teaching of the classics, leading up to one of her best novels.

Our conversation began with her schooldays. She went to Badminton School in Bristol, a good, progressive girls' boarding school which expected its pupils to be sort of universal people. Two of the subjects which she studied were Latin and Greek, which helped to instill in her a lasting love of languages.

"I like languages very much, I like grammar, I like reading a grammar, I dabble in various languages. But I think that to know Latin and

Greek is a very great felicity for one in so many ways and I was always very happy as a schoolchild to find this treasure house of another world."

We agreed that Latin in particular helped in learning other modern languages, but Iris Murdoch also felt that Latin helped with English prose style.

"We were also taught English grammar at school but I know that a lot of schools now not only don't teach Latin but don't teach English grammar either. But Latin gave me a kind of pleasure in grammar and in the construction of sentences and so on which I think improves the instinctive construction of sentences in English.

"I do in fact feel anxious about English prose style and the ordinary use of prose. I don't know whether you saw John Carey's article in one of the Sunday papers reviewing the prose of three political party manifestoes. What he quoted was absolutely abysmal. It really frightened one to think that in these very serious political statements they couldn't write English . . . I think that unless people write lucid prose and there's some standard of what clarity in prose is the whole area of thought becomes fuzzy.

"I think that knowing several languages is very helpful to thinking and to writing, apart from being very enjoyable. To be able to read poetry in several languages is a great joy. Poetry in one language can inspire poetry in another language. If one thinks how much Horace, for instance, has inspired English poets one can see exactly why."

"Which other languages do you enjoy reading?"

"Well, Greek, though my Greek isn't by any means as good as my Latin, but I read Homer still, in Greek, with help from a crib, and find immense pleasure in that. It's alas true that it's very difficult to translate poets from one language to another and translations of Homer are very different from Homer. The tragedians I find so many difficulties in that I don't read them very much for pleasure; I sometimes look at parts that I know anyway."

She then mentioned that she could read poetry with varying degrees of ease in French, German, Italian, Spanish and Russian and that the great lure about learning a language was to be able to read the poetry.

"And do you still read Latin. Horace, perhaps?"

"Yes, I read Horace, but in a selfish kind of way; I read bits of Virgil from time to time. I write poetry myself in a very modest fashion and I find that I feel a great affinity with Horace, and also with Catullus, but particularly with Horace. It somehow or other spurs one on. And I have done translations of a few things, but mainly I read it just for fun and to make me write poetry myself.

"And Homer particularly belongs to the whole deep area of my imagination. One assimilates a great poet. I'm not meaning that I'm in any sense a scholar, I'm not; but one's imagination can take on aspects of a poet's great vision."

"Do you turn to the Iliad *and the* Odyssey *equally?"*

"Well, I like the *Iliad* better than the *Odyssey,* but of course there are parts of the *Odyssey* which one has known since childhood. Before I started to know any Greek I knew about Odysseus' adventures and they are indelible. But I feel very much closer to the *Iliad.*"

"Achilles, I suppose, is the key character."

"I'm very attached to Achilles and Patroclus, yes. I think my two favourite characters in literature are Achilles and Mr Knightley in *Emma.* Perhaps that represents two sides of one's character, or something, but I find that I identify with both of them."

We then reverted to the question of language learning.

"I very much used to enjoy doing proses. I miss that. I recall the enormous pleasure I got in writing particularly Latin prose and Latin verse. I was never very good at verses but the task of constructing these things is very pleasing. I'm afraid that my style was rather Tacitean when I was an undergraduate."

*"I was wondering whether you were Golden or Silver."**

"I think that I was wrong. I'm very fond of Cicero and I think that he's a better stylist than Tacitus and one should model oneself on Cicero and not on Tacitus. (A point of some interest in connection with her own rich prose style.) But Tacitus is very tempting to young persons, for obvious reasons I suppose, because of the opportunity for witticisms and tricks."

---

* According to the *Oxford English Dictionary,* 2nd ed., the term "golden age" is "often applied to the finest period of Latin literature (Cicero to Ovid), in contrast to the 'silver age' which succeeded."

"From Bristol you came to Oxford to read classics."
"Yes, during the war (1938–1942), when one worried about one's
exams and the fate of England. I wish my Greek had been better. I was
always in a state of great anxiety. I used to go to Eduard Fraenkel's
classes, the great *Agamemnon* class which went on for years and years.
(Fraenkel was Professor of Latin.) Ken Dover was sitting next to me
and you can imagine how nervous I felt. I was terrified that I'd be
asked a question which would show that I'd made a grammatical mistake in understanding a passage, instead of going into deep matters
straight away as Dover did. However, I got by and I learned an enormous amount from that class and not just about the *Agamemnon*, but
about Greek, about literature and poetry and all kinds of things. I saw
quite a lot of Fraenkel and he was a marvellous teacher, a wonderful
man."*

Iris Murdoch was also very interested in classical art history. She did
a lot of archaeology at Oxford and wanted to go on with it. Indeed,
Beazley, the Professor of Classical Archaeology, took her on as a personal pupil. [. . .]

But philosophy which she had done as part of her classics course
also fascinated her and provided her with an initial career. [. . .]

She has published two interesting philosophical works which are in
open debate with Plato, *The Sovereignty of Good* (1970) and *The Fire
and the Sun* (1977), the second arguing against Plato's denigration of
art as against philosophy.

"I wasn't a Platonist at all when I was an undergraduate. I didn't
really discover Plato until much later. I think Plato was just not very
well taught. He was regarded as a fantasist, or some sort of poetical fellow."

"A spinner of myths," I interjected, in the hope of drawing her out.

"Somebody who was teaching philosophy in Oxford actually said to
me, 'Of course, there's nothing much about moral philosophy in Plato,
is there?,' which is, considering that Plato invented moral philosophy
and we're still living in the shadow of his thought, a pretty fantastic way

* See Bayley, *Elegy for Iris*, 60–61, for an account of Murdoch's memories of working
with Fraenkel.

of looking at the matter. Of course the fact that Plato is a great poet and a great writer puts some people off; they think that it's all so poetic that it can't really be saying anything serious.

"But I gave the Gifford Lectures in Edinburgh in 1982 and I'm try-ing to write a book based on them which will be a very Platonist book."*

"What was the theme of the lectures?"

"Well, they're supposed to be about Natural Theology. But that can be anything. It's partly about Kant, partly about Plato, partly about Schopenhauer and Wittgenstein. But I was really trying to say what I think, which is a very difficult thing to do."

Finally I brought up the question of the classical element in her novels. I chose to avoid her Platonist preoccupation with the search for Truth and Goodness, suspecting that she was tired of pointing out that she does not write philosophical novels.

"Might we talk about The Black Prince? *After all one of the charac-ters is called Loxias, which is a name of Apollo."*

"Yes, very few people who read *The Black Prince* make anything of this at all. Even critics writing comprehensive accounts of these things think that the Black Prince is Hamlet. Of course I had that picture of the statue of Apollo on the cover, and I thought, well really I'm laying it on with a trowel if I've actually got him on the cover. But nobody bothered. They didn't think that the cover meant anything, they didn't recognise the picture. . . . Mostly they just thought Loxias was a funny name.

"This is really in a sense private mythology, but then I find it hard to imagine what people actually believed about the Olympians, even when Greek mythology was flourishing. Whereas mystery religions, of which Plato was no doubt an initiate, are easier to understand in a way because they're more like what we think of as religion; but what believ-ing in the Olympian gods was like in the ancient world, I can't imag-ine."

"I certainly think that there's something very Greek in the book, in the real, sometimes demonic powers which move people around like

---

* Murdoch's *Metaphysics as a Guide to Morals* (1992) is based on the 1982 Gifford lec-tures.

counters on the board. It's very important that you don't simply write about internal psychological forces."

"Yes, the feeling of being in the hand of power which is not necessarily always friendly, and which also attaches itself to certain localities, and takes on powers of more primitive gods. This is all something which one's imagination can enter into.

"But talking of private mythology, in a way a religious believer always has a private mythology, so that my private mythology about the Greek gods is something which needn't be thought of as too alien from Greek ways of thinking about them.

"The distinction between Apollo and Dionysus has always interested me; well, it interests everyone who comes across it, especially from Nietzsche onwards. Many people, in a casual way, prefer Dionysus because he's jollier and more comprehensible and he's taken to represent the emotional part of the soul which people tend to prefer to the rational part. Whereas Apollo is regarded as a kind of god of light and reason. The fact that he's a most terrible murderer and rapist and so on, like Mr Loxias in the story, is passed over. He's become a symbol of a kind of cold rationality. I would want to reverse this for my own mythology. I regard Dionysus in a sense as a part of Apollo's mind, and I would want to exalt Apollo as a god who is a terrible god, but also a great artist and thinker and a great source of life. An ambiguous figure, certainly."

"As Cassandra's speech in the Agamemnon shows, when she rails against Loxias for having betrayed her. That's presumably one of the evocations of the name Loxias."

"Yes, that's probably one of the roots of it. (She paused.) Yes indeed, Cassandra's speech was one of the things I had to do for Fraenkel's class; at least part of it was. You can imagine the number of difficulties there were in that.

"But this thing to do with the nature of art—that art is terribly deep and dark—it's not to do with getting drunk or with unbridled emotion; it's to do with emotion which cuts much deeper than that. So that Dionysus doesn't cease to be; he's part of the scene, and to make an opposition between Apollo and Dionysus seems to me to be a mistake."

We then talked about Bradley, the central character of *The Black Prince.*

"The poor old hero is full of illusions. He's not to be thought of as a great writer manqué. He's just a man who's obsessed with the idea of art, but can't actually do it. And Arnold, whom he constantly denigrates, is probably a far better writer than poor old Bradley. But Bradley is somehow destroyed by art; he's also destroyed by the black Eros, whom I identify in a way with Apollo. But the voice of Apollo is very much there—a cold, ambiguous voice."

She then rose to go to another appointment. I managed to remind her of the cover of the Penguin edition of *The Black Prince,* which features a figure who combines the attributes of Eros with the body of Apollo. She rather approved of the design. Then, after confiding to me about the miracle at Delphi, she was gone into the dazzling sunlight.

15

JO BRANS

Virtuous Dogs and a Unicorn: An Interview with Iris Murdoch

At the time of this interview Jo Brans was a member of the English department at Southern Methodist University in Dallas. Now living in New York, Brans has won numerous grants and awards for her work. This interview was published in *Southwest Review* 70 (1985) and in Brans's *Listen to the Voices: Conversations with Contemporary Writers* (Dallas, Tex.: Southern Methodist University Press, 1988).

BRANS: I went to the Tate yesterday, and saw the Gainsborough portrait of the Pomeranian bitch and puppy, I suppose you're familiar with it. Seeing it made me think of Zed, the little Pomeranian in *The Philosopher's Pupil,* and the goodness that he exhibits in the book. His tact, for example. He pretends to like water, pretends to like swimming. I began to think of all the other dogs in your books—Mingo [*The Nice and the Good*], for example, and the big Alsatian in *Under the Net.* I wondered why these dogs often seem to be a lot better than some of your people.

MURDOCH: Yes, they're virtuous dogs. There's a very virtuous dog in *An Accidental Man,* that black Labrador which Charlotte acquires. I think dogs are often figures of virtue. Of course, there are bad dogs too. There are bad dogs in *The Sacred and Profane Love Machine,* you remember, who pursue and attack—they're like the hounds of Acteon. Dogs are very different from cats in that they can be images of human virtue. They are like us.

BRANS: Is there any significance to the fact that Zed is so tiny?

MURDOCH: I do not normally portray my characters from life, but in the case of Zed, he is actually copied from an individual dog I know. But his being very small is of course part of the drama. The dog is a character in the book and interacts with the other characters, he is a very important figure.

BRANS: So that he's much more vulnerable because he's small, and you're much more frightened for him?

MURDOCH: Yes, indeed. He is fragile.

BRANS: His size doesn't have anything to do with the shrinking of virtue?

MURDOCH: Nothing like that!

BRANS: Good. I thought I might be overreading. Do you think Americans react differently to your work from the British, or read you differently?

MURDOCH: I don't know enough to say. What do you think?

BRANS: An American friend told me recently that he thinks a lot of Americans read you for a certification of what they consider to be the social and intellectual superiority of the British, and that in a way it's satisfying to them to find this superiority in book after book that you write.

MURDOCH: I think some people—but this wouldn't be only Americans by any means—might read my books because there is a kind of assertion of old-fashioned values, of the reality of virtue. Of course this also annoys other people who regard it as something not proper to be said.

BRANS: Not proper for aesthetics' sake, I suppose.

MURDOCH: There's positive critical warfare on this subject between, as it were, the "old-fashioned" critics and writers, and those who want fiction to deny the traditional idea of character and the traditional notion of absolute guilt or of the reality of virtue, which they regard as "bourgeois" or "religious" in some unacceptable sense. These are partly very deep matters and partly things to do with immediate style and what attracts people to a book.

BRANS: For some people, if a writer doesn't espouse the highest morality he knows, doesn't attempt to write morally, he's writing badly.

I guess that's the kind of position that Tolstoy took when he wanted to destroy *Anna Karenina,* for example. Where do you stand?

MURDOCH: A writer cannot avoid having some sort of moral position, and attempting to be nonmoral is in a way a moral position, an artificial one. I think that a novelist, a storyteller, naturally portrays his own moral judgments. But these very judgments are not just a small area of human discourse; they're almost the whole of it. We are always making value judgments, or exhibiting by what we say some sort of evaluation, and storytellers dealing with persons must constantly be doing this. It's Tolstoy's great apprehension of the whole moral scheme which makes his novels great, not his artificial, censorious feeling that he had to burn *Anna Karenina;* that's an incidental thing. But the moral perception and depth of the writer is something very important. It's a kind of realism— seeing what the world really is, and not making it into a fantasy.

BRANS: In *The Sovereignty of Good,* you say that the ordinary person does not, "unless corrupted by philosophy," believe that he creates values by his choices.* He thinks that some things are really better than others and that he may get it wrong—make the wrong choices. I wanted to ask you about this phrase, "unless corrupted by philosophy." How do you think philosophy can corrupt? I think you might be thinking of pragmatism and "whatever works is good"—a very American attitude, I suppose.

MURDOCH: That would be one example certainly, but I was talking more of various kinds of existentialist philosophy and Oxford philosophy, which attempted to explain value judgments as emotive statements or arbitrary acts of will. This has distorted moral philosophy in recent years by suggesting that one has got to make a sharp decision between fact and value; and if something isn't factual, in the sense of scientific fact, and so presentable in some way, it belongs to a shadowy world, of private will and emotion, so that moral attitudes would simply be private emotional attitudes of one sort or another. There are refined versions of this which suggest that moral statements are really commands—that through moral language we attempt to influence people and alter the world.

* Murdoch, "The Sovereignty of Good," 380.

BRANS: So philosophy corrupts by making moral decisions simply a matter of preference or taste?

MURDOCH: Yes, you can just choose. You just choose your attitude, there's nothing behind it. Now it's perfectly true that one cannot prove that moral statements are right in the sense that one can prove ordinary matters of fact or science. But this is true of a whole world of value, of art for instance. And the fact that you can't "prove" a painting or a book doesn't mean that it isn't in some sense true or significantly connected with reality. It seems to me obvious that morality is connected with truth, with rejection of egoistic fantasy, and with apprehension of what's real; that the ability and the wish to tell the truth are a very fundamental part of morals. Morality is connected with the real world in innumerable ways, and is something that goes on all the time. It isn't a kind of special activity that you suddenly take up.

BRANS: To follow your idea that ordinary persons and even dogs can readily be exemplars of virtue, let me ask this: Do you think as Tolstoy seemed to imply with his peasants and children, that behaving rightly, behaving correctly, is easier for simple characters? Are there levels of sophistication, let's say, that make behaving correctly, doing good, more difficult for some than for others?

MURDOCH: Well, I think that some people are blessed with happy friendly temperaments. I think that what Freud says about these things is roughly true, one is influenced by one's history, one's own early life, so that some people are calm, some people are excitable or easy to anger, by temperament. The question of sophistication is another one, a complicated one, and I don't think I hold any special view on that. A simple person can be either good or bad. I think that goodness at every level of sophistication demands the ability to face life and be truthful, and the ability to be honest and faithful and loving, and the ability to give help. Facing life honestly at every level of sophistication.

BRANS: Without illusions or fantasies.

MURDOCH: Yes, I think "fantasies" is the name of a very important tendency to protect oneself by imagining that things are other than they are.

BRANS: But aren't we all damaged too by others' fantasies about us?

MURDOCH: That could be the case too. People often like to build up other people through fantasy or destroy them through giving them pictures of themselves which are false.

BRANS: I once had a good friend who kept telling me what I was like.

MURDOCH: Yes, this can be very damaging. I mean, people some-times, as it were, damage the being of other people, as if they were actually scratching it away.

BRANS: I felt myself stripped of the freedom to change, to try to be better. Suppose I were to come to you as a child would come to a par-ent or a disciple to a guru, and say to you, I want above all things to be good. What would you say? What would be your instinctive response to that?

MURDOCH: I'd want to find out something about the question. It would matter whether or not you were in some kind of tangle. I mean, if there was an immediate thing, then one might want to talk about that, particularly about truthfulness.

BRANS: Suppose I just wanted a beautiful life—"I want my life to be good."

MURDOCH: There are many aspects. I think getting hold of work, which is good, which you want to do, which you think you can do well, and which you feel does something for yourself and perhaps for other people is important. But then of course everyone is the victim of cir-cumstances. That's what's so tragic in our country and even in your country—people can't find work. Why isn't some statesman brave enough to grasp the problem and say, "Well, look, there isn't going to be work for everyone in the future. We've got to try and see how we live in a society where people can't all work"? But I think work is good and if you can find a work which connects you with the world and allows you to use your talents, I think this is quite a large part of the good life. But there are all sorts of ways whereby our natural selfish-ness can be checked. I mean, if one has a religious belief—do you have one?

BRANS: My beliefs are vague and undefined.

MURDOCH: How were you brought up?

BRANS: In a fundamentalist religion, scared of hell for years, night-mares about hell.

MURDOCH: You must have felt you'd gotten out of something when you broke free. It's an awful thing to bring up young people like this. But if one has some religion, if one is in any sense at home there even as a lapsed believer, this probably can help, because one has the idea of how to pray. Not in the sense of asking God to do things, but in the sense of retiring from the world into a different dimension. Actually anyone can do this. I think meditation is important. I would like meditation to be taught in schools, the ability just to be quiet, and to see what is worthless, to distinguish between what's important and what isn't important.

BRANS: You've written a lot about selflessness, about getting rid of the self in order to love the world, in order even to see the world. You define humility as getting rid of the self. All of this makes me think that you might intend a specifically Christian vision in your work. Let me turn the tables. Do you have a religion?

MURDOCH: Oh, yes, I believe in religion, in the sense in which a Buddhist believes in religion. My background, as it happens, is Christian. But I don't believe in God and I don't believe in the supernatural aspect of religion, I don't believe in life after death, or heaven.

BRANS: How can it be religion if you strip it of the supernatural?

MURDOCH: Ah, but religion is everywhere, religion is breathing. It's connected with the deep aspect of one's life at every moment, how one lives it all the time, and with truth and love and all these things we've been talking about. I mean, this is what any sophisticated Buddhist or Hindu would say; he doesn't believe in God, or heaven. Though obviously in any religion there's imagery which is understood by different people in different ways. Some hold very literalistic beliefs about God, but many people can't hold such beliefs now. It's too contrary to their own perceptions of truth and reality. But this doesn't mean they can't be religious. I became a Marxist when I was young, and I thought I had given up religion. Then I gave up Marxism, though it's very enlightening to have been a Marxist. But I thought when I gave up believing in God that religion was gone out of my life. Then I realized that this wasn't so after all. Religion is still there, even if one holds no supernatural or dogmatic belief.

BRANS: You said you prayed. To whom do you pray?

MURDOCH: I don't exactly pray to anyone. I retire into myself, perhaps have a conversation between the higher self and the lower self or something of that sort. It sounds rather pompous. But all I mean is an ability to withdraw from immediate concerns and to be quiet and to experience the reality of what's good in some way. But one is doing this all the time, through beautiful things, through art, through music, and of course very much through other people, apprehending their reality and their goodness or wanting to help them and so on.

BRANS: Yes, you've written about these stairsteps to the good, art, relationships with people—

MURDOCH: Intellectual studies also. We can learn about truth through any sort of craft or study or work—

BRANS: Which imposes a discipline on the life, is that the idea?

MURDOCH: Yes, if you don't have ordinary work, try to learn something, learn another language for instance. Of course, it's all very well to say this to people, people have such terrible troubles. But at least one can picture a society where people don't have ordinary work but are always learning something.

BRANS: I almost instinctively reject that; maybe it's the American in me. I feel terribly sorry for people without work.

MURDOCH: Well, exactly, yes, if one assumes that we can come back to full employment in Western society. But I don't think we can. We've never had *full* employment here in England, and everything to do with modern technology suggests that computers will take over all sorts of jobs which they can do more efficiently than we can. People feel very concerned with this. I'm not an expert, but it looks to me as if it is all going to be very difficult.

BRANS: So we'll have all these energies that aren't being used unless we think up a way to use them.

MURDOCH: Yes, people get demoralized. I think education helps enormously, and so one must spend more money on education. People can be taught how to learn, and can learn to enjoy things which are worthy, like art, and creation, and helping other people, and can use their energy in this way.

BRANS: In a number of your books you have women who are more or less imprisoned by the expectations of the men in their lives. I'm thinking of Hannah in *The Unicorn* who's both idolized and imprisoned, of Dorina in *The Accidental Man*, with Austin's adoration of her which really serves to keep her separate from him and to keep her enclosed, and of Crystal in *The Word Child*, whose brother's definitions of her entrap her or imprison her. There do seem to be a number of them, and I wondered if it were deliberate on your part for some reason.

MURDOCH: I don't think it's deliberate. The three women you mention are very different from each other. Crystal seems to be a sort of redemptive sufferer, who gives herself over to love for her brother, and I don't think she feels trapped.

BRANS: But the reader feels that she is trapped, and that this man is not really worth her attention and her love.

MURDOCH: All the same, she is right to love him and that love makes her happy. Dorina is more of a victim, more of a wispy figure without much strength. And Hannah is entirely different because the whole story has an allegorical aspect, and it's much more mythical and less logical. Hannah is a figure who is either spiritual or demonic. The spiritual and the demonic are very close together. She's seen either as a kind of noble victim or as a sort of *belle dame sans merci,* a *femme fatale.* She doesn't know herself really, and it's not clear which she is. She's a power figure as well, with a great deal of effect on all these people, and they in turn build her up. It's like a case you mentioned earlier of somebody's fantasy building somebody else up into something which perhaps they are or are not.

BRANS: But she is trapped, because Effingham realizes that he could have sprung her, but he chooses not to.

MURDOCH: Yes, partly because he's afraid of the consequences, partly because he likes her to be there shut up and sort of kept a prisoner for him.

BRANS: There, you see. And in *The Sea, The Sea,* remember, Charles kidnaps Hartley and shuts her up.

MURDOCH: That's a much more realistic situation. Charles is suffering from a delusion that the first love is the great one and that people don't change.

BRANS: You said you think there's something to what Freud said about early experiences. Does that mean you're somewhat in agreement with Charles?

MURDOCH: Oh, no, I think Charles is making a mistake, but it's a natural mistake. I mean it's not totally absurd. He feels so sure that this thing meant so much to both of them at the time that it must retain its meaning for her as well as him. But then, he fails to do what a more sensible person would do, having looked at the situation to drop it.

BRANS: And this is what you mean by not facing reality, his inability to imagine that she feels differently.

MURDOCH: And his arrogance too, because he's so grand, he can't help feeling, How much she must regret that she didn't marry Grand Me, and that she married this absolute nonentity.

BRANS: And it would have been such a good thing—

MURDOCH: She would have had such a happy life!

BRANS: But actually, as she tells him quite frankly, he would have been too grand for her. She would have been hopelessly out of things.

MURDOCH: She might have had some regrets sometimes, but on the whole I think not.

BRANS: Do you think people can ever serve as solutions for other people? Often in the books I've mentioned men will offer themselves as solutions for these women, and of course the reverse is true. Several women in various books, like Hilda in *The Nice and the Good,* think of themselves as solutions for these muddled males who clearly need to have their socks washed and their sitting rooms tidied.*

MURDOCH: Yes, I think people do solve each other's problems. In happy marriages people do that and in long friendships one's supported by other people all the time. I mean this can go wrong, but it can go right as well. That's quite often what one's looking for, someone to love one and be with one in some permanent way.

BRANS: So that's a way of coming to a sense of reality about the world?

MURDOCH: I think so, though of course any love relationship can be full of delusions. You may wish a person to be what he really is not, but a long relationship then becomes more truthful.

BRANS: We were talking about the discipline of art and work. What's the connection, do you think between discipline and visions? I'm thinking of that glorious vision that Effingham has when he is sinking in the swamp in *The Unicorn.* He imagines himself dead, and he says that if *he* were to die, what was left was everything else, and this vision

---

* There is no Hilda in *The Nice and the Good.* Hilda is a character in *A Fairly Honourable Defeat.* I suspect Brans intends to refer here to Kate in *The Nice and the Good.*

shakes him and enlightens him. Do ordinary people get visions like this, and how do these visions relate to life as it has to be lived in the discipline of the day?

MURDOCH: In the case of Effingham, he has a truthful vision of the world without the self, but of course he cannot sustain it, it disappears from him.

BRANS: And the same thing happens to Cato in *Henry and Cato.* He's had these visions of goodness and he's gotten increasingly separated from them.

MURDOCH: Yes, though with Cato, it's more connected with religion and with a sort of orderly life. But it's something very odd for Effie. I don't know how often people have such visions, but I think they do come in one way or another, through art or other people, sometimes rather suddenly or remarkably and at other times more gradually. And then one drifts away from the vision, but it can also remain as something that you remember, like having a good dream. Sometimes in a dream something extraordinarily real can happen.

BRANS: Your books are full of dreams. I once heard a psychiatrist remark that a criminal who doesn't dream can be regarded as beyond redemption.

MURDOCH: What we invent in dreams is astonishing. Sometimes there are very beautiful symbols in dreams. Religion is a kind of formalization of such matters. We have all sorts of ways of experiencing things which are pure and sort of out of the world. But then anything can become like that; in certain states of mind we see all sorts of things as full of grace.

BRANS: Do you believe that grace touches your life?

MURDOCH: Oh, yes, though again not in the dogmatic, supernatural sense. But I think there are forces of good that you suddenly can find, streams flowing toward you, whatever the metaphor would be. Yes. And I think sometimes people try for a long time in a rather dull way to do what they think is right, and then they're suddenly rewarded or cheered up. Some sort of vision holds the world together, and this is part of the subject matter of literature.

BRANS: There's Lisa, that wonderful girl in *Bruno's Dream,* who's going to give herself over to the starving millions in India. Then all of a sudden at the end of the book you see her in a sports car and she's married and she's cut her hair and she's bought clothes. Was this a kind of grace? I was surprised that Lisa didn't have to live the rest of her life in suffering poverty to be good. No one reading the book could have predicted what would happen to Lisa.

MURDOCH: I dare say she might have chosen a much nobler life if she'd gone off to India, and in some sense a better life. But I think happiness is important too. That's part of this thing about finding work and finding the right place for yourself in the world. One has a right, even a duty, to be happy. For some people, happiness is part of organizing a good life. Making other people happy is part of that, but very often making other people happy is a happiness of one's own. Lisa's end has something to do with Danby. Danby is the happy hedonist. He makes happiness for other people too.

BRANS: Is she reciprocating when she marries him and lives in a way that will make him happy?

MURDOCH: I think she is infected by his particular kind of life energy, which he's been lucky in.

BRANS: I was terribly thrilled that you allowed them to have this happy ending.

MURDOCH: Yes, I'm glad you felt that. I liked it too. I was fond of Danby and I think it was probably a good thing.

BRANS: Another one of your characters with a shocking contradiction for me was Tallis Browne. Here is this supremely good man, and I was horrified when I read the description of his house. It's so dirty! Julius King comes in and cleans up for him, and he has to scrape the kitchen floor because there's this sticky substance all over it, and the dirty milk bottles in which various things are growing, and really just this sort of horrifying filth.

MURDOCH: I must say, I don't mind filth as much as you do.

BRANS: But his was an exaggeration of filth. Why, for such a good man?

MURDOCH: That book too has an allegorical background. Tallis is not only a good man, he should be seen as a high incarnation, a holy man, something like Christ, arriving in the world. And it's symbolic of the situation that nowadays the holy man is sort of shaky, hopeless, muddled, he hasn't got a place. Somebody else has to clean up his kitchen and so on. Julius should be thought of as the devil. The conflict between the two is really what the book is about. They recognize each other as two spiritual beings, of opposing kinds, though Julius doesn't recognize Tallis at once. And Julius has been in a concentration camp, so perhaps the devil suffers too. But, then, all this is part of the struggle between good and evil that lies behind ordinary life. Because of course at the same time they are ordinary characters. One doesn't have to know these things to read the book and understand the drama.

BRANS: Your books are so full of meaning. Would you be disappointed if people only read them for the stories they tell?

MURDOCH: I would like the reader to see everything in the book. But I'm glad if people like those stories, it gives me pleasure, because stories are a very good way, you know, of getting away from one's troubles. Now let's have a drink.

16

RICHARD TODD, EDITOR

Discussions from *Encounters with Iris Murdoch*

Richard Todd has written books on modern British novelists, including Murdoch and A. S. Byatt, and teaches at the Free University in Amsterdam. An informal symposium on Murdoch's work was held on 20 and 21 October 1986 at the Free University. This chapter contains excerpts from discussions that followed the presentation of various papers at that symposium, which were published in Amsterdam by Free University Press in 1988. Participants in the symposium include John Fletcher and Cheryl Bove, joint compilers of the major bibliography on Murdoch; Peter Conradi, Murdoch's biographer; and W. Bronzwaer and Diana Phillips.

John Fletcher. "Iris Murdoch: The Foreign Translations"—Discussion.

MURDOCH: I was fascinated by what I heard from Professor Fletcher, and dismayed by a lot of things I didn't previously know. One of the things I did know was that the American editions actually alter some of the words . . .

FLETCHER: Only at the beginning. Later on I think Chatto must have said "don't."

MURDOCH: Yes; to begin with they altered the names of underclothes, suspenders and braces, things of that sort, which I objected to very much. And I was shocked to discover that in *The Sandcastle*, Rain Carter's green Riley had become a Jaguar! But I am afraid that one does surrender oneself to a foreign publisher. I mean, I was so grateful to begin with that anybody should want to publish me in another language that I didn't really attempt to keep any control over their activities, so they did what they liked. On the other hand, beyond a certain point you can't go on objecting. I can only really read easily French and Italian, and although I could have a go at some of the other languages, it would be laborious, and one hasn't the time at a given moment to check a translation, so that the translator is free, really, to do his worst with the text. And I am very upset at the idea that they could translate from German into French.

FLETCHER: Yes. I may have been maligning Maria Wolff, but . . .

MURDOCH: Well, I did hear one or two horror stories, actually, from Germany, about how one translator was told: "Look, this book is too long. You must shorten it. Leave out a few passages." This sort of thing really does fill one with dismay. And then there's the matter of the titles. This is good advice, I think, to anyone who's here whose books are likely to be translated into other tongues: you must keep hold of the titles. Again, as far as this is concerned, I didn't care: I was just so filled with emotions of gratitude that anybody should want to translate me that I didn't settle down to worry about the titles. But if one's books are known, say, in two or three countries, it is important that they should be identified. It produces great confusion if all sorts of fancy titles are then put on, quite apart from the fact that the titles themselves may be terrible, as in the examples you quoted. *Under the Net* first appeared in, I think, Swedish as "Escapade": you know, senseless titles are very often put on. And the same novel first appeared in Italian as "I gatti ci guardano" ("The cats are looking at us"). This was a joke made on the basis of *The Children Are Looking at Us,* which was a book that was popular, apparently, just at the time that mine came out. All kinds of local interests can suddenly appear in this way, as with the title of the French translation of *The Nice and the Good,* which was "Les demi-justes." This was quite an interesting title, but it was based on the idea that it would remind people of *Les justes,* which had just been published. Incidentally, there is an explanation for the French title of *The Bell,* when I caught up with them on that, because there is a good reason for not using "La cloche." It has a slang meaning related to "clochard" and being "de la cloche," that is somebody who is a sort of tramp. But this piece of advice is that you must get your home publisher to put a clause into the contract to say they've got to consult with the author about a change of title.

As to the value of the translation, this is a question that is extremely important, but something that again you can't control. I think novels are especially difficult to translate, and I've been told that English novels are particularly difficult in this respect, because of the ironical nuances and the kind of funniness: the way something which is funny in English is, if translated in a rather dead way into another language, just dull. One is lucky if one has a translator of talent who can deal with that.

JOHN BAYLEY: It is true of all languages.

MURDOCH: Well, it is true of all languages, yes.

BAYLEY: They all have their own kind of funniness.

MURDOCH: I know exactly, and it's particularly true of novels, of course, where all these nuances are so important.

RICHARD TODD: We do have at least two translators in the audience, James Brockway and Heleen ten Holt. Heleen ten Holt has translated the most recent novel, *The Good Apprentice*, which has just been published by Contact here in Amsterdam under the title *De Leertijd*.

HOLT: Well, I'd like to say something about the titles. I think in many cases a wrong title is not so much the fault of the translators as of the publishers, because they want a title that will sell. What happens to the poor translator is that he or she gets the book, often in typescript, and before he or she has even had a chance to read it, the publisher says: "Well, could you come up with a title by next week? And a blurb for the cover?" That's very hard on the translator, because it's often only when you're working on a book, and sometimes even when you've finished it, that you suddenly think: oh, that's the right title. Certainly not when you're starting. And of course titles are very difficult. I always try to keep as close to the English as possible, but a literal translation isn't always possible. In the case of this latest one, *The Good Apprentice*, it was extremely hard, but in Dutch we don't really have a word for "apprentice." We have the word *leerling*, which can mean both "apprentice" and "pupil," but "De goede leerling" just doesn't sound right.

TODD: What was the Dutch title of *The Philosopher's Pupil?*

HOLT: *Een leerlingfilosoof.* That was a difficult one too, because we can't really use this genitive construction. It doesn't exist in Dutch, or at least not so much as in English. And "Leerling van de filosoof" would have sounded very peculiar indeed, or at least I think so, so that's what we came up with.

BROCKWAY: I think Professor Fletcher would like to hear that Iris's fourteenth novel, *An Accidental Man,* was translated in Holland by half a dozen students. Which student did which part I don't know, but they did it under the guidance of Cees Buddingh'. I did go through it as a matter of fact and I must say that Buddingh' did rather a good job because I checked various parts and I didn't find anything in the translation of which I thought: this demonstrates that this book has not been carefully translated. However, one mistake was made, I think, with the title of *The Nice and the Good:* it has an abstract title in Dutch, "Het Aardige en het Goede," or something like that, an abstract title that doesn't refer to the people as the English one does.

MURDOCH: Well, it's ambiguous in English, of course.

Peter Conradi. "Iris Murdoch and Dostoevsky"—Discussion.

MURDOCH: I want to thank Peter very much for what he says. I think literature does feed on literature. I don't agree with some of the connections that he's made, but I agree with many of them. I think it is a mysterious thing how one writer casts a shadow on another, but the man who is influenced may be re-creating something quite different, and this is a good kind of relationship. As in—these are just two speculations on my part—it seems to me that *The Queen of Spades* must have influenced *The Aspern Papers.* That is, it is possible, it could have happened; and I think that *La Cousine Bette* is influenced by *Les liaisons dangereuses.* But of course these books are entirely different and re-created, and yes, the narrator in *The Philosopher's Pupil* is certainly a Dostoevskian narrator, and I think he is an awfully useful sort of narrator, I mean somebody who can be both knowing about the characters and also in some doubt about them. And, in a sense, a comic figure who hovers on the brink of the action.

TODD: And yet it is made quite clear in *The Philosopher's Pupil* that N is not the voice of any of the characters.

MURDOCH: Ah, well, you could speculate that he actually *is* one of the characters . . .

TODD: Yes?

MURDOCH: It is quite possible that N is the psychiatrist, Sir Ivor Sefton.

BAYLEY: I was very interested by some of Peter Conradi's points. They suggested to me that where fiction is concerned you can make a sort of rough-and-ready distinction, perhaps, between the minor fiction writer and the major one, which has something to do with one's response to their personality. Philip Larkin, the poet, who died recently (himself rather a good novelist: he wrote two novels), said that the first thing we require of a novelist is that he make a separate world for us. Well, I think this goes with the way in which a minor novelist, and I think Larkin himself was one, is also one who shows us, in perhaps a very engaging way, his own personality. I think it may be true that the greater the writer, the more we feel the personality is not present in this sense at all, in the sense in which we encounter somebody in life. Dostoevsky himself made a very interesting remark when he was young. He said something like this: "I promise you won't see my ugly mug in my writing." And in a sense it is true that we don't see his ugly mug in his writing. And I think, if I may say so (it is a little difficult to criticize in a fully independent way Iris's writing), but I think it is true with her also that in this sense her novels do not present personality in the way those of a minor writer can do. This rather interesting conception, in the context of a novel of Tolstoy's would be the idea of self-satisfaction: *samodavolstvo* is the Russian word. It is true, I think, that where all novelists are concerned, self-satisfaction is the great enemy. They are like us, so to speak, in the sense that they are very apt to indulge themselves.

Now I think a writer with personality may be a very good writer, but he or she is often indulging his or her personality. I feel that with— again this is very invidious, but a minor writer like (say) Margaret Drabble is simply being herself, but it is not the real thing. It is not the big thing the novel can do. It is also true, I think, that comedy, which Peter Conradi was speaking of very interestingly, has two sides in the novel. It can be an aspect of self-satisfaction. I think so-called black humour in the novel, in for example the novels of Evelyn Waugh in

English, is very often simply a form of release and relief for the author, and for the nastier side of the author. Again the amazing thing about Dostoevsky—why he is so great, I suppose—is that he doesn't seem to indulge in black humour in this way, though we can speak of it as dark comedy, as Peter did. So I think that (to go back to my only point, really) if self-indulgence is the great sin of the novelist, a great novelist—and I would count Iris and Dostoevsky among them, myself—does manage to avoid it in some way.

TODD: You do regard comedy as in some ways a higher form than tragedy? I think you have said things along these lines?

MURDOCH: I think that the novel is a comic form in that it is concerned with the accidental aspects of life. Tragedy is a very peculiar and limited form (as I would put it), being really confined to the theatre and poetry—poetic theatre—and there are very few writers of tragedy. Of course, there are many writers who portray the miseries and sorrows of life mixed up with what Peter was saying: the wit of deep feeling; and I think this is a very important literary form. It's something Shakespeare does very well, and the other writers you [Conradi] were speaking about.

CONRADI: I perhaps didn't make this point: now what my sense was, certainly I think in both your work and Dostoevsky's, is that it is *beyond* dark comedy. It is not *simply* dark comedy.

FLETCHER: I would just like to say that the overwhelming impression I get from Iris Murdoch's novels, particularly in the comic or outrageous *skandal*-scenes, is that they bowl along, as it were, at a tremendous pace and are extremely funny. So much so that one is often aghast with amazement at some extraordinary event that has happened that, in another novelist, would be purely melodramatic, but that in her work seems to have a sort of remorseless logic about it. This goes on quite a long time and then after a while one is aware of something rather curious, and that is a somewhat steely look that comes across as well, and *that,* even though these scenes are very funny, and very touching, and so on, tends to be the abiding impression. And I think that other writers, and since we've said it, lesser writers, such as Kingsley Amis perhaps, can be extremely funny, but what one misses is that steely look. I think one gets it in Dostoevsky in the same way.

QUESTIONER 1: The matter of personality was mentioned and it always interests me. Do you think your own work is realized, by readers, or by critics and reviewers, as being your own, or rather in terms of the theories or philosophies behind it?

MURDOCH: I'm sorry, do you mean how far have the critics been right in the things they've said, or do you mean is there a philosophy which I am trying to propound, or put forward?

QUESTIONER 1: The former.

MURDOCH: Well, I don't read the critics, really [laughter]. I mean, naturally I occasionally read a review, if it comes my way, but I don't collect reviews, and I don't think novelists should worry about critics. It's very unlikely that one would learn something deep from a critic. Though one might learn something from reading general observations about literature by a talented critic. So I don't know. I think critics obviously have a tendency, or feel compelled, to find something clever to say, and very often a reviewer is writing very fast. I mean he has been reading several books at once, or something like that, and the notion that one has got a philosophical position which is being propounded in the novel is, I think, an idea which many critics latch on to (about many novelists), where this is not so, where insofar as there is a philosophy it's something which is diffused into the whole object.

QUESTIONER 1: And if one talks then about translations, as Professor Fletcher did, and you see the title "The Sandcastle" translated as "Built on Sand," the translation could convey something entirely different from what you had intended?

MURDOCH: Yes, thank you for making this point. Yes, I think this was early times, when I didn't think I had any power to stop people from calling my books what they pleased. I imagine there is a simply Dutch term for "sandcastle," and that it's a metaphor which is slightly different from the English. I mean, the ideas overlap but the metaphor is slightly different.

QUESTIONER 2: On the subject of comedy and tragedy I noticed that you admired Shakespeare greatly, and I would be very interested to hear your response to this quotation from Samuel Johnson: "The irregular combinations of fanciful invention may delight a-while, by that novelty of which the common satiety of life send us all in quest; but the pleasures of sudden wonder are soon exhausted, and the mind can only repose on the stability of truth."* Do you think that in novels it's more difficult to get that deep impression of "stability of truth" across, or is the one who dedicates himself or herself to theatrical and poetical things maybe more fortunate?

MURDOCH: I agree that something to do with truth is fundamental to good art. If one thinks of what critics rightly say, as when in adverse criticism of writing and painting and music they may call it superficial, or sentimental, or fantastic, this is accusing the work of a kind of untruthfulness; and I think that it is some sort of truthfulness that is particularly fundamental to the novel. This doesn't mean that the novel must be realistic, but that there must be an intelligent just judgement in the portrayal of the story. But I think Dr Johnson may be being a bit hard on the fantastic side of the matter. If one thinks of Shakespeare, and not only the comedies, there's an awful lot of extraordinary play and fun and fantasy going on, and there is a play attitude to all of it, which is very important too. I think stern critics have sometimes been wrong, and I think Dr Johnson possibly was at some points, in looking at a work (say) of Shakespeare and regarding it simply as a pantomime. *The Tempest* was said by some critics to be a sort of pantomime, but there is a very deep, even religious, truth in that play. I'm told that many critics in the past thought that *Così fan tutte* was just a joke of some kind, so that I think critics must beware of becoming too solemn.

Cheryl Bove. "America and Americans in Iris Murdoch's Novels"—Discussion.

MURDOCH: Well, that's a very interesting talk. I think this could be picked up in various ways, that is I want to defend myself against some of these charges!

BOVE: Oh, I wasn't attacking!

MURDOCH: I think I have a lot of strong feelings about America, mainly affectionate ones. I have a lot of American friends, and I've quite often been to America. The novels cover a long period from my being unacquainted with America to my being well acquainted with it.

---

* Samuel Johnson, "Preface to Shakespeare," in *Johnson on Shakespeare*, vol. 1, ed. Arthur Sherbo (New Haven: Yale University Press, 1968), 61–62.

Of course Henry James is the great exhibitor of the European-American myth, I mean the way in which either side of this vitally important relationship, which on the whole has been a very good relationship, tends to romanticize or darken, or at any rate produce a mythological picture of, the other side of the Atlantic. Henry James's characters very often regard Europe as a wicked, dark place whereas America is a place of innocence and clarity and moral goodness. One could of course make the picture the other way around, and I'm sorry about these remarks about American academics, which are really joke remarks and not to be taken at all seriously! Of course such colleges as Henry's in the Middle West I think do exist, but they are not to be confused with the great American institutions of learning such as Stanford, where Giles Brightwalton [in *The Good Apprentice*] was, and from whence he wrote an important letter to Stuart Cuno, saying that Stuart should come to America!

Now I notice that the most important American character in the novels is not mentioned, and that is Ludwig Leferrier in *An Accidental Man* who is, I think one of my most engaging characters. He is a good man who is in a political dilemma about the Vietnam war.

I think that the amount of criticism which I've heaped on a lot of my minor characters on this side of the Atlantic would probably equal that which may appear to be attached to the Americans, but my Americans are usually mythical figures and America is not for example treated as a place of awful exile. I think there's nothing more terrible in Henry James than the end of *The Golden Bowl* where Charlotte is pictured as now being exiled from Europe and as having to go back to America. This really does count as exile, but I don't see my characters who go to America as being exiles; rather, they are going towards some kind of freedom, towards a new life. Admittedly this is the other, the good, open, as it were *white* European myth of America, that it's the land of the free; that you left tormented, sinful, awful, cruel, constricted Europe for an open space where you could renew your life. This I think is the feeling with which Anne Cavidge [in *Nuns and Soldiers*] leaves for America, and I think that other characters who go to America do so having similar feelings.

I think that Cheryl was a bit unfair about Russ Fischer [in *Henry and Cato*] because I think that in Henry's friendship with Russ and the relationship between Henry and Bella there is a characteristic kind of Anglo-American joke: I have lots of American friends who go on and on about how different we are, and we're like this and you're like that, and the Fischers play this game. But it is a game, because after all these are human beings dealing with each other, and what Russ and Bella do in, as it were, abandoning Henry is what they would *have* to do. They've got to look after themselves; they couldn't stay in this inferior college when they could go to a good academic institution where they'd been offered tenure; how *could* they sacrifice themselves to Henry by staying in that place? I think Russ Fischer's little postscript to Henry should be read as something very touching; there's a very deep affection between these three people, and Henry is waiting for them to come and see him. I think that if you look at the detail of these cases you see that there is a great deal of affection involved.

In the novel I've just finished [*The Book and the Brotherhood*], there is a very beneficent American, a good American [Conrad Lomas], who arrives and rescues people from difficulties. So, well, that's what I think, and I should say that I'm very deeply fond of America and my American friends. I do regard America as a big open scene to which many Europeans go with a sense of relief; and this thing about letting their hair down is very true of many academics. I've known people, English academics, who were very constricted and unhappy and neurotic in England and who, when they went to America, felt that they were in the open air.

BAYLEY: I think we might just take up what Iris said about Henry James for a moment. I think, though Iris is not influenced by him at all, that she likes Henry James very much; his is a remarkable case of a writer who inaugurated in his fiction what she calls this mythology of the difference between Europe and America, particularly England and America. Ever since then I think all novelists have tended to follow it to some extent. It's a very good, ready-made difference, like the difference between the Cavaliers and the Roundheads, or something like that. Yet I think Iris would agree that in spite of the way in which we talk about James's point about American innocence and European decadence, if you look at his early stories about the American scene, that distinction is simply not borne out. Those early stories actually do insist just as much on certain kinds of American corruption and weakness which are really no different at all from what we find in Europe, although we do on the other hand also find the characteristic American virtues. It's true that in his story *The Europeans* he does make one feel that there is a certain kind of innocence involved in the daily existence of being an American, which is rather notably absent from the daily existence of being a European. But I don't think we can really insist too much upon that as critics; you see, it's much more important really for James to admit that because we speak the same language—and he is writing with one foot as it were in each continent—that gives us an enormous advantage.

QUESTIONER 1: I wondered if it was fair to draw a comparison between stereotypic criticism of the aristocratic closed circles of those European tea-parlours where so much seems to happen in James, and recourse to the role of the analyst in American society as a kind of European stereotype.

MURDOCH: Do you mean that the futility of James's high society might be compared with people in America resorting to psychoanalysis? And that these would be two bad things, of different kinds? Yes, I see that an American parody of England might be that everything important happened in a fairly closed circle of people who thought very well of themselves, and had some money, and that kind of thing. And that the parody of America would be that everybody had a psychoanalyst. Well, I think these are ideas which novelists play with obviously, and of course neither idea is true. But I think that in reading a writer's work, one should take note of the status of the character making a given judgement, since it is fictional characters very often who say things, and the status of a given character will determine whether one should regard the statement as true or not; so that a lot of prejudiced remarks about psychoanalysis, how people resort to it in America (say), and *vice versa* what Americans might say about Europe, could well be made by people who perhaps haven't got a very wide knowledge of the country they were speaking about. I think it's probably roughly true that psychoanalysis *is* a more popular and ordinary resource in America than in England; and that this is partly because there's more money in America than England; we can't afford it. But I think such notions are generalizations, which may be used in a frivolous sense, but of course they can be misleading.

TODD: I'd like to ask you a question about something you said earlier, where you talked about your lack of direct acquaintance with America in the earlier novels. I've noticed that America, or indeed Australia, was often a way, a place for characters to just leave at the end of the novel, to exit or as you said to start a new life. But it is also a way of getting them out of the world of the novel, isn't it?

MURDOCH: Yes, certainly. Yes, I mean you don't want to kill them all, you know, you send them to Australia.

TODD: But in a sense you began to move away from that, and I suppose it's that as your knowledge of America became greater, your treatment of America and Americans becomes more interesting and sophisticated and joky; it isn't any longer just a place where they're living in limbo. Yet I noticed in *The Good Apprentice* that you've done something very similar to your earlier manner of disposing of the Wilsden family.

MURDOCH: Well, I sent the Fitches to Australia [*The Sea, The Sea*]. Yes, but there's nothing particularly odd about this. I mean after all, people have disappeared from my life to America, and it's a long way off; the idea of emigrating is quite a deep one, full of emotional resonance, and so on. Of course, we've lived through a good deal of enforced emigration in our lives, or I have, and it's something which is a familiar part of life. Many people do leave England to go to Australia because they feel that they'll have a better climate and more work and a better life, and so forth. And people go to America with the same expectations, or to Canada. I mean it can be in a particular context symbolic and it's also, as you say, a literary device, but it's also something that just happens, and quite a good feature of a novel.

BAYLEY: I thought that Cheryl was very perspicacious in what I took to be her suggestion about the way English people understand each other. It is vitally important in your novels, isn't it, for certain kinds of people to understand each other in silent and (as Henry James would say) equivocal sorts of ways. Whereas of course the English characters can't understand the Americans like that. It seems to me that, in a way, you were suggesting that her version of the Americans reflects back on the way in which the other characters understand each other, if you see what I mean.

MURDOCH: Well, yes, it's just a fact that if you're writing a novel you put people of other nationalities into it knowing that they're people you don't entirely understand. I think that national differences are very deep. And the national differences between English and American people are particularly puzzling, because on the one hand we all speak English, that great language, and on the other hand the origins of people in America are very diverse, and American life is very different. In a way the English and the Americans can play about with these things easily because they share a language and because they assume that they're brothers and cousins; and then there are family difficulties when you find that you don't understand each other, but I think that in fiction this can often be a source of pleasure, something which you play about with.

But do let me say that I love America, and I want to stress too that one has partly a romantic feeling about it. I'm thinking of Stanford and Berkeley, and, you know, these are great romantic homelands. When John and I were in Berkeley, we could hardly bear to leave, and we still talk about going back to Berkeley and living in the Women's Faculty Club!

[DIANA] PHILLIPS: You suggest in your novels that visiting psychoanalysts and psychiatrists is not a good thing; most of the characters usually make fun of them. Cheryl said that psychoanalysts are on the whole theorists, and I am also remembering the remark "all theorizing is flight:" I connect all these things. Now my problem is, if it is true that psychoanalysts don't solve people's problems but just tidy things up (which is what you said), I wondered why at the end of *A Fairly Honourable Defeat* Peter [Foster] finally goes to see a psychiatrist and it is actually Tallis who suggests early in the novel that he should see one?

MURDOCH: Well, that's just real life, as it were, that one has mixed feelings about these important institutions. There are analysts and analysts, of course, and plenty of them here, it's not just an American institution. After all, the analyst whom Gunnar Jopling [in *A Word Child*] consulted might have helped him, and Thomas McCaskerville [in *The Good Apprentice*], after all, is capable of helping people. This is my own personal feeling, but I feel alarmed by the notion of people going into deep analysis, where they spend literally years, and a great deal of money, trying to solve problems, which perhaps *are* solved, I don't know, but I think it can very often be like taking some kind of drug. That's just my outsider's view, and I know other cases where analysis has helped people very much. I think in desperate cases you might go to a priest or to an analyst, to somebody who's going to shake up your whole mind in some way, and this can be beneficial.

PHILLIPS: I was just very much struck by the fact that it was Tallis, whom you described yesterday as one of the only really good characters you've created, very perceptive and so on, that it was exactly Tallis who said Peter should see a psychiatrist; it struck me as very odd.

MURDOCH: Well, I think there's a difference between going to a hospital and seeing a psychiatrist, and going into analysis, and I don't think Tallis meant that Peter should necessarily settle down with a psychoanalyst, as he in fact does at the end of the novel.

Diana Phillips. "The Complementarity of Good and Evil in *A Fairly Honourable Defeat*"—Discussion.

MURDOCH: Well, that's terrific. I don't think I can . . .

PHILLIPS: You recognize the book in it, don't you?

MURDOCH: Yes [laughter]. I think that your thoughts about it are very good, ingenious, deep, and altogether splendid. I think that a novel is allowed to be ambiguous, I mean it's not surprising if people interpret a novel in different ways. And the author is very likely to be tolerant to different interpretations—or, at least, I am, because I see a pattern in the book which I may have only partly realized, and which is mixed in with other patterns. That's to say one could read the book without bothering about the refinements which you've drawn attention to. At one level it's a perfectly straightforward story about a decent chap and a rotter, and marital love and mistakes and confusion, and so on. But there is also this aspect to it, that you've brought out very well.

I think that Arthur Fisch [*A Word Child*] has more or less got it right, that it is the defeat of good that one is speaking of, that the good is defeated, but only by evil. But in a way this is slightly contradicted by the sort of religious allegory which is in the book also. You rightly identified Julius as the devil: one may as well regard him in this light. Tallis then is not exactly a Christ-figure, I think, but what in the East would be called a "high incarnation." He is a good person who's turned up, as they perhaps do every now and then, in the world, but he is also a spiritual being. I think you might say that Julius doesn't recognize this at the beginning. It isn't until the scene in the kitchen that he says to Tallis: "I didn't realize who you were"—something to that effect. He then realizes that it is his opponent whom he is meeting, and the sympathy between them is the sympathy felt by two spiritual beings in a human scene. And they will meet again, and so on, but then Julius will go on to do something else. You might think of the devil as being omnipresent, that's to say incarnate in different places, both because it amuses him to be so, but also out of a perverse desire to suffer. Of course, this is all really a wild quasi-theology that's as it were behind the book rather than clearly expressed in it: that the devil might also want to suffer, and that it's not just the prerogative of the gods.

BAYLEY: That's very ingenious; I mean the devil is not normally portrayed as suffering, is he?

MURDOCH: Well, I don't know. He does suffer in *Paradise Lost.*

BAYLEY: Ah, you're quite right; he does.

MURDOCH: He suffers from being banished from God. So that if he decides to go to a concentration camp it is a symbolic gesture, it's something that he's chosen to do, a chosen manner in which to suffer. The concentration camp idea came to me as some sort of aspect of Julius, and then the thing on the arm, the concentration camp number, for Tallis to see. And also there is dear old Leonard who, if you want to carry the allegory a little bit further into a kind of absurdity, is God the Father. He's Tallis's father, and he's constantly making the remark: "It all went wrong from the start."

PHILLIPS: I think possibly the funniest page I've ever read in any novel is your description of Leonard's views on sex. I think they are hilarious.

TODD: How seriously are we to take this idea that there is an allegory of the kind you've just mentioned to be read in the novel? It's just that you don't seem very enthusiastic about it.

MURDOCH: Oh no, I'm very enthusiastic about it. I think it's part of the creative urge of the novel to picture this; but then as I say it's made into an ordinary story, so I don't mind if nobody notices it except a special kind of reader.

TODD: But I'm worried about Leonard. I mean, if he is supposed to be an allegory of God the Father, then he's obviously a highly parodic one.

MURDOCH: Yes, he is a funny one.

TODD: Is this to be reconciled with your beliefs concerning the idea of God the Father?

MURDOCH: Well, not especially, no. I mean, that would be a separate thought. It's true I can't believe in a personal God. But it's partly Tallis's *position* that interests me: as a high incarnation he is a very tattered, bedraggled figure who can't really find a good foothold or home in the world, and his father is even more bedraggled, and this is a sort of picture of creation.

TODD: You really would be quite firm about separating that novelistic fact from your own instincts to demythologize the idea of a personal God?

MURDOCH: Oh yes, I think so, but they might be leading to the same conclusion. I mean the old idea of God the Father is difficult to believe in now, whereas the idea of holiness, of goodness incarnate in people, is not a lost idea.

TODD: But it does seem as though you're quite explicitly keeping the novel separate from the thought or philosophy.

MURDOCH: Yes, there's nothing in the novel to do with the philosophy. After all, it's a novel.

TODD: I understand that, but are you not still saying the same kind of thing in the novel, or using a joke to make the same kind of belief operate in the novel?

MURDOCH: Yes, but making Leonard into a joke would be different from arguing why the idea of God the Father is not tolerable now.

BAYLEY: Isn't one of the troubles about trying to discuss the novel that explanations of a cut-and-dried kind aren't really applicable to its form? You have to criticize it in terms of other kinds of art, don't you? D. H. Lawrence said that there is nothing absolute about the novel, and I suppose he meant by this that its relativity is exceedingly difficult to get hold of, and as Iris has often said, it's the presence of jumble and rubble that's part of its charm.

MURDOCH: It's open-textured, yes. The world comes in and out of it. You might think of it as a sort of pot with holes in it, lying on the floor of the sea, with the fish swimming through it. Human life as we understand it, and the things that concern us at the moment, and how we see the world at the moment: these things all have to be seen in relation to a novel which endures. If you go on reading (say) *War and Peace* throughout your life, then it is like a different book at various times. But I was very touched by the care you've so kindly given to *A Fairly Honourable Defeat*.

PHILLIPS: Well, what I feel at the moment is that it is my favourite novel.

FLETCHER: I found it went down very well with some students I taught in Germany about eight years ago, particularly its moral complexity. Could I perhaps ask Diana a question about Morgan? For this particular reader, who may be prejudiced, you know, Morgan is an exasperating person, and I suppose she's meant to be, and to be self-indulgent and have all the worst features, and so on. But on the other hand, I didn't feel very strongly hostile towards Julius: I could see his charm shining through his wickedness. But it seems to me that Morgan is entirely without charm.

PHILLIPS: I don't know. She's only the enchanter's accomplice, so she doesn't have to charm, whereas he's evil and has to charm too, so that one's fascinated by him. But she's also *closer* to us than Julius is, I think.

FLETCHER: Yes, in some ways perhaps that's my point. Although she provokes this strong reaction in me, which I'd be interested to know if other readers share, she would of course be more sympathetic.

PHILLIPS: She's much more human. I don't think one necessarily feels that she's more sympathetic, but she's more like us (if we care to admit it) than is Julius. Julius is a success at everything he does, whereas she's not, so in a sense she's a pitiable character, and Julius never is. She speaks of herself and Julius living like gods, but that's not the way she comes across. I feel sorry for Morgan. She is exasperating, and so on, but I think she also exemplifies the tolerance of the novelist towards the characters, so that one's first reaction is indeed to think that she really is awful, but then one starts to see other traits in her and to pity her. I don't know whether other people react in exactly the same way.

BAYLEY: I agree with John [Fletcher]. I think that men perhaps find Morgan exasperating. Perhaps all women secretly want to be a little like Morgan.

PHILLIPS: Well, not necessarily, but I think I can see the hidden positive things in her. I think for example she is genuinely distressed at the end of the novel, when she says that it all started as a game, and how can we be responsible for something if we don't know how awful it is going to turn out to be? I think she really means that.

MURDOCH: But I think actually it's possible for one to take a simpler view here, which is that she's just not a very successful character [. . .] a great novelist would have *animated* all these people. The difficulty is that one may be able to animate some of the characters, but then they steal the power from the other ones, and if Morgan had been a much more eccentric, interesting character, it would have been a far better book. And I think the same applies in a way to Rupert and Hilda, who are just not interesting enough, I mean they haven't got enough individuality to pull the thing even more apart, to open up the texture even more. So their drama ends up being underplayed, and Morgan ends up much more of a conventional character than she should have been, because I didn't manage to make her strong enough to be herself, to be something quite odd. She should have been much odder.

TODD: Is this problem one you feel you've become more successful in dealing with as time has gone on?

MURDOCH: A little bit.

TODD: Are there characters you're prouder of having created in the later novels?

MURDOCH: I don't know. I think in novels with a great many characters one just has more successful ones because they have a larger field to play in. The danger with a very strong plot and a few strong characters is that other characters, perhaps, haven't got any space in which to develop themselves. I think there's more detail in general in the later novels. They are longer novels, and there's more opportunity for descriptions of all kinds, and I think they are more realistic. The characters are better, and I think this is the main thing, to be able to invent characters who have a life of their own, who seem to exist, and who may not be obviously like ordinary people at all, but then they may be what ordinary people are like in the eyes of God, as it were. I think the advantage of the novelist is that he can see into the soul.

BAYLEY: But in general it's an interesting question, isn't it, whether the novelist is more fond of a given character than the reader becomes, to the extent that one feels that the novelist has a certain feeling for a character which the reader perhaps can't share.

PHILLIPS: I'm sorry, I don't agree, not about Julius, anyway, that there's something appealing about him that the reader doesn't share. I think he is brilliantly done, in that he is fascinating yet repulsive. Then all of a sudden the reader finds out this thing about his having been in a concentration camp, and I think that is a perfect example of where the reader sees that he has been cruel to this character, and accused him, drawn him in black and white, whereas Julius has a life of his own which we've never known about. We just accept that he's bad, thoroughly evil, until we hear that he's been in a concentration camp, and it's only then that we become more charitable. I think it's not just the novelist, but the reader too, who has constantly to be tolerant to the characters. I find this very, very difficult.

MURDOCH: Yes. I'm thinking of the way writers sometimes really are unjust and cruel to their characters. I'm thinking of poor old Clifford Chatterley in *Lady Chatterley's Lover,* which is admittedly not my favourite book by that author, and he's not my favourite author either. [Laughter.] I think that it is very much spoiled by Lawrence's veiled contempt for this poor chap, whom he's made into something horrid and contemptible. It would have been a much better book if Lawrence had made Clifford an interesting and curious character with some dignity and status of his own.

TODD: Could I relate what you were saying earlier about Julius and Tallis as spiritual beings to your treatment of Jesse Baltram in *The Good Apprentice?* It seems here that we have a character who's almost totemic, or something: he's most powerful in his absence and in the minds of others, so that when he does appear, the situation becomes anticlimactic and even farcical.

BAYLEY: He's rather a decayed Prospero, isn't he? Prospero gone to seed.

MURDOCH: Yes, well, I daresay I do think of Jesse as a supernatural figure. But of course you can also regard him in an ordinary way, as just a harmless, decrepit old man. Or you could indeed think of him as a sort of junior god, a kind of magician who comes back to earth at different times (perhaps there are many of them). In the story, his power has become exhausted, so perhaps he has to retire somewhere for three thousand years before he comes back again.

TODD: The trouble is, I feel, that it's the characters whom one's least inclined to pay much heed to, such as Ilona, who tells us that.

MURDOCH: Well, Mother May also refers to it, doesn't she? And of course Bettina. And Edward calls him a magician at the end.

TODD: Yes, the idea that he goes away and comes back.

MURDOCH: But this is just one way of looking at him.

TODD: So it's a view that's not really endorsed by the most forceful characters in the book, or the most trustworthy, perhaps.

MURDOCH: Well, this is an ambiguity, and it could be compared to the position of Julius if you like. You could look at it either way. Things may not be perceived as supernatural; one feels this about the presence of what looks like magic in the world, strange things or paranormal things. But lots of ordinary human relationships, too, may move into an area of mystery.

TODD: What attitude are we to take to your characters, such as Bradley Pearson in *The Black Prince,* who clearly have difficulty in perceiving things in the way most of us perceive them? He tells us, for instance, that he has certain sensory defects or abnormalities, that he's slightly deaf but has an unusually acute sense of smell. How important are these things to our view of the truth his story tells?

MURDOCH: I think it's quite easy in the case of Bradley Pearson to tell when he's got a just idea and when he hasn't, as it would be in the case of a real person telling you the story of his life. I mean you'd assess this person, wouldn't you, and you'd soon get a jolly good idea of when he was exaggerating, when he was lying even, and when it was the truth. This is a much more realistic business. The business about Jesse and how you look at Jesse is an oddity, it's something in the novel that contains a bit of magic, but that magic is absent, I think, from *The Black Prince,* where Bradley Pearson narrates real events even though he is, of course, only partly reliable. But he's reliable in the most important respects: the author does not intend us to imagine that he murdered his friend.

TODD: No, I understand that. But I suppose there is magic in the figure of the editor Mr Loxias, even though it's pushed on to the periphery.

MURDOCH: Yes, it's in the periphery, where it's an obvious myth in the sense of a jest. But of course in another sense it's not a jest because Mr Loxias is Apollo, he's the god of art and the inspirer of the artist. And one is here to imagine him, just as one imagines Julius, coming back to the earth and making himself mortal and incarnate. Apollo himself is sometimes sorry for his adherents who can't make it, and for people who are devoted to him who never manage to achieve anything, so that there is a curious relationship between him and Bradley which is worked out in this tale of Mr Loxias as Bradley's literary executor.

TODD: Are we to assume that Rachel, who actually says something "true" about Loxias when she says that Loxias made the headlines some considerable time ago with the particularly gruesome murder of a fellow-musician, is aware of having said something true, that she's privy to the knowledge that you as author are privy to?

MURDOCH: No, Rachel doesn't know anything about Loxias and all those episodes that Apollo is associated with, flaying Marsyas, raping girls, and so on.

TODD: But she has stumbled on a truth?

MURDOCH: No, this is just what we are to imagine, that if Mr Loxias, Apollo, appears in human form he might do the kind of things he used to do in the Elysian fields. But this is all, you know, a kind of play; I mean although it's serious play, it doesn't matter if the majority of persons who read the novel don't know who Mr Loxias is. The majority of reviewers didn't, even though his picture is on the cover.

QUESTIONER 1: May I ask you another question in connection with these postscripts? On the one hand they do seem to upset the narrative rather severely here and there, but on the other hand all the four people actually writing the postscripts seem to have had private motives for writing the postscript they've written; and if they do, then that wouldn't necessarily invalidate the story such as it is, would it?

MURDOCH: Yes, I think that's the right way to look at it. I mean it's pretty patent in all the postscripts that the writers are protecting themselves, that they're putting themselves into some kind of more dignified situation. I think too that Bradley, for all his self-importance, and his mistakes such as when he imagines that Julian must be writing him a letter with all sorts of cryptic messages and so on, and his way of blundering on through life, does have an honesty such that one must at certain points obviously believe him. But all these kinds of things must be indicated by details in the tone of the writing.

QUESTIONER 2: And then one does get Bradley's point of view over an extremely long period, in comparison with the postscripts, so that in that way one's completely biased, one has the whole detailed analysis of Bradley's view of things.

MURDOCH: Yes, but then it would be an entirely different kind of novel, if one divided the space up equally between the different versions.

FLETCHER: May I ask you, in connection with my experience of teaching this novel, about the very interesting postscript by Julian which is, as you say, like all the postscripts, self-defensive. However, right at the end, before pronouncing Bradley's story "a literary failure," she says that in fairness she should add that she thinks the child she was loved the man Bradley was. In other words, when I was discussing this with my students, it did seem to us that this was the truth shining through all the obfuscation, there she is saying: it was a true love affair, before the mask comes back on again.

MURDOCH: Yes, she does say casually, actually it's all true.

FLETCHER: It's all true! Ah, you did intend it to be that!

MURDOCH: Yes, I mean she evades the question of whether she believes her mother or not, but then she says, well, yes, all this did happen, you may take what you've just been reading about as true; but the implication that *she* could have told it better, perhaps, except that of course she's a poet, so she's not going to write a long baggy thing like a novel.

TODD: She might have written a crystalline novel.

MURDOCH: Yes, she could have written a very short novel [laughter].

BAYLEY: Or a small haiku [laughter].

FLETCHER: It did seem to us, in discussing the novel, that in the end the reader is the jury; you've got several versions, equally plausible, and you've got to make a choice, but what would give it all away and convince me as a juryperson would be just that one sentence of Julian's.

TODD: Yes, but why is that? Is it because of where it's placed?

FLETCHER: Yes, I think its place as well; but it strikes me as the kind of thing a good counsel would elicit from the witness, and the jury would see it as confirmation.

TODD: Shouldn't the jury really say that where it comes doesn't matter, that it's got to be a truth, not a rhetorically-placed statement?

MURDOCH: I think the way somebody tells a story, and the way they utter certain sentences, would be what would convince you that the voice of truth is suddenly speaking. Of course, it may be a fault of the construction, but those postscripts do come at the very end, and they're not supposed to be a kind of counter-balance to this long story, which Bradley Pearson together with the author must put out as being something which is largely true. Where it isn't true, this will be indicated in the text, just as in that example I gave where Bradley imagines that Julian is looking for him and sending him secret messages, and it's perfectly clear to the other characters and to us that this is not so. Whereas at other points, it's quite clear that he has got things right.

W. BRONZWAER: But what would you think about the reader who at the end still can't quite make up his mind, but for whom at the end certain ambiguities must remain? Would you welcome that kind of response?

MURDOCH: I don't mind, provided they are a small number of readers. I mean this is one of the interesting paradoxes of works of fiction, that the author must, I think, feel that his work convinces in a certain important sense, and that the story is clarified. There could be and indeed are wilful mystifications in some books, where the author is positively trying to upset the reader by putting in contradictory constructions, and so on, but this is not my desire. If some people did feel mystified, however, it would show at least that they'd entered very deeply into the imaginative structure of the thing, but I would not start out with that intention. I would want mystification to be something of a further intensification of the story: not a contradiction of it, but a kind of shadow hiding the story which people could see if they could unveil it.

TODD: Is this also true of the little games such as the way in which Septimus Leech, whom Julian has invented as a pretext for not going with Bradley to the opera, actually reappears in *The Sacred and Profane Love Machine* as a patient of Blaise Gavender's?

MURDOCH: Well, it's just that I like the name.

TODD: So we needn't think it is the same person?

MURDOCH: No, you can think of it as the same person, but this is just a little game to amuse a small number of kindly readers.

PHILLIPS: There was an example in *The Bell* as well. The bell was cast by Hugh Bellyetere, which is actually Belfounder, who also appears of course in *Under the Net* and is described as having died in *The Philosopher's Pupil.* So there's obviously something there, I think.

TODD: Would you see that kind of thing as mystification or just play too?

MURDOCH: No, it is all play. There was a character called Peter Topglass in *The Bell,* he was an ornithologist, and his son appears in the novel I've just finished writing [*The Book and the Brotherhood*]. As a minor character I mean; it's just fun stuff.

FLETCHER: I've always assumed these things were games rather than the Balzacian idea of having the same characters coming up in different guises.

MURDOCH: Oh no, it's certainly nothing like Balzac.

FLETCHER: But your way is more or less a wink at a faithful reader.

BAYLEY: But it's a different kind of wink, isn't it? I think Iris is actually much closer to Balzac than she is, say, to John Fowles or David Lodge who obviously make the new fashionable point that they are not really writing novels, but making something up, playing around in a completely radical sense, and we shouldn't believe their story as being in any sense true. I think Iris's technique is always to make the story true, in the old-fashioned sense.

MURDOCH: Of course there are many more kinds of experimental novel, and I think some of the young people feel that they've got to write in a completely new way, which I think is wrong. There are many ways of writing, and the traditional way is still alive.

TODD: Do you think the historical novelist is faced with this issue in a particularly acute form? I mean, you wrote one historical novel; would you do it any differently now?

MURDOCH: That was a very special case, the novel about Ireland, because it was something I knew about and felt very deeply about. But

I certainly couldn't write it now. That novel, *The Red and the Green*, was written before the IRA emerged onto the scene. But it is written in the same sort of style as the others.

TODD: You didn't feel you were doing anything distinctively different, apart from just setting it in another period?

MURDOCH: No, but the thing was very close to me emotionally. I knew what it was like, whereas if somebody were to set me as a task to write a story set in 1810 or the time of Shakespeare or whatever, I wouldn't have the faintest idea how to do it: I think it's very difficult to write a good historical novel, though some people manage it, but I think it's very hard because of the sensibility.

BAYLEY: Yes, I think the trouble is indeed that if you really refuse to accept the convention, if you refuse to go along with the idea that inventing fiction is a way of getting at the truth, then I think you become frivolous.

FLETCHER: *The Red and the Green* has been criticized by hostile critics for mixing what appears to be frivolous, such as Millicent's antics, with the serious and courageous actions, say, of the men defending a humble post office against the British Artillery. Is there a problem here, that it's sometimes a bit difficult to marry or match the rather grotesque comedy of life to events such as the 1916 Easter Rising?

MURDOCH: I don't think there's any problem about that. As Peter Conradi was saying, it happens all the time in Dostoevsky and Dickens and Shakespeare; while vast destinies are being decided, the fate of Ireland or the fate of the major characters, whether they live or die, and so on, somewhere else quite close by something small and frivolous and quite ridiculous is happening. I think that's the mixture; the question is: exactly how to do it. I think the novelist must just have some kind of intuition as to how to do it. People may have been a bit more censorious just because it was a historical novel, and because I was talking about real people, who died, and so on. So perhaps they may have thought a more solemn tone would have been appropriate. But I wouldn't have dreamt of adopting the solemn tone. It would have been a very bad novel. I really did put a lot of work into that book The Bodleian Library did wonderful things: to my amazement I was able to get hold of all sorts of pamphlets that were written at the time, and references to newspapers, and, you know, the smell of the whole business.

I've got all this atmosphere anyway from my childhood and from when people talked about it, and knowing Dublin and so on, and I wanted to express all this in the novel. And what might be called the frivolous parts are also very carefully done in terms of the atmosphere of Ireland; but one can try and fail, and if the stuff looks frivolous in an incongruous way, one has failed.

FLETCHER: Well, no-one ever reproaches Flaubert for doing the same kind of thing in *L'éducation sentimentale,* and I think it's interesting that you have been reproached in that way.

BRONZWAER: I remember in an interview with me in 1971 that you got bored to hear critics say that *The Bell* is your best novel, and I wondered if you could express your views on that point seven or eight novels later?

MURDOCH: I think *The Bell* is the best of my earlier novels, but I think that all the novels since and including *The Nice and the Good* are certainly as good as *The Bell,* and I think the later ones are better, but this is a hope that any novelist must have, of getting better. Somebody told me this morning that they thought *Under the Net* was the best one, which I found very distressing!

BAYLEY: Curiously I think *Under the Net* is the only one of your novels where you can feel that the novelist doesn't know how it's going to end, if you see what I mean. Actually, this is an important criterion about novels, historically speaking, that a great many novelists did write quite genuinely not knowing how to end the thing; when novels came out in instalments, of course, it was quite common. I may be quite wrong about *Under the Net;* you probably did know how it was going to end, but it has a kind of freshness that is very mysterious, and that we strangely associate with something that is not planned.

MURDOCH: Well, yes, I did know how *Under the Net* was going to end. But I think this is a matter of style. It is quite an interesting point, isn't it, that some novels can seem like that, and it may be better if you have that feeling. I mean there can be a sense of too much presence of the author, a feeling that the author is going to bring the thing through to the end, come what may, in a particular way.

QUESTIONER 3: I know we have touched on this already, but what do you think is the relationship between your criticism of your work and our criticism of your work? And how far is what you say about your intention, what you want your books to do, more valid than what we think comes out of them? Or is it rather that there are two different points of view that are equally valid and equally important?

MURDOCH: Yes; people can have different interpretations, and there are some interpretations I would welcome, in a way, because they would show that a reader had been thinking about the work. Other interpretations I think would be mistaken, but of course this is just what the author thinks, and in the end it's persons other than the author who are going to decide what the work means. On the other hand, one wants to think that when one's confronting a work of art, one's confronting something which is not the victim of any sort of thoughts about it. But this is a paradoxical business, just as it is to talk about absolute values, or anything of this sort; however, I suppose one does feel that there are standards, and there [are] good and bad readers, and some people have views about the work that are better than others'. That's one point. The other point would be how far the individual writer is actually influenced by critics, and I doubt if writers are, I mean serious writers. A writer could be influenced by seeing what sells, or what most people praise, but I think that a serious writer is totally self-absorbed really, and although he may find it enjoyable to discuss his work with other people, I doubt if the critics help him. Of course, one would be glad of help, I mean if someone could tell me how to make my novels much better, I would be very glad. But I think the help that comes, that makes one's work better, comes from very deep inside the soul and the unconscious mind.

17

BARBARA STEVENS HEUSEL

A Dialogue with Iris Murdoch

Barbara Stevens Heusel is president of the Iris Murdoch Society and teaches at Northwest Missouri State University. She has written two books on Murdoch, the most recent appearing in 2001. This interview took place on 27 July 1987 and was published in *University of Windsor Review* (21 January 1988).

HEUSEL: In your letter you expressed warm feelings about Ireland. Do any of your earliest memories involve Ireland?

MURDOCH: Well I was born in Ireland, but I was removed at the age of one to London. I was born in Dublin. Yes, I went back; almost all my childhood holidays were spent in Ireland. I have warm feelings about the past, yes; I'm not so sure about the present.

HEUSEL: Do you consciously use certain metaphors in your work to represent Ireland?

MURDOCH: No.

HEUSEL: I had an experience with a bog while I was there, and I immediately thought of you and thought of *The Unicorn.*

MURDOCH: That's set in Ireland. It doesn't say so, but it is set in County Clare, where there is a limestone desert, and black cliffs, as described in the book.

HEUSEL: I went to Powerscourt, near Dublin, and saw those great beech trees, and they seemed so magical. Do you have feelings like that about Ireland?

MURDOCH: There are many magical places in Ireland. Clonmacnoise for instance. But the Ireland I know is mainly Dublin, the Wicklow coast, parts of the far west, and Belfast.

HEUSEL: Have you spent much time in Sligo?

MURDOCH: I've been to Sligo. It's not a place I know well.

HEUSEL: As a child, or even now, have you observed the strong Irish reactions, such as curses, that outsiders might describe as primitive?

MURDOCH: Plenty of primitive things are going on at present in Ireland. I mean the IRA. But not much, no, I didn't get to know the country people in the West.

HEUSEL: Is it in the West that one might hear Irish curses and experience mystery?

MURDOCH: Well, there is plenty of mystery there. I don't know. I have been to the West, but it's not a place I've lived in. I know Dublin best and Dun Laoghaire and the Wicklow hills and Belfast.

HEUSEL: But you don't speak the language?

MURDOCH: No. I think it would be a waste of time. I think it's unfortunate that people are forced to learn it, as in Wales. It's good to keep an old language alive, but that should be a voluntary matter. Precious school time should be given to languages such as French, German, Russian, Latin, Greek.

HEUSEL: Do you see the Irish as having an unusual attitude toward death—simultaneously realistic and bizarre, such as standing up the corpse at a funeral?

MURDOCH: I think these things belong to a peasant society. I'm not an anthropologist on the subject of Ireland. I don't know how the rites of that peasant society compare with those of others. There are still peasants in Ireland and this is interesting.

HEUSEL: Do you see Ireland as less westernized than other European countries? Is that perhaps why there are vestiges of the primitive?

MURDOCH: Yes, but perhaps I should qualify this. Of course Ireland is westernized and is part of Europe. I think that partly because of the dominance of the Roman Catholic Church the traditions of peasantry and countryside may have endured more than they have done in countries where the Church hasn't had a continuous presence.

HEUSEL: Do you see any relationship between your Irish heritage and the frequency with which death is a theme in your fiction?

MURDOCH: No.

HEUSEL: Is either of your parents still living?

MURDOCH: No. My father died many years ago, and my mother died about 18 months ago. I had wonderful parents.

HEUSEL: You write so much about death. Do you think your mother's recent death will affect your fiction? Does it change your perspective?

MURDOCH: I don't think so. My father died in 1960. My mother died, as I said, more recently. (Pause) Thinking about death is something fairly constant if you're a reflective person.

HEUSEL: Is there magic about being born in Ireland like Joyce, Swift, Shaw?

MURDOCH: Not specially. There's magic all over the place.

HEUSEL: Why are there so many great Irish writers?

MURDOCH: A majority of well-known Irish writers, in the past, were Anglo-Irish. I am Anglo-Irish. This in Ireland is very important. I didn't think this until approximately 1968, when the troubles started. Since then I've got used to it. When I say I'm Anglo-Irish, people sometimes say: "Oh, I see then, you're not real Irish. Not Celtic." My family is Protestant. My mother's family were settled with land in County Tyrone in 1610. They were landed gentry from the South of England. My father's family must have been, from the name I should think, yeoman farmers living in Scotland, in Galloway, and a lot of those were settled in Ireland, as protestants, about the same time.

HEUSEL: So then Swift and Joyce and Shaw you consider Anglo-Irish?

MURDOCH: There's nothing mysterious about all that talent. Those people were the top dogs. They were the people with education and leisure to read and write books. There are plenty of all sorts of Irish writers now. There is very strong literary activity in Ireland.

HEUSEL: Do you consider yourself a satirist? Do you think that you follow in this line of Irish satirists?

MURDOCH: No. I'm not interested in satire, and I would not like to be a satirist. Irony is something different. I think satire is a dangerous game unless you are frightfully good at it and have a particular end in view. If you are writing an ordinary work of art in the tradition of the

English, French, and Russian novel, you're not likely to be a satirist. You're likely to be ironical, to make fun of people and institutions. Satire goes with allegories and fables and a kind of story telling which is not like the novel. I don't feel any affectionate leanings toward satire.

HEUSEL: And you are not trying to change anything?

MURDOCH: Except in the sense that anybody who writes a serious novel is putting forward a point of view and expressing certain values, so that one might if pressed say that one wanted the values one hopes one is successfully expressing to be seriously attended to.

HEUSEL: You've mentioned at some point that you've been influenced by Dostoevsky.

MURDOCH: Yes, I've been influenced by Dostoevsky and Tolstoy—and Homer and Shakespeare and Dickens and—! There are people that one *hopes* one has been influenced by; they are the gods—such as Shakespeare. There are others whom one is very consciously influenced by, and certainly Dostoevsky is one. Yes. And Tolstoy is in some ways a greater writer than Dostoevsky. His influence is less pointed, less easy to pick up. I have certainly picked up influences from Dostoevsky.

HEUSEL: You are often considered a writer of comedies of manners. Do you agree with that description?

MURDOCH: No. I don't think so.

HEUSEL: Am I wrong in seeing your criticism of society as much more harsh than that, say of George Eliot?

MURDOCH: No. I don't think I write harsh criticism. Of course, I'm in the second league of writers, and George Eliot is in the first league. It would be the same kind of mistake to use "comedy of manners" to describe Jane Austen's work.

HEUSEL: Would you consider George Eliot to write comedies of manners?

MURDOCH: No. She'd faint! She is hyper-serious.

HEUSEL: But she is also very funny.

MURDOCH: Yes, she is very funny. Comedy of manners suggests something more like Noel Coward than George Eliot. And I think I'd want to be more like George Eliot.

HEUSEL: I remember reading years ago a no doubt oversimplified discussion of the way Henrik Ibsen went about creating the actions of his characters. Supposedly he sat in the park each morning and allowed the characters to work out their motives and actions in his head, to live out their lives—then he went home and wrote down the scene. And Flannery O'Connor writes that she didn't know that Manley Pointer, in "Good Country People," was going to steal Hulga's wooden leg until he did it. You have suggested in interviews that your goal might be to let characters help invent themselves or assist at their own births. You have said that you do not like to control your characters. How do you create them?

MURDOCH: Here is a slightly different question—How soon do you start to write? I don't write anything until I have invented the whole thing. Until it is all there, I would not write the first sentence.

Some people prefer to start writing the first sentence and then say, "Oh, is it going this way? Oh good heavens, it's going that way." I would have "Oh good heavens, it's going that way" in my mind very early on. But I think the period of reflection—when one has nothing, except notes, of course, to remind one—is very important; it's a kind of deep free reflection which may be more difficult later on.

HEUSEL: So during that time the characters might more or less invent themselves?

MURDOCH: Yes, if you get hold of a good character, he will invent himself, will invent his mode of speech and his past, make his jokes, and so on. The thing is to get the fundamental patterns right, the basic idea of what it's all about and who the people are. It begins for me with a very small, but one hopes a very powerful, nucleus of two or three people in a situation. This might be anything, but I want these people to be very real to me so that I can see them and think them and understand them, because I'm going to be with them for two or three years. Gradually, then, I develop the situation.

HEUSEL: As the characters begin to have language, are you parodying particular individuals' language?

MURDOCH: No. I don't put real people in. That would be death to my kind of writing. I have no instinct to copy people I know. I couldn't do it anyway, and I think it's horrid—if you can invent people, why copy? It is much more entertaining to invent people.

I wouldn't use the word *parody*. It's an interesting thing about modern writing that dialect speech is very difficult to manage. In fact people don't usually do it now the way Scott or Dickens do it. Their "simple folk" are allowed to talk a kind of blunted, broken-down dialect, perhaps ungrammatical, sometimes funny, sometimes wonderfully eloquent, as in Scott, for instance. Now unless you are going to make a great point of this, I think it is difficult to do this now because people feel those characters are being treated as inferior. It is not something taken for granted. If I have an uneducated character, I am very careful about his speech. He's got to have reasonably blunted speech but not made into anything that could be laughed at.

For instance, in *The Philosopher's Pupil* there is a servant called Ruby who is a gypsy. Her speech is rather simple and laconic, blunted. For instance, at one point she says, "I went a walk." Now my kindly publishers changed that to "I went for a walk." I said, "No, this is Ruby speaking, and she went a walk." Something like that you can do, but it is very difficult to reel off, as people used to, yards of Yorkshire or Cockney.

HEUSEL: I'm going to begin a new line of questioning. Have you responded in print to Dorothy Winsor's statement in "Iris Murdoch's Conflicting Ethical Demands: Separation Versus Passivity in *The Sacred and Profane Love Machine*"?* The article focuses on the differences between "the ethical standards" in your essays as opposed to those in your novels. I will paraphrase most of this statement: Murdoch's essays "voice only the rejection of solipsism"—but in the novels, separation and recognition of another as a separate reality is impossible.

MURDOCH: I'm not sure what she means. The essays reject egoism, and command openness to what is other than oneself. That is what ought to be. The novels deal with what is: the selfishness which is more natural to us, together with how this is sometimes overcome. The novels are not moral tracts. They are works of art. But obviously there is a moral orientation, which is the same as in my moral philosophy. Any story, any traditional novel is about such conflicts, about how to treat other people, about power, about misunderstandings, about authority, about love.

* Dorothy Winsor, "Iris Murdoch's Conflicting Ethical Demands: Separation Versus Passivity in The Sacred and Profane Love Machine," in *Critical Essays on Iris Murdoch*, ed. Lindsey Tucker (New York: G. K. Hall & Co., 1992), 148–60.

HEUSEL: So there are very few people in the novels who achieve goodness?

MURDOCH: None that I can think of. How many people do we know who achieve goodness? I think it is extremely rare. Even so-called saints are imperfect. But to come back to the ideal, the human task is to become unselfish, to unself.

HEUSEL: This unselfing happens only momentarily?

MURDOCH: If it happens momentarily, it is not happening. It's something that's got to become a way of life. This is an interesting topic. Some people sit in halls of meditation for years, and then perhaps find that they haven't really changed themselves. On the other hand, "invisible" people can be very good. I think of school teachers, for instance. I went to a high-minded school with lofty ethical standards. I think some of the teachers there did exemplify a kind of goodness. They weren't pursuing wealth or fame or power; they were really unselfish people.

HEUSEL: Please respond to this quotation also from Ms Winsor: "Implied in the novels is the view that goodness comes through allowing or even promoting destruction of oneself in order to prevent oneself from destroying others." Is it masochistic to destroy oneself for others?

MURDOCH: I wouldn't use the word *masochistic*. That suggests that there is something self-regarding in this pursuit. What is to be "destroyed" is one's egoism, not oneself. The problem is to cease having selfish desires. This is very difficult. In the novels this problem is sometimes in the foreground, sometimes not. Sometimes there are goodish people in books. More often there are various kinds of egoists, as in life.

HEUSEL: At the end of *The Good Apprentice*, are all three men good apprentices?

MURDOCH: No, only Stuart. The other two are nowhere near having the concept at all.

HEUSEL: Peter Conradi, in his recent book . . .

MURDOCH: Such a nice boy. Do you know him?

HEUSEL: I have corresponded with him. In *Iris Murdoch: The Saint and the Artist* (New York: St Martin's Press; London: Macmillan, 1986), he suggests that your use of classical myth is sometimes "consciously disposable and provisional." What do you suppose he means by that? I see your use of classical material as absolutely integral to your purposes. Considering your thorough knowledge of Greek and Roman literature, how do you see your stories as different from those of your contemporaries?

MURDOCH: I don't know; I don't read contemporary novelists much. Certainly, I think having had a classical education is a deep part of me. I don't know what exactly Conradi means without the context. I would certainly regard myths as more than mere ornament. Allusion to myth is a complicated matter.

HEUSEL: Do you take for granted all this knowledge that many of your readers don't have? Is that sometimes a problem?

MURDOCH: I don't think so. Obviously there will be some things that the reader doesn't pick up.

HEUSEL: I have mentioned the classical material to lead into a discussion of the ideas of Mikhail Bakhtin, the Russian Formalist critic. The Iris Murdoch Society is conducting a session at MLA in San Francisco called "New Readings of Iris Murdoch." To your knowledge, isn't this the first whole session MLA has had on your work?

MURDOCH: Yes.

HEUSEL: My paper at that session argues that *The Philosopher's Pupil* celebrates the carnivalesque and that this novel is the clearest and most useful place to begin illustrating a pattern that applies throughout your fiction.

This spring I mentioned Bakhtin to you in a letter. As you probably know, he traces the genealogy of the carnivalesque from the Greek satyr play through the comic mystery play to the sacred parodies to Dostoevsky's work. One of his most popular works right now is *The Problems of Dostoevsky's Poetics*.

Will you comment on the appropriateness of the following interpretations of *The Philosopher's Pupil* and your fiction in general? Do you consider the novel to be, as Bakhtin calls carnival, "a profanation of every thing sacred"—an overthrow of what is sacred?

MURDOCH: What would lead you to apply it particularly to *The Philosopher's Pupil*?

HEUSEL: Because it is so funny and because you seem to be going back to some ancient society for a serious purpose, to write serious comedy. Is your choice of a Bath-like setting carnivalesque? Bakhtin suggests that in Menippean satire the square and bathhouses were traditionally scenes of free and familiar contact among different levels of society. Also, in *The Philosopher's Pupil* I think especially of the contact of generations—Alex the grandmother is able to hold and understand her grandson only in the water. *Do* your novels "turn things inside out"?

MURDOCH: In relation to Dostoevsky, I don't think one can explain great literature by reference to minor literature. How would one apply this stuff to Shakespeare? The moral content of great literature and its funniness and tragedy lie at a deeper level. *Satire* and *carnival* seem superficial concepts by contrast, and I would connect them with cruelty and artifice.

I don't feel, myself, that I have any connection with the satyr plays, or Attic comedy in general. My connection with the Greek world runs through Plato, of course, and through Aeschylus and through Homer and belongs to a very much more solemn, god-ridden world.

I don't own any connection with what you've been saying until you come to Dostoevsky, and then of course I do. I know what you mean in regard to him. Dostoevsky has scenes which I think exhibit what you say and which is sublime. I mean, for instance, the long scene in *Karamazov* where Dmitry pursues Grushenka to the inn, and the riot at the fête in *The Possessed*. These are great scenes which are funny and absurd and terribly sad, sort of festivals of contingency. This mixture in Dostoevsky is wonderful.

HEUSEL: You don't think you have that same kind of mixture?

MURDOCH: I hope so! I wouldn't myself connect Dostoevsky with Attic comedy. But then maybe that's because I don't know a great deal about late comedy. My ancient world ends with the death of Plato.

HEUSEL: Do you feel your wonderful set pieces are similar to Dostoevsky's? For example, the saturnalia or mardi gras or ceilidh scene at the Slipper House in *The Philosopher's Pupil*? Isn't that the same sort of thing?

MURDOCH: It's a scene in a novel. I feel the same about Dostoevsky; but after all, I'm just a novelist and critics are critics. If people want to explain something by saying that it is like something else then okay. Anyway we can't stop them, so they will. I would find it deadly to my imagination if I thought I was trying to create something which was like something else in that sense. I would like to create something which was like Dostoevsky, but then I'm doing a different thing from Dostoevsky. Something about those wild scenes in Dostoevsky fed my imagination very deeply. There is nothing in Greek comedy about which I feel this; but there is plenty in Greek tragedy and in Plato and in the myths.

HEUSEL: In *The Good Apprentice* the comedy rolls on and on and becomes more and more absurd when the couple ride to Seegard and get stuck in the mud and the mad artist descends from the stairs.

MURDOCH: It's a use of an absurd situation, the breakdown of order, the unexpected—and how in the midst of all this some awful thing can be taking place. As it was perhaps at Seegard, as it was in *Karamazov* and in *The Possessed*.

HEUSEL: Bakhtin emphasizes the "overthrowing of the order" in carnival, the importance of decrowning. Would it be accurate to say that George McCaffrey decrowns Rozanov and that Tom decrowns him? Is there a series of decrownings in *The Philosopher's Pupil*?

MURDOCH: Not that I know of. That would seem to me an arcane, artificial way to describe relationships which are clearly stated in the book.

HEUSEL: Reading Bakhtin, I discovered a connection between him and a real Rozanov. In *Problems of Dostoevsky's Poetics* Bakhtin refers to Vasily Vasilievich Rozanov (1856–1919), a Russian philosopher and literary critic who wrote *Dostoevsky and the Legend of the Grand Inquisitor.*

MURDOCH: Yes, how interesting. I didn't know that, but I knew that there was a painter named Rozanov.* That's where I picked up the name.

As for this "decrowning," I wouldn't have thought that George did any harm to Rozanov or to his reputation. George is a half-mad person,

---

* A Russian painter, Nikolay Vasilyvich Rozanov (1869–1940), is mentioned in *The Dictionary of Art,* vol. 30, ed. Jane Turner (London: Macmillan, 1996), 299, although he does not have an entry under his own name in that work.

living in a magic world. One of the original ideas in the creation of that novel was the fate of Schlick, who is mentioned in it, a philosopher of the Vienna School, who was murdered by one of his pupils.* The notion that you kill your teacher is deep in various situations in education [laughing], just as you may kill your analyst. And the illusion that George is under is one I have seen in many cases. It can be funny, it can be almost tragic: the pupil thinks that the teacher is deeply interested in him, has gone on thinking about him, is delighted to see him again, will eagerly read any stuff he has written—when this is not the case.

I can remember when I was a pupil at Oxford I thought that my teachers spent the week wondering what I would write next. Of course, when I was a tutor I realized that one rather tended to dismiss such things from one's mind.

HEUSEL: Are you suggesting incest in the student/teacher relationship?

MURDOCH: No, that's different.

HEUSEL: Is it a profanation to bring in the incest theme at the end of the novel?

MURDOCH: No, it's part of the story. Have you written novels? Are you going to? You should. It's a matter of will power—trying and failing, trying and succeeding.

For me a novel begins in a great cauldron of ideas and images, impulses and feelings. For instance, I invented Hattie early on and I'm very fond of her, and Tom appeared early, too.

HEUSEL: Tom and Hattie are very likeable.

MURDOCH: Yes, they are sweet. I'm very attached to them. George, of course, was fundamental to the story. The incest theme wasn't a deep, original theme but came up because of thinking about Hattie and her relation to her grandfather. It then became an integral part of the tale.

HEUSEL: You don't think that novel seems Greek? It is a celebration of marriage which ends in hope. Bathing scenes are integral.

MURDOCH: No. The bathing is modern bathing—there *are* such establishments. I wouldn't have formulated it in that way in my own

* Moritz Schlick (1882–1936).

mind, but if it enlightens the picture for you, okay. Since we are on the novel, there is the case of N. I don't know whether we should bring that up?

HEUSEL: Yes, I am very interested in N.

MURDOCH: Dostoevsky does that, too, for instance in *The Possessed*. I think it's a good device to have the narrator as not omnipresent, though he could have been; and at the end the lady that helped him might have been Pearl rather than me. So he could have known all these things. There is no reason why people should know who he is, but he might well be the psychiatrist Ivor Sefton, who is mentioned a few times, and at certain moments speaks directly.

HEUSEL: Who narrates the first section before N arrives?

MURDOCH: Well again Dostoevsky does this in *The Possessed*. He just charges along and writes as if it's all part of one narration and then introduces the narrator in certain contexts. So I've just done that. All right—the narrator wasn't present, presumably, when the car went into the canal, but he knows what happened, and he's just going to tell.

HEUSEL: But there's some narration in that first section, in addition to dialogue.

MURDOCH: There is plenty. The narrator moves to and fro between things which N could have written and some things he couldn't possibly have written.

HEUSEL: Is it accurate to say you are mocking a version of a Christian utopia in *The Bell* and in *Nuns and Soldiers*?

MURDOCH: No, not mocking. Certainly not! There is a certain amount of mockery—*mockery* is not exactly the right word, but ironical treatment—of the hangers-on of such communities who are often eccentric and far from holy. No, I'm not criticizing religious houses. I have friends who live that life of austerity. One faints when one thinks of what they give up. But I wouldn't mock at *them*—no, never. Anne in *Nuns and Soldiers* is a very serious person. She was trying to be selfless. She goes back to another religious community in America.

HEUSEL: Do you parody cliché and journalese in those newspaper accounts in *The Philosopher's Pupil*?

MURDOCH: Yes, it is imitation.

HEUSEL: There are no serious implications here? It's just that communication breaks down?

MURDOCH: It is quite realistic, and also, I hope, funny.

HEUSEL: A few writers have criticized your novels for containing tricks or for being sensational.

MURDOCH: What tricks? What sensations?

HEUSEL: Well, while you're on Anne, does she have a dream vision? Does she see Jesus?

MURDOCH: One does not know. Perhaps.

HEUSEL: I would argue that these devices have a serious purpose.

MURDOCH: Yes. Comedies can be tragi-comedies. Good novels are tragi-comedies. Why should it be called a trick if it is an integral part of the story? It's a drama. I think the word *ordeal* is relevant here, like Effie falling into the bog in *The Unicorn*. There are startling episodes, like Ducane and the cave [*The Nice and the Good*].

HEUSEL: But they do happen in real life.

MURDOCH: Yes—but I do not like all this formalism. Dostoevsky or any novelist likes to have a great scene now and then. Having the novel and the narration going on quietly, and then suddenly rushing over some rapids.

HEUSEL: Is there a trick in *Henry and Cato*? You certainly took me in. I felt for a time I was reading a John Hawkes' novel before I discovered that Cato was not being imprisoned by a gang.

MURDOCH: But still something awful happens.

HEUSEL: Some people might call that a trick, though.

MURDOCH: I don't know why it should be called a "trick," if this suggests something frivolous or superficial. Art is full of trickery. The artist is a trickster, and these seem perfectly legitimate tricks, absolutely embedded in the story, performing a function in it. They have got elements of surprise and funniness. And if one wanted to generalize about them, we could say they can represent an ordeal which a character undergoes and is changed by. Going to Seegard was an ordeal for Edward. One's life can change by a particular drama.

HEUSEL: Wouldn't the long serio-comic tradition in which Bakhtin finds comedy "turning things inside out" more clearly explain the seriousness and comedy in what you are doing? Instead of your fictive ordeals being negative, don't they clear the way for rebirth? For example, the change in Tim in *Nuns and Soldiers*, all of it ending in a rebirth.

MURDOCH: It is an ordeal that suddenly changes this situation for Tim. After that he can go back. But it is also absolutely realistic. Such things can happen. There are places in the south of France where canals enter tunnels. In fact, I've swum through one myself. Of course it wasn't as dangerous as in the novel. Such places can be frightening. It is quite plausible that Tim could have fallen in and been swept through this tunnel.

Tom McCaffrey's ordeal is, in a way, odder because what would the machinery of such an installation be like? I was obviously not copying any real machinery but making a fantasy. But I think that is fair enough, too.

I don't see what the objection is to the so-called "tricks." If they were absolutely out of key and if they meant the situation was changed by a kind of magical jump without any explanation, then that would be another device, but I don't use such things.

HEUSEL: One more line of questioning: May I ask you about your female characters? None of them seem to have your strengths. It is interesting to list the number of women whom might be considered to fit this quotation referring to Harriet in *The Sacred and Profane Love Machine:* "just a piece of ectoplasm" (272)—"empty, floppy, disjointed . . . and this was for her really a form of being happy" (12). I think of Rachel in *The Black Prince* and the wife in *The Unofficial Rose.*

MURDOCH: Yes, often that is an aspect of—not of being good, because nobody is totally good—but being the same as some of the people mentioned earlier like teachers who lack identity. They're not self-assertive. I think that a lot of such people who are goodish may *seem* like that. Incidentally, it isn't a remark made by me, but by one of the characters. It's a very unjust description of someone who is not self-assertive. It's true that women don't lead the stories, but there are very strong characters—Anne, for instance. *Nuns and Soldiers* is really about two strong women. People sometimes ask, "Why don't you write about women's problems?" Women's problems are problems among other problems, and I write about them also. I just don't write only or mainly about them. Unfortunately, it's still a man's world. A man doesn't have to explain what it's like to be a man but a woman has to explain what it's like to be a woman.

HEUSEL: Yes, you do write about women's problems; it's just that there are no women like you in your novels.

MURDOCH: If you portray an intellectual woman, part of her role in the book is to be an intellectual woman, but an intellectual man can be just a man. The same question arises for black writers. People expect black writers to write about blacks and black problems, and some are persecuted by their fellow blacks if they don't. I think this is very unfair. In literature writers *may* want to write about their own problems of being black or being Jewish or being female, but they may also want to write more generally about human problems.

HEUSEL: Is it simply that intellectual women don't often invent themselves as you are in the process of creating a world in a novel?

MURDOCH: There are intellectual women in the novels, but not usually as main characters.

HEUSEL: And not as narrators?

MURDOCH: Only six of the novels have first-person (and male) narration. But most of the other novels have very important female narrators.

18

JONATHAN MILLER

My God: Iris Murdoch Interviewed by Jonathan Miller

Jonathan Miller (b. 1934) is a British opera and theater director, author, and physician. He was a coauthor and actor with Peter Cook, Alan Bennett, and Dudley Moore in the satirical review *Beyond the Fringe* in the early 1960s and has since become well known for his sometimes controversial interpretations of classic plays and operas. This interview, which focuses on Murdoch's religious attitudes and beliefs, was broadcast by Granada Television on 3 April 1988.

MILLER: How old were you when you first encountered God?

MURDOCH: Well, I can't remember a time before that. My parents were, well, my mother was Anglican, my father a Quaker, a sort of Quaker. And they assumed that I would learn Christianity, and be religious and pray, and I think I could pray as soon as I could speak. And I knew that God was present.

MILLER: What form did the prayers take in childhood? I mean, was it kneeling by the bed every night?

MURDOCH: Yes . . . I think there were certain routine prayers which I said but also I had a feeling of communing with God—as if there was somebody present to whom I could address myself.

MILLER: And were you addressing yourself to God at the level of requests and petitions, or was it a private conversation?

MURDOCH: Well, it was partly petitions, asking him to look after my parents and see that they are all right and so on. But there was also a feeling of vast space and a presence, and of course the figure of Christ, who was very much a part of this first apprehension.

MILLER: And was it a two way conversation, a two way address? Was there ever a sense that something came back?

MURDOCH: Well there was a sense of reward in a way. I mean there was a sense of relief, from one's trouble, and a feeling of . . . space.

MILLER: And was that immediate at the time of the prayer or was it a sense of relief that extended through the day?

MURDOCH: It had a certain extension, yes.

MILLER: And these were the prayers that you undertook at night, say? Just before going to bed? And of course the Sunday services?

MURDOCH: Yes. Yes.

MILLER: And was there a moment then—or did it gradually fade away?—was there some crisis?

MURDOCH: Well, it faded away as I grew up, and remained vaguely with me until it was abruptly removed by the image of Karl Marx, and I became a Marxist, and then felt that Christianity was a kind of illusion, or that religion was an illusion.

MILLER: But how did encountering the figure of Marx, or the writings of Marx, actually succeed in replacing what was quite clearly an extremely valuable private sense of consolation, solace, and of renewal?

MURDOCH: Well, it may have been fading in any case. I think it was replaced quite abruptly by a sense that the world could be changed very much for the better, made more just, and happier, reasonably easily by the adoption of certain techniques.

MILLER: But at the same time as these improvements were possible by using certain social techniques recommended by Marx, there must have been some idea that what was going to count as a direction of improvement might itself be derived from sources other than the secular and the purely social, so that you presumably retained standards of what in fact would count as an ethical improvement, something in society from something which was, as it were, pre-Marxist?

MURDOCH: Possibly. Yes. But I don't see any particular problem there. I mean, one was then involved in the most immediate political matters concerning justice and happiness and poverty and so on, and these things seemed quite instinctive.

MILLER: But this after a while presumably proved unsatisfactory and Marx was replaced by something else? Or was it replaced by a sense of void which had to be filled by something else?

MURDOCH: Well, I gradually became aware that it was very much more difficult to change society than I had thought, and I became aware of what practical Communism meant in existing states, and so on. I think I was then perhaps gradually influenced by moral philosophy and by an interest in Plato—and the feeling that, although I never felt any impulse to come back to God the Father, and have never done so (I mean, I don't believe in a personal God, and I don't believe in the divinity of Christ)—I began to feel, partly as a philosopher and partly generally in life, that the place of God, being empty, needed to be filled by some more positive kind of reflection, a kind of moral philosophy, or even neo-theology, which would explain very fundamental things about the human soul and the human being.

MILLER: And what were the most fundamental things about the human soul which you felt required explanation, which were not supplied, for example, by the traditional practices of academic Oxford philosophy at that time, nor by science?

MURDOCH: Well, nor by science! Oxford philosophy, I think, has done a good job. I mean, the linguistic philosophy has done a good job in removing certain philosophical mistakes, for instance the Christian mistakes, as it were. Wittgenstein said he was ending the Cartesian era. The notion that you can start philosophy from the notion of a thinking ego. I mean there are many reflections in modern philosophy which I think have been very helpful, but I think that one effect of the development of linguistic philosophy was to diminish the central area of moral philosophy, where it could possibly connect with religion, as it did, say, in Hegel and Bradley, and, of course, does in Heidegger. This area was, as it were, parcelled out, I mean partly given to science, partly given to linguistic studies, and partly to utilitarianism, which I think has become, in a sense, the philosophy of the planet.

It's something which does us a great deal of good, and now spreads everywhere—as it does into the new theology, as practised in South America and so on—the notion that the most fundamental thing that human life should be doing is to ameliorate the situation of unhappy poor people and to promote justice. And the reflections upon, as it were, the technicalities of justice and the meaning of happiness, and the study of utilitarianism, I think, has taken up a lot of this central area, and is certainly a kind of moral philosophy—well, it is moral philosophy.

But I think that the more positive notion of goodness and virtue, the notion that it is the duty of the human being, it is the function of the human being, his form of being demands, a kind of change, a pilgrimage (like the pilgrimage in Plato's cave where the people go through a period of realizing that what they took to be real objects are actually shadows or icons or images, and then they emerge into the daylight, into reality), this image of the human pilgrimage, which is a pilgrimage from illusion to reality, and falsehood to truth, and evil to good, and that this tension in human affairs is something which cannot be explained by science and can't be dismissed by philosophy and now, of course, in my view, cannot, is not in fact, being explained by theology, Christian theology, because it is still bound to the idea of personal God which I regard as an image. I mean, one must pass beyond the image of the personal God, and this I think is something which Christian mysticism has always been hinting at, the notion that you go beyond the image of God towards godhead or divinity, and is expressed in mystics, like Eckhart for instance, where the notion of the personal God dissolves at a certain point.

And this is something which is a kind of Platonism and of course Platonism, through Saint Augustine, was a very important element in Christian theology and of course is shared with Buddhism, where the Buddhists have no problem about a personal God—the notion of Buddha who was a real person is taken up into the notion of Buddha as a mystical figure, as a vehicle of grace or a vehicle of spiritual power. And it's the feeling, the notion that there is an orientation between good and evil in human life which is unique. The ontological proof suggests not that God has to exist because existence is a predicate or quality which everything perfect must have, but rather that the idea of God is that God is a unique entity. He's not an entity actually. He's not a thing among things but that the contingency of the world contains a great jumble of things but God is separate from this, God is not a thing among things.

And I think that Buddhism recognises this (and this is true of Hinduism too, I think that they recognise the basic contingency) and I think this is something that is itself a part of religion—that we are accidents, our existence is accidental, our historical circumstances are accidental, the whole background of human life is a jumble, but nevertheless, in the midst of this jumble, there is still this particular orientation which is unique and special and belongs to us and is a part of our being. And how one expresses this in the imagery of metaphysics—if metaphysics is still going to be allowed to exist, or whatever one calls this form of philosophy—I think is very difficult, but the function of this is very important.

MILLER: But do you think this reflection, and this orientation, can survive the disappearance of some personal God, and can it also survive if, in fact, we dismantle the complex liturgical apparatus that we have previously used in order to concentrate the mind on such things?

MURDOCH: Well I should be very sorry if . . . well, we're already dismantling the liturgical apparatus by banishing Cranmer's prayer book and the great words that it contains, which it seems to me are perfectly understandable and can play their part without believing in a personal God, or the divinity of Christ, because these things are about the fundamental orientations and realities of human life—the way in which we pass beyond egoism towards more open recognition of the reality of other people and the importance of other things, and beyond illusions to reality, and beyond falsehood to truth, that the idea of truth, I think, is a great binding factor here which ties—this is very much part of Plato's philosophy—that in the recognition of truth there is also the recognition of virtue.

MILLER: And yet I get the impression that, although I agree with you that the Cranmer prayer book and the original King James version of the Bible are admirable as literature, and also they have a numinousness which is not contained in the Welfare State prose of the New English Bible, but nevertheless they are attached, and given their legitimacy as forms of prayer and forms of contemplation by virtue of the fact that they are attached to the idea of a personal God and to the notion of a Trinity. And if that is dismantled, in what sense are they anything more than, as it were, picturesque objects to be visited and enjoyed for their purely literary value?

MURDOCH: Well, I think that human beings are always moving with the greatest ease through imagery to what lies behind it. After all, again, Eastern religions have no problems with this sort of. . . . I think it's difficult for Christianity (because of the historical nature of Christ's mission, that we know a lot about—that he was a historical person and so on) but . . . the survival of Christianity (unless you mean that God didn't arrange it) is in a way surprising. And I think Saint Paul played a great part in this, that Saint Paul wasn't concerned with the details of Christ's life. He immediately took hold of the notion of the Mystical Christ, that Christ is in the soul and a Buddhist will say Buddha is in the soul, that it is part of the nature of the human soul to want—this word which is so unscientific I think is important—to have this sense of a kind of "otherness" which is connected with everything one knows about what is real and true.

MILLER: But much of what we find is so attractive—and I as a Jewish atheist see it from the outside and still see it as attractive—is connected with a calendar, a Christian calendar, that marches steadily and elegantly through the year, marking off the episodes of Christian events. And if in fact one withdraws belief in the existence or in the divine significance of those events it is very hard to see what in fact is different from—I was going to say Asterix, but . . .

MURDOCH: (laughing) Really!

MILLER: But, nevertheless, they are, in some sense, merely exotic stories unless, in fact, one supplies belief.

MURDOCH: But we live by stories. I mean, we interpret stories; we are always using metaphors and stories. I don't myself see any problem there at all. I still myself use the Christian mythology. I am moved by it and I see its religious significance and the way in which ordinary life is given a radiance. You used the word "numinous" yourself about the prayer book and so on. There is a numinous aspect to life. And that if somebody says . . . well, a child I know just recently suddenly decided (in this family where people were not religious) that she wanted to be confirmed. People said to her "But it's not true." Well, now, about Christianity, in a sense, all right. *I* don't think it's true that there is heaven, or God, and so on, but this seems to me not at all to touch the sacredness and the numinousness and the truth-bearing properties of the Christian mythology. As it happens if we lived somewhere else we'd have Krishna and we'd have Buddha. A sophisticated and (perhaps this is a bad word to use here) a *devout* believer knows that these images (he may even have literalistic views too), he knows that these things represent something real in his life and that they are a refuge from evil.

MILLER: In that case can you find yourself participating, with anything more than touristic enthusiasm, in any form of religious service today?

MURDOCH: Good heavens, yes, I do. I mean, I don't actually take communion, I don't receive the sacrament. Something inhibits me from doing this—I'm not quite sure what. But I certainly attend Christian services. Religious experience is something we should be having all the time in fact. Because—this is an aspect of religion which, I think, differentiates it from ordinary, segregated ideas of morality, as some (kind of) part-time occupation—that religion is something that fills the whole of one's life. It's to do with every moment in one's life.

MILLER: But is it then merely a familiarity and an old pedigree in Christianity which makes you gravitate towards church services rather than, say, synagogue services or services in a mosque, since all of them, as you say, express numinous otherness?

MURDOCH: Well, I've certainly participated in Buddhist services and Hindu ones but . . . this is an accident, I mean that I'm familiar with Christianity is an accident of my life. We live in history, and in the midst of our own accidents. I mean, somewhere else the same thing probably would be brought to me by a different medium. But this is our local medium, and I think it's extremely important that Christianity should survive in the West. But it may be said that the chances are rather small but it would be necessary . . . somebody said that Christianity has always been changing itself into something that people can believe. I think it's important that this change should be going on now—I mean that people should be able to realize that they can have Christian religion without literal dogma, that they can have a religious dimension in their lives without having to subscribe to beliefs that now seem to them impossible.

MILLER: Do you think it is possible to remove dogma and retain what, for many of us, is still the attractive aspect of Christian iconography—pictures, for example, of the Virgin and child, of the Adoration, of the Visitation, all of which somehow have a numinousness—but is it possible for them to retain that numinousness if in fact one fundamentally and finally says "It is only a story, it has no divine significance"?

MURDOCH: Well, the word "only," you see, would have to be removed here. The human race has fortunately manufactured for itself, or been vouchsafed, great stories, great images. The notion of virtue and goodness itself immediately has its own imagery, whether it's Platonic or that of a mystic or that of a saint. These are images but they are life-giving images, and they're natural to us, and provided one is not misled . . . I mean, I would feel that one would be misled in thinking, for instance, that there would be life after death, or anything like that—heavens elsewhere, where Jesus is sitting on the right hand of God—I can, as it were, discarding *these things*, still see that the iconography is part of something true and important in human life, that it is something which points to (and perhaps this is the more fundamental thing) what the ontological proof is about: the fact that in human beings (and this does make us unique; we're not like any other creatures that we know of) there is this permanent orientation and this permanent magnetism (one might put it like that: the form of the good, Plato's image, is magnetic), that there is something which pulls us and checks us. And you might say "Well what's the proof?" or "Is it true?" or "How can we investigate it?" This is what I think serious moral philosophy and theology should reflect upon, to find a mode of speech which will enable one to say something about it, while recognising its reality.

MILLER: But in a way, of course, you're fortunate in that you start with, as it were, a history of an involuntary commitment to Christianity. You grew up with the belief in a personal God from which you gradually rid yourself, but nevertheless retained enough link with the belief to still be committed to the iconography, and to the calendar, and to the liturgical forms of Christianity. How would you advise a parent who himself or herself no longer believes and is going to start with children?

How could a child, starting from scratch, as it were, be introduced to the virtues and the galvanising powers of Christianity while being told at the same time that the story is completely untrue?

MURDOCH: Well, yes, but you are using this terminology which I don't like—"The story is completely untrue." The story of Christ's life is perhaps partly true. It's a story about a man. The notion that he rose from the dead is perhaps untrue. I have no children, but if I did have children I think I would put them into the situation of learning about Christianity and regarding it as religious. And a child can take in anything. If you tell a child all about sex when it's four or something, it's not going to worry, it'll draw its own conclusions.

MILLER: But you were told by people who actually held these beliefs rather than someone who, as it were, is going to pretend to hold these beliefs in order to introduce the child to religious views.

MURDOCH: Well, I think that a knowledge of Christianity in childhood is very important.

19

JEFFREY MEYERS

Two Interviews with Iris Murdoch

Jeffrey Meyers, a Fellow of the Royal Society of Literature, taught for thirty years at universities in the United States, England, and Japan, and he has written a number of literary biographies. The background to these interviews is recounted in Meyers's book *Privileged Moments: Encounters with Writers* (Madison: University of Wisconsin Press, 2000). Meyers recorded an interview in July 1988, and Murdoch revised and expanded the text. For the first publication by the *Paris Review* 115 (1990), additional material was added by the editors and some of Meyers's original material was omitted, against his wishes. The omitted material was published in 1991 by the *Denver Quarterly* (26, no. 1). Extracts from both publications of this interview are also reprinted here.

The Art of Fiction CXVII: Iris Murdoch

Iris Murdoch was born in Dublin on July 15, 1919 and grew up in London. She was educated at Badminton School in Bristol and studied Classics at Somerville College, Oxford, from 1938 until 1942, receiving first class honors. She was Assistant Principal in the Treasury from 1942 to 1944 and an Administrative Officer with the United Nations Relief and Rehabilitation Administration in England, Belgium and Austria during the years 1944 to 1946. She held a Sarah Smithson Studentship in philosophy at Newnham College, Cambridge, in 1947–1948,

and became a fellow of St. Anne's College, Oxford, and a university lec-
turer in philosophy the following year. [. . .]

Murdoch and her husband live in a house in academic north
Oxford. In its comfortably untidy rooms books overflow the shelves and
are piled high on the floor. Even the bathroom is filled with volumes on
language, including Dutch and Esperanto grammar books. Her paper-
strewn second-floor study is decorated with oriental rugs and with
paintings of horses and children. The first-floor sitting room, which
leads out to the garden, has a well-stocked bar. There are paintings and
tapestries of flowers, art books and records, pottery and old bottles, and
embroidered cushions on the deep sofa.

Additional questions were proposed to Murdoch by James Atlas in
front of an audience at the YMHA in New York last spring.

MEYERS: Do you think you could say something about your family?

MURDOCH: My father went through the first war in the cavalry; it
now seems extraordinary to think there was cavalry in World War I.
This no doubt saved his life, because, of course, the horses were
behind the lines, and in that sense he had a safer war. My parents met
at that time. My father's regiment was based at the Curragh near
Dublin and my father was on leave. On his way to church he met my
mother, who was going to the same church on the same tram. She sang
in the choir. My mother had a very beautiful soprano voice; she was
training to be an opera singer and could have been very good indeed,
but she gave up her ambitions when she married. She continued
singing all her life in an amateur way, but she never realized the poten-
tial of that great voice. She was a beautiful, lively, witty woman, with a
happy temperament. My parents were very happy together. They loved
each other dearly; they loved me and I loved them, so it was a most
felicitous trinity.

MEYERS: When did you know you wanted to write?

MURDOCH: I knew very early on that I wanted to be a writer. I mean,
when I was a child I knew that. Obviously, the war disturbed all one's
feelings of the future very profoundly. When I finished my undergraduate career I was immediately conscripted because everyone was.
Under ordinary circumstances, I would very much have wanted to stay

on at Oxford, study for a Ph.D., and try to become a don. I was very anxious to go on learning. But one had to sacrifice one's wishes to the war. I went into the civil service, into the Treasury where I spent a couple of years. Then after the war I went into UNRRA, the United Nations Relief and Rehabilitation Administration, and worked with refugees in different parts of Europe.

MEYERS: You were a member of the Communist Party, weren't you?

MURDOCH: I was a member of the Communist Party for a short time when I was a student, about 1939. I went in, as a lot of people did, out of a sense which arose during the Spanish Civil War that Europe was dangerously divided between left and right and we were jolly well going to be on the left. We had passionate feelings about a social justice. We believed that socialism could, and fairly rapidly, produce just and good societies, without poverty and without strife. I lost those optimistic illusions fairly soon. So I left it. But it was just as well, in a way, to have seen the inside of Marxism because then one realizes how strong and how awful it is, certainly in its organized form. My association with it had its repercussions. Once I was offered a scholarship to come to Vassar. I was longing to go to America—such an adventure after being cooped up in England after the war. One did want to travel and see the world. I was prevented by the McCarren Act, and not given a visa. I may say there was a certain amount of to-do about this. Bertrand Russell got involved and Justice Felix Frankfurter, trying to say how ridiculous this was. But the McCarren Act is made of iron. It's still here; I have to ask for a waiver if I want to come to the United States.

MEYERS: Even now?

MURDOCH: It's lunatic. One of the questions sometimes asked by some official is, "Can you prove that you are no longer a member of the Communist Party?"

MEYERS: I should think that would be very difficult to do.

MURDOCH: Extremely! I left it about fifty years ago!

MEYERS: Could you tell me a little bit about your own method of composition and how you go about writing a novel?

MURDOCH: Well, I think it is important to make a detailed plan before you write the first sentence. Some people think one should write—"George woke up and knew that something terrible had happened yesterday"—and then see what happens. I plan the whole thing in detail before I begin. I have a general scheme and lots of notes. Every chapter is planned. Every conversation is planned. This is, of course, a primary stage, and very frightening because you've committed yourself at this point. I mean, a novel is a long job, and if you get it wrong at the start you're going to be very unhappy later on. The second stage is that one should sit quietly and let the thing invent itself. One piece of imagination leads to another. You think about a certain situation and then some quite extraordinary aspect of it suddenly appears. The deep things that the work is about declare themselves and connect. Somehow things fly together and generate other things, and characters invent other characters, as if they were all doing it themselves. One should be patient and extend this period as far as possible. Of course, actually writing it involves a different kind of imagination and work.

MEYERS: You're remarkably prolific as a novelist. You seem to enjoy writing a great deal.

MURDOCH: Yes, I do enjoy it, but it has, of course—I mean this is true of any art form—moments when you think it's awful, you lose confidence and it's all black. You can't think and so on. So, it's not all enjoyment. But I don't actually find writing in itself difficult. The *creation* of the story is the agonizing part. You have the extraordinary experience when you begin a novel that you are now in a state of unlimited freedom, and this is alarming. Every choice you make will exclude another choice, so that it's rather important what happens then, what state of mind you're in and what you think matters. Books should have themes. I choose titles carefully and the titles in some way indicate something deep in the theme of the book. Names are important. The names sometimes don't come at once, but the physical being and the mind of the character have to come pretty early on and you just have to wait for the gods to offer you something. You have to spend a lot of time looking out of the window and writing down scrappy notes which may or may not help. You have to wait patiently until you feel that you're getting the thing right—who the people are, what it's all about, how it moves. I may take a long time, say a year, just sitting and fishing around, putting the thing into some sort of shape. Then I do a very detailed synopsis of every chapter, every conversation, everything that happens. That would be another operation.

MEYERS: Which tends to come first—characters or plot?

MURDOCH: I think they all start in much the same way, with two or three people in a relationship with a problem. Then there is the story, ordeals, conflicts, a movement from illusion to reality, all that. I don't think I have any autobiographical tendencies and can't think of any novel I've written that is a copy of my own life.

MEYERS: And you write by hand?

MURDOCH: Oh, yes, yes, yes.

MEYERS: No machines, no computers?

MURDOCH: No.

MEYERS: And then take them up to your publisher who's terrified because there's only one copy?

MURDOCH: Yes, at the end there's only one copy. I know that some people like word processors, but I do a great deal of correcting as I go along. I think if one had the green screen in front of one, one would be so fascinated by the words on it one wouldn't want to change any of them!

MEYERS: What are your daily work habits?

MURDOCH: I like working and when I have time to work, I work. But I also have to do other things like washing up and buying food. Fortunately my husband does the cooking. I sometimes have to go to London or I want to see my friends. Otherwise, I work pretty steadily all the time. I go to bed early and I start work very early. I work all morning, and then I shop and write letters—the letters take up a lot of time—in the afternoon. Then I work again from about half-past four until seven or eight. So I work steadily when I've got the open time, which is more days than not.

MEYERS: How many words a day do you usually write?

MURDOCH: I've never thought of counting words. I'd rather not know.

MEYERS: A moment ago you mentioned the names of your characters. How do you choose them?

MURDOCH: They have to choose themselves; one just waits. If you make a mistake there, this can be quite a serious matter. The character has to announce his own name. I make lists of names; I often invent names. I once invented the name Gavender; I thought, "Nobody's named Gavender." Then I got a letter from someone in America saying, "How did you know about our family?" It is fun inventing names. Names are very important because a lot of atmosphere comes with a name. The way a person is going to be addressed by his fellow characters is important, too.

MEYERS: How do you find specific details about experts, like Bruno and his spiders, in your novels?

MURDOCH: I'm very interested in spiders. I like spiders. Spiders are my friends, and I have read books about spiders. So that part of the book was just part of a spider lore which I happen to possess.

MEYERS: But if a man has a job like a wine merchant or a soldier?

MURDOCH: I ask my wine merchant friends to help me. As for soldiers, my brother-in-law is a soldier. Everything to do with guns my husband, John, supplies because he is very interested in weapons. He knows all about weapons from the early Greeks up to the latest machine guns. One's friends can help. And of course there are books.

MEYERS: What's your most difficult technical problem?

MURDOCH: It's the one I mentioned earlier, the beginning, how to start and when to begin structuring the novel. It is this progression from complete freedom to a narrow cage, how fast you move and when you decide what the main things in the book are going to be. I think these are the most difficult things. One must consider what one's characters are like, what jobs they do, what religion they have, what nationality they are, how they are related to each other, and so on. Here at the beginning one has infinite possibilities, this choice of what sort of people they are and what sort of troubles they are going to have, who wins, who loses, who dies. Most of all one must reflect upon their values, their morality, their moral dilemmas. You can't write any novel without implying values. You can't write a traditional novel without giving your characters moral problems and judgments. That is what is most difficult of all.

MEYERS: You've said that "one constantly takes prototypes from literature who may actually influence one's conduct." Could you give specific examples?

MURDOCH: Did I say that? Good heavens, I can't remember the context. Of course, one feels affection for, or identifies with, certain fictional characters. My two favorites are Achilles and Mr Knightley. This shows the difficulty of thinking of characters who might influence one. I could reflect upon characters in Dickens, Dostoyevsky, Tolstoy; these writers particularly come to mind: wise moralistic writers who portray the complexity of morality and the difficulty of being good.

Plato remarks in *The Republic* that bad characters are volatile and interesting, whereas good characters are dull and always the same. This certainly indicates a literary problem. It is difficult in life to be good, and difficult in art to portray goodness. Perhaps we don't know much about goodness. Attractive bad characters in fiction may corrupt people, who think, "So that's okay." Inspiration from good characters may be rarer and harder, yet Aloysha in *The Brothers Karamazov* and the grandmother in Proust's novel exist. I think one is influenced by the whole moral atmosphere of literary works, just as we are influenced by Shakespeare, a great exemplar for the novelist. In the most effortless manner he portrays moral dilemmas, good and evil, and the differences and the struggle between them. I think he is a deeply religious writer. He doesn't portray religion directly in the plays, but it is certainly there, a sense of the spiritual, of goodness, of self-sacrifice, of reconciliation and of forgiveness. I think that is the absolutely prime example of how we ought to tell a story: invent characters and convey something dramatic which at the same time has deep spiritual significance.

MEYERS: If your fictional characters are not based on real people, as they are for most novelists, for example Hemingway and Lawrence, then how are your characters created?

MURDOCH: Just by this process of sitting and waiting. I would abominate the idea of putting real people in a novel, not only because I think it's morally questionable, but also because I think it would be terribly dull. I don't want to make a photographic copy of somebody I know. I want to create somebody who never existed, and who is at the same time a plausible person. I think the characteristics gradually gather together. The first image of the character may be very shadowy; one vaguely knows that he is a good citizen or a religious sort of chap.

Perhaps he's puritanical, or hedonistic, and so on. I must have some notion of the troubles he's going to be in and his relationship to the other characters. But the details on which the novel depends, the details of his appearance, his peculiarities, his idiosyncrasies, his other characteristics, his mode of being, will come later—if one is lucky—and quite instinctively, because the more you see of a person the more a kind of coherence begins to evolve.

MEYERS: Your characters are not necessarily innocents. They're able to commit violence and all sorts of misdeeds, and yet there exists this imperative within them toward the good. Does philosophy apply here?

MURDOCH: I don't think this connects with philosophy. The consideration of moral issues in the novels may be intensified by some philosophical considerations, but on the whole I think it's dangerous writing a philosophical novel. I mean, this is not a thing writers can easily get away with. Take the case of Thomas Mann, whom I adore, for instance. When his characters start having very long philosophical conversations, one feels, "Well, perhaps we could do without this." My novels are not "philosophical novels."

MEYERS: Well, your characters also have long philosophical arguments.

MURDOCH: Well, occasionally, but not very long.

MEYERS: You once wrote, "A great artist is, in respect of his work, a good man and in the true sense a free man."* I wonder if you could interpret this?

MURDOCH: The important phrase is, ". . . in respect to his work," because obviously great artists can lead less than perfect lives. Take Dante for instance. Or Shakespeare. We know very little about Shakespeare's life. You could name almost anybody who has written a great or good novel and see that their lives are imperfect. You can be unselfish and truthful in your art, and a monster at home. To write a good book you have to have certain qualities. Great art is connected with courage and truthfulness. There is a conception of truth, a lack of illusion, an ability to overcome selfish obsessions, which goes with good art, and the artist has got to have that particular sort of moral stamina.

* Murdoch, "On 'God' and 'Good,'" 352.

Good art, whatever its style, has qualities of hardness, firmness, realism, clarity, detachment, justice, truth. It is the work of a free, unfettered, uncorrupted imagination. Whereas bad art is the soft, messy, self-indulgent work of an enslaved fantasy. Pornography is at one end of that scale, great art at the other end.

The reading of great books, the contemplation of great art, is somehow very good for one. There's a truthfulness of great art which one sees in the great nineteenth-century novels. It is very difficult to attain, to create something which is not a fantasy. I'd want to make the distinction between fantasy and imagination, not the same as Coleridge's, but a distinction between the expression of immediate selfish feelings and the elimination of yourself in a work of art. The most obvious case of the former would be the novel where the writer is the hero and is always succeeding. He doesn't succeed at first, but he's very brave, and all the girls like him, and so on. That tends to spoil the work. I think some of D. H. Lawrence's work is spoiled by too much Lawrence. What is important is an ability to have an image of perfection and to expel fantasy and the sort of lesser, egoistic cravings and the kind of imagery and immediate expressions that might go with them, and to be prepared to think and to wait. It's difficult, as I say, to make this into any sort of program, to overcome egoism and fantasy.

MEYERS: What would be an example in the novel?

MURDOCH: There would be very obvious cases—the whole tradition of the English novel from Jane Austen, Charles Dickens, Emily Bronte, George Eliot and, of course, Henry James, whom I love. I also love the Russian novel. In a curious way English-speaking people feel a great affinity with the Russians. Somehow, the works of Tolstoy and Dostoyevsky in translation seem very natural to us. It's as if they were already writing in English. I think we have the same feeling about Proust—that he's really an English writer! He speaks to us very directly . . . whereas Stendhal and Flaubert are more remote. We know they're French. It was the great age of the novel. One can always return to them and find marvelous wisdom.

MEYERS: Should the novelist also be a moralist and teacher?

MURDOCH: Moralist, yes. Teacher suggests something more didactic in tone. A novelist is bound to express values, and I think he should be conscious of the fact that he is, in a sense, a compulsory moralist. Novelists differ, of course, in the extent to which they set out to reflect on morals and to put that reflection into their work. I certainly do reflect and put this reflection into my works, whether or not with success. The question is how to do it. If you can't do it well, you had better not do it at all. If you have strong moral feelings, you may be in difficulties with your characters because you may want them to be less emphatic than you are yourself. In answer to your question, I think a novelist should be wary of being a teacher in a didactic sense, but should be conscious of himself as a moralist.

MEYERS: In your work you consider what religion means for people who do not believe in God. Can you say something about this?

MURDOCH: This question interests and concerns me very much. Looking at western societies I think that if we have religion, we shall have to have religion without God, because belief in a personal God is becoming increasingly impossible for many people. It's a difficult question actually to know what believing in a personal God is. I know that I don't believe in one. I don't want to use the word "God" in any other sense. I think it's a proper name. I don't believe in the divinity of Christ. I don't believe in life after death. My beliefs really are Buddhist in style. I've been very attached to Buddhism. Buddhism makes it plain that you can have religion without God, that religion is in fact better off without God. It has to do with *now*, with every moment of one's life, how one thinks, what one is and does, about love and compassion and the overcoming of self, the difference between illusion and reality.

MEYERS: In your book on Jean-Paul Sartre, you write of a kind of breakdown of moral authority, the disappearance of religion and a sense of chaos that's ushered in and reflects itself in your work.*

MURDOCH: Well, it's a long way back to the Sartre era. His popularity immediately after the war was extraordinary. People who had nothing to do with philosophy felt that a philosophy had been invented for them. The war had been so terrible and so destructive, and the Hitler era had been so unimaginably awful. People wanted to find a way of having some kind of spirit come back into their life. Sartre's existentialist

* Murdoch, *Sartre* (1953).

ethic with its notion of complete freedom, and the notion that you should get yourself into a state where you can make a choice which transcends conventions and the dull feeling of being contained, submerged, and so on—this (and his novels, too) reflects a, in a way, heroic ethic. It did cheer people up a lot. I don't particularly go along with this myself, but it had a great revivifying effect.

MEYERS: I wondered how you feel about your own achievements and what you've done?

MURDOCH: Well, one is always discontented with what one has done. And also, of course, one's always afraid that even the things one has done can't be done again. I don't know. I think artists live in the present, really. I mean, forget about the past and what you've done because it's what you think you can do *next* which matters. For any writer it's terribly discouraging if somebody says, "Oh, I loved your first novel!" My heart sinks when they say that, because that suggests it's been downhill all the way!

MEYERS: What were you able to accomplish in the play, *The Black Prince*, that you did not accomplish in the novel?

MURDOCH: Well, the theater is such a different game. Writers of fiction, of novels, are pleased when they can see something of their work on stage and hear people uttering their lines and so on. But a play is made of lines, and it's got to be . . . I mean, the miracle about the theater is why people stay there. Why don't they get up and go? It's not at all easy to write a play. There's a special kind of magic involved. My first adventure in the theater was a very pleasant one because I worked with J. B. Priestley on making a play out of a novel of mine called *A Severed Head.* He said to me, "Duckie, this is a difficult game; a very few people can succeed at it. If it was all that easy everybody would be doing it." It is very difficult to compress the reflections of one's characters and the great pattern of a novel into a drama where it is a matter of lines and short speeches and actual actors and so on. The forms are so different that they can't possibly be compared. A play is much more like a poem.

MEYERS: Could you say something about your use of painters and painting in fiction? I'm thinking of Max Beckmann in *Henry and Cato,* Bronzino in *The Nice and the Good,* Titian in *The Sacred and Profane Love Machine.*

MURDOCH: I am very interested in painting. Painting appears more frequently than music, for instance, because I know far more about painting than about music. The only music which tends to appear is singing, which I know about because of my mother. I love painting. I love looking at pictures, and I did once very much want to be a painter. I understand painting in a way I don't understand music, though I am moved by music. I know a lot of painters. I know what painting is. I enjoy bringing in painting. I admire Beckmann very much and I've seen a lot of Beckmanns in St. Louis and other places. With a bit of luck, one's own interests and feelings can run straight along with those of the character. But there is also the challenge of inventing characters with alien interests. This can be a dangerous business.

MEYERS: Do you see a painting you are particularly interested in and think, "I might be able to use that some day in a novel," or "I'd like to use it because it attracts and interests me"?

MURDOCH: The novel often indicates a painting during the process of creating the characters. Somehow the character will lead to the painting. A great painting which I have only recently seen—it lives in Czechoslovakia—is Titian's *Flaying of Marsyas*. He was over ninety when he painted it. This painting gives me very much, though I have only referred to it indirectly.

MEYERS: Does your husband read and comment on your works before they're published?

MURDOCH: No, he doesn't see them until they're printed. I talk to him occasionally about things where he can help me, about how a revolver works or something like that.

MEYERS: Do you show parts of your novel to your editor at Chatto and Windus before it's completed?

MURDOCH: No, I don't show it to them until I've finished it. I don't ask for advice.

MEYERS: Do you think children limit the freedom needed as a writer?

MURDOCH: Oh, no. There are innumerable examples of their compatibility. Women have obvious problems about family life and doing jobs. But, in a way, being a writer is one of the easier choices because you can do it at home. I don't think there is an awful problem there.

MEYERS: Which contemporary writers do you respect?

MURDOCH: I don't really read contemporary writers very much. For instance, I enjoyed reading Kundera's *The Unbearable Lightness of Being*, Ishiguro's *A Pale View of Hills,* and A. S. Byatt's wonderful novel, *Possession.*

MEYERS: Do you read the works of writers you know?

MURDOCH: Yes, sometimes. But I don't read much contemporary fiction. I particularly admire John Cowper Powys. I particularly liked *Wolf Solent, A Glastonbury Romance* and *Weymouth Sands.* They are very long novels, full of details which novels should have. I think he is very good on sex. Sex is a complicated, subtle, omnipresent, mysterious, multifarious business; sex is everywhere. I think Hardy is a far more erotic writer than Lawrence. John Cowper Powys is really interested in sex, just as keen on it as Lawrence, but he understands and portrays it far better. He sees so many different aspects of it. He treats it with reverence and respect. He finds it very strange, and funny, and mysterious.

MEYERS: What effect would you like your books to have?

MURDOCH: I'd like people to enjoy reading them. A readable novel is a gift to humanity. It provides an innocent occupation. Any novel takes people away from their troubles and the television set; it may even stir them to reflect about human life, characters, morals. So I would like people to be able to read the stuff. I'd like it to be understood too; though some of the novels are not all that easy, I'd like them to be understood, and not grossly misunderstood. But literature is to be enjoyed, to be grasped by enjoyment.

MEYERS: How would you describe your ideal reader?

MURDOCH: Those who like a jolly good yarn are welcome and worthy readers. I suppose the *ideal* reader is someone who likes a jolly good yarn and enjoys thinking about the book as well, thinking about the moral issues.

MEYERS: Do you think a good yarn is essential to the novel?

MURDOCH: It is one of the main charms of the art form and its prime mode of expression. A novel without a story must work very hard in other ways to be worth reading, and indeed to be read. Some of today's anti-story novels are too deliberately arcane. I think story is essential to the survival of the novel. A novel may be "difficult" but its story can carry and retain the reader who may understand in his own way, even remember and return. Stories are a fundamental human form of thought.

An Interview with Iris Murdoch

[. . .] MEYERS: How did your postwar refugee work affect your fiction?

MURDOCH: I don't think it affected it very much, except for a strong feeling about refugees. I've never attempted to portray anything that happened to me either during the war or afterward in the refugee camps. I don't think I have an impulse to use my life in that way. [. . .] Some sort of feeling about homelessness and exile came out of that experience.

MEYERS: Did you have any contact in England with the refugees you worked with in Europe?

MURDOCH: Only two or three. Most of these people didn't want to go back to their homeland. They'd had enough of Europe and wanted to go to America, and some of the younger ones did. The older ones, of course, just got left in the camps. Nobody wanted them and God knows what happened to them. One was very much concerned with helping people to go where they wanted to go and some of these refugees wanted to go to England. In fact, there were several cases where I managed to help people who wanted to come over here. But the most successful long-standing contact was a Yugoslav.*

I was working in Graz, in Austria—I worked in several different camps in several parts of Austria—and Graz University set up a camp for students. They had refugees who were studying and the university gave them facilities. This young Yugoslav chap was a medical student, and when we first met our common language was German, which we both spoke badly but with great mutual comprehension. He wanted to come to England and I did help him to get into medical school. Now he is a head consultant in Bristol and has had a very successful career. But he was one of the lucky ones.

MEYERS: [. . .] Why did you begin to teach at the Royal College of Art in the mid-1960s?

* Jože Jančar. See Conradi, *Iris Murdoch.*

MURDOCH: That was really for fun. I decided that I would give up teaching at Oxford, which was a hard decision; I didn't want to, but I couldn't go on doing quite so many things at once. [. . .] At the same time a friend of mine who was running the General Studies department at the Royal College said, "we're looking for someone to teach some philosophy to our students," so I thought, "why shouldn't I?"* It was a day-a-week job. I am very interested in painting, I really wanted to be a painter at one time, and it was a very nice job to teach these kids. Many of them were painters and sculptors, and very intelligent, but had never read a book. It was a challenging, exciting operation talking to these lively young people who were much wilder than Oxford students and very picturesque. It gave me insight into the art school world and I was interested in seeing painters and sculptors at work.

MEYERS: What were the effects of your move from Steeple Aston, a country village, to Oxford?

MURDOCH: Convenience, shopping, no long car journeys. I miss the big garden and the lovely house, but it was getting too difficult to cope with. It's a more convenient life here. I see more of my Oxford friends.

MEYERS: Who are your closest literary friends and what have you learned from them?

MURDOCH: I don't think I learn anything literary from them, but I may learn a lot of other things. Kingsley Amis is an old friend, I've known him since we were students. Also, for instance, A. S. Byatt, A. N. Wilson, Andrew Harvey, Bernice Rubens, Vikram Seth. I think I have more friends who are scholars or painters or do other things.

MEYERS: How do you use your travels in your work?

MURDOCH: Not much, really. One of my novels, *Nuns and Soldiers,* has a scene in a French landscape, the Alpilles, north of Marseilles, but that is a landscape that I know very well and have a strong feeling about.

MEYERS: What are the benefits of attending international cultural conferences?

MURDOCH: Fun, travel, friends, occasionally thoughts. I met Vikram Seth at a conference in Delhi. One sometimes meets someone one

* Christopher Cornford. See Conradi, *Iris Murdoch,* p. 469.

really wants to know, and one meets one's old friends. One may even, actually, get some ideas out of the discussion. It can be valuable. Yes, I think that one gets a lot out of traveling to another place, meeting a lot of intellectuals and just collecting one's wits, thinking of something to say and thinking about what people think about what you have to say. I think there is some value in this. I feel very strongly about Europe, that it's important for Europeans to get used to being in one another's pockets. I feel this very much about France and England, that we should be closer than we are.

MEYERS: Could you tell me specifically how any one of your novels was conceived? What idea, plot or characters you started with, and how you planned the book before writing?

MURDOCH: *The Book and the Brotherhood* obviously came out of an interest in Marxism and the way in which people's ideas changed, out of having a lot of friends at the university. It concerned the way in which differences of opinion define people; the notion of a book which at one time everyone felt was going to express their views and later on realized it wasn't. So it's got some sort of connection with Oxford and Marxism.

[. . .]

MEYERS: What is the function and meaning of the homosexual characters who appear quite frequently in your novels?

MURDOCH: I think it depends on the context. They play different parts in different stories. I know a lot of homosexuals. I have homosexual friends. I'm very much in favor of gay lib, and I feel very strongly that there shouldn't be any sort of prejudice against homosexuals, or suggestions that homosexual love is unnatural or bad. I hope such views are tending to disappear from society.

MEYERS: How are your political beliefs, about Ireland, for example, expressed in your fiction?

MURDOCH: My book about Ireland, *The Red and the Green*, was written before the IRA started up again, so that it was, as it were, an innocent, optimistic book which assumed the troubles were over. [. . .] But now, of course, one's heart is broken over Ireland. I don't think we can go on talking about this because I have such strong emotions about it. The activity of the IRA exhibits the extreme of human wickedness.

It is an example of how a few evil people can maim a whole society. It is a tragic situation, often misunderstood by people in other countries.

MEYERS: You have been described as an idealist without illusions. Would you agree with this?

MURDOCH: I'm an idealist, I suppose, yes. Whether one is without illusions is difficult to say. I should think I probably have illusions. I think there are a lot of half-illusions which one has where one is half-deceived or half-deceiving oneself. Being an idealist suggests that one has certain hopes, and I have lots and lots of hopes, and, I suppose, ideals. I feel very optimistic in one way and very pessimistic in other ways, and this may sometimes be difficult to adjust. One hopes that one is going to be able to partake in or witness some good change in the world or in oneself. Then someone comes along and says, "you're not looking at the facts, you're not being realistic, it can't happen like this, you just think it would be nice if it did." But hope and optimism can be justified. Consider the recent changes in eastern Europe. Hope is said to be a virtue, a kind of attention which may illuminate the way to the good.

[. . .]

MEYERS: Do you think your books have been generally understood?

MURDOCH: I don't know. I get letters which I value from people who say that my books have helped them in some way. That's pleasing news.

20

ROSEMARY HARTILL

Flight to the Enchantress

Rosemary Hartill, a British writer and independent broadcaster, was the BBC's religious affairs correspondent from 1982 to 1988. This interview first appeared in *Writers Revealed* (London: BBC, 1989) and was based on a broadcast on BBC Radio channel 4 on 20 July 1989.

[. . .] At eighteen, partly due to the influence of her left-wing, progressive school, Badminton, she [Murdoch] gave up religion for Marxism: "Indira Gandhi was there when I was there, and a lot of left-wing people and German Jewish refugee girls, so we were very politically conscious." [. . .]

She still retains many of her old feelings about social justice, and voted Labour until quite recently. But some of her views about socialism have changed, and she is currently voting Conservative.

"I couldn't accept the Labour Party's doctrine on defence, or their reluctance about belonging to Europe—I feel strongly that we must make ourselves into Europeans—I don't like the line many of them take on Ireland, and I think that Margaret Thatcher's government has done a number of good things. There are a number of good things it has failed to do, but I think it's done some good."

[. . .] Why has the search for goodness in [a] fallen world come to absorb her so much? One answer is the immense influence of Plato in her life.

"Plato is king. Plato established the notion that human life is about the battle between good and evil. A. N. Whitehead said that all Western philosophy is footnotes to Plato. He set up the first great philosophical picture of the human soul and of this mysterious business we're all involved in, and when I really started studying all Plato's dialogues, I was absolutely enchanted and taken over by this extraordinary mind."

Plato broke away from the pre-Socratic philosophers who thought in terms of a general rhythm or harmony of nature, rather like Taoists. Such thinkers esteem harmony rather than virtue. A modern example of this sort of thinking is the twentieth-century psychologist Carl Jung. She [Murdoch] says Jung is a magician; that he wants people to come to terms with the dark side of their soul and to recognise the great archetypal images and to harmonise themselves into some sort of serene unification of the soul.

"That's the opposite of what I think. If one's looking for philosophical pictures, I would follow one which makes it very clear that human beings live on a line between good and evil, and every moment of one's life is involved in movement upon this line, in one's thoughts, as well as in the things one does."

[. . .] In several novels, Iris Murdoch explores figures like Julius [in A Fairly Honourable Defeat], ranging around with an extraordinary, deadly, wasting, dangerous power like jokers or wild cards. Does she actually know such people?

"Well, I've known very powerful people. In all sorts of ways, people often find themselves under a spell—whether it's through their work, or through religion or through falling in love and so on. . . . One might say that magic is the enemy of religion, that religion degenerates into magic. . . . But persistent religions do have magical elements, and it's a short step from loving God, or wanting to save one's soul, to wanting power. You feel you are going to transcend the ordinary human state, and be in some higher state. And there are people who achieve, or at any rate exude, this kind of aura of magical power. I mean ordinary people, people who are teachers or artists . . . many, many kinds of people in ordinary situations. And other people want this. It is a very familiar human situation that people are fascinated by a magician, a man who seems to be either very good (it sometimes takes this form), or (more often) simply very powerful and frightening."

In A Fairly Honourable Defeat, Julius emerges as particularly frightening and powerful. He is able to set up the trap for each person so perfectly because he judges their weaknesses correctly—that Morgan wants to eat all her cakes and have them too, that Rupert is fond of holding forth about goodness in a self-satisfied sort of way, and so on. At the end of the book, he asks Tallis whether he concedes that he is an instrument of justice. Tallis just smiles. Does the author concede that Julius is an instrument of justice?

"Well, no, because what he sees is only part of the picture. Besides, it's not for him to go round punishing people, so he's not a proper instrument of justice."

"So it's justice without mercy?"

"Yes."

"I suppose if Christianity is about anything it's about justice with mercy?"

"I think the concept of justice is a very difficult one unless you use it in a secular context—relating to courts of law and how they operate, and what you blame people for. Ideas of justice alter, and people used to be blamed for things they are now not blamed for. This would be a tempering of justice with intelligent understanding. But if you think of justice belonging to a personal God, then this is a much more difficult question. I think there can be perverted ideas of justice involved in a religion. If one thinks of all the pictures in churches of the Last Judgment, with people going up to heaven and other people being trampled on and cast down, this is a very grim idea of justice. I personally don't believe in a personal god, and I don't believe in the Last Judgment or anything of the sort."

"I suppose it could be said that many Christians understand justice as the recognition of truth?"

"I think the concept to hang on to is truth. Let justice look after itself. Justice suggests judging other people, and punishment and so on. Truth and love are much more fundamental concepts and these are the matters we are primarily dealing with." [. . .]

"Why is stealing wrong?" That is the simple moral question Hilda's shop-lifting, but intelligent, drop-out son asks of Tallis. Tallis, taken by surprise, replies unconvincingly. Others fail the question too. Why is stealing wrong?

"That's a good question. One good reason is that if you steal, you get into trouble, you may ruin your life, you may make your parents very unhappy and so on. But I think, basically, stealing is a kind of lying, you're not in the open, you're not in the clear, you're not being truthful if you're a thief, and stealing usually damages a lot of people. It will damage the person from whom you steal. Of course, some shoplifters will say, 'Well, I only steal from Marks and Spencers, that's all right. They can afford it,' and so on. But it's a very bad kind of thing to do, because it is a kind of lie, and if your life rests upon a lot of lies of this sort, then it's a very bad sort of life."

"In the novel, there's the constant idea that lying ruins relationship . . ."

"Yes."

"Do you ever tell lies now?"

"Well, I sometimes tell social lies, but I think I would not be too stern upon that. . . . One very often says something which is not quite what one thinks in order not to hurt people. Kant thought you should never ever tell a lie. Even if somebody comes to murder someone else and says, 'Where is he?,' he thought you should appeal to the nobler aspect of the would-be murderer and tell him the truth in the hope he'd change his mind! Well, I think most of us would not be quite as strict as that." [. . .]

"Do you allow people to edit your books?"

She looked startled. "Well, no . . . but I don't think anyone has ever tried to." I wasn't a bit surprised. We both laughed. "I think that with one of my very, very early novels, someone suggested that I should leave a character out. But I refused to do so." Her back straightened. She chuckled. "Quite rightly. My publishers are very kind and nice." [. . .]

"Do you ever stop being a novelist? I mean, when you write to your bank manager, do you write an ordinary straightforward business letter?"

"You mean, do I produce a rather flowery letter to my bank manager?" We both laughed again. "No," I said, "I mean an imaginative, creative letter . . ."

"Well, one likes to write a clear and elegant letter. I like writing letters and I write a lot of letters. I think there are different styles for different relationships." [. . .]

In a number of her books—for instance, *The Sea, The Sea, The Good Apprentice* and *Nuns and Soldiers*, water seems to be used as a symbol of cleansing. She said she did this instinctively, rather than consciously. She loves the sea and swimming. Water is a deep symbol—frightening, and murderous, and also cleansing and forgiving. But she thinks there is a danger in symbolism. "I think a writer of a traditional novel is wise to rub out or fudge over a piece of symbolism that is coming out too clearly."

Writing such books, and keeping up such a high output, seemed to me to be potentially exhausting, both mentally and emotionally. She's absorbed in a novel almost continuously, and sometimes writes philosophy as well as fiction. She relaxes by listening to the radio or to music, reading and sewing. She also likes conversation very much, but doesn't get as much as she would like, because she works all day.

She loves singing, and was once trained by a singing teacher. At home during her childhood, her mother would play the piano. "We would sing all those marvellous popular songs of the 1930s, which are great songs compared with what's called the popular song nowadays. And lots of other songs, folk songs and opera. But when does one get a chance to sing now, unless one belongs to a choir? If one starts singing when you're with friends, they begin to look a bit shifty—"she laughed"—and I think they'd rather you stopped—however charming one's voice may be, which in my case is getting rather rusty. People who don't like singing resent it very much."

Sometimes people say of Iris Murdoch's work that it is obsessed with the moral and spiritual problems of the same group of middle-class intellectuals appearing in different guises in different books, and that they would be all much less anxious and better adjusted if they had to do a decent day's work in the rough-and-tumble of the world outside university cities. I threw this into the hat.

"Good heavens, people work very hard in university cities. The notion that there isn't any serious work which belongs to intellectual people is a very dangerous and misleading idea. People work extremely hard, as people in the civil service work hard. When I was a civil servant, I was filled with the greatest respect for the people I knew there, who were not only very clever, but extremely hardworking, extremely conscientious. Few of my characters don't work. They are teachers or painters or civil servants. Some of them are servants. So the notion that they are all idlers, just sitting round examining their conscience, is not just."

"But they tend to be middle-class intellectuals with a certain standard of living?"

"Well, not all of them. But I don't think this is important. One has got to write about what one knows. If I knew a lot about coal mining, I would write about coal mining. If I knew what it was like to be a sailor, I'd write about sailors. I very much wish I did know about other things. An aspiring novelist should take note—the more you know about anything is a help to you in writing a novel. I don't know about physics and chemistry for example. I wish I did. But there it is, one's life has certain limitations." [. . .]

Iris Murdoch has now published twenty-three novels. Dickens published fifteen. What keeps her writing? Is it because she wants Christian ideas to work without God, and they just don't?

"No, I don't think so. I write because I like it, this is my art form and I want to write better, and I want to create works of art. It's very dangerous to write as a pedagogue. I think good novelists, for instance Sartre, are damaged by a desire to put across a philosophical creed. You have to follow your instinct as an artist, I think, and not try to be a teacher in art."

"What do you think you would need so that you wouldn't need to write any more?"

"I can't imagine not needing to write. I should be very unhappy if I couldn't write."

21

MICHAEL KUSTOW

Boundary Breaker and Moral Maker

Michael Kustow is a former associate director of the National Theatre and the Royal Shakespeare Company. He was the first arts commissioning editor for BBC Television channel 4. This interview first appeared in the *Guardian* (Manchester) on 8 October 1992.

[. . .] I ask Iris Murdoch what she thinks when people say what a good person she is, as people frequently do. She has blue eyes of an extraordinary calmness and candour, which look at you with a steady and quite unthreatening gaze. "I'd rather they didn't. I'm not a good person," she says, turning her gaze to the carpet. "I'm far too . . ." and her voice trails away.

Does she know any good people? What are they like? There's an immense pause. "Yes I've met some good people. Mostly in religious houses. They exhibit goodness in a particular way, that of giving up the world. Of course there are an infinite number of degrees of doing so. There are a lot of ordinary pleasures which one might be better without."

Art? "No, not art. Bad art, perhaps." Food, alcohol, sex? "Things about sex. Clearly sex is a great ocean of temptation, all sorts of goodness and badness."

But to be good and not to give up the world, isn't that the acid test? No, she still can't come up with a name, a description of a good person's goodness. Yet she's been thinking and writing about morality for

10 years, and the outcome is her new 500-page book of philosophy, reflection, polemic and testament, *Metaphysics as a Guide to Morals*.

Later, walking back to her Oxford house, I ask about her neighbours. "Now there's a good person," she says emphatically about her neighbour's wife. "She always has fresh-baked pies for me when I come home."

Two days later, I get a letter from her. "Re goodness, a basic constituent is courage. I think here of those dissidents under tyrants who will continually shout out the truth. One I knew: Vladimir Bukovsky, who was imprisoned, let out, went on shouting, knowing that he might be put into a mental home—where he could be deprived of his sanity. What a case of pure courage and goodness."

At 73, Murdoch lets autobiography and memory seep into her talk, giving me a sudden glimpse that, had it not been for Jean-Paul Sartre, she might have become a Mother Teresa of the post-war refugee camps. In 1942, 10 days after getting a first in Greats at Oxford, she was in the Treasury, following in her civil servant father's footsteps. When the war ended, she went to Belgium and then spent two years working in a Displaced Persons Camp in the French zone of Austria.

"I hadn't read a book in all this time. I was pretty exhausted by the camps. But I got a great whiff of philosophy on the way out. I was in Brussels, Sartre was there, I met him . . . beautiful. There was a wonderful bookshop man who had all the philosophy books. He pressed *L'être et le néant* into my hands. I read it with the greatest interest, it was wonderful. People were liberated by that book after the war, it made people happy, it was like the Gospel. Having been chained up for years, you were suddenly free and could be yourself.

"There's a lot that's quite objectionable about it, but it was a thrilling book. So then I thought, I want to go back. The satisfaction of helping other people, I had a lot of that in those camps. Everyday one was helping someone, every single day and all that day. Well, almost: I remember the wild joy when, after months of toil, the French brought some wine for us. I loved that work, I even thought I'd like to spend my whole life with refugees. I wasn't saintly enough."

The sense of that moment being a crossroads for her, of the almost terrifying possibilities of choice in any direction, comes across vividly

50 years later, after a career teaching philosophy and the production of 24 novels. [. . .]

Born a Protestant in Dublin in 1919, educated in the thirties at Badminton, she studied philosophy at Cambridge under Elizabeth Anscombe, then taught it as a Fellow of St Anne's College, Oxford, "where I worked through all the basic stuff, Descartes, Hume, Kant. I loved the tutorial system, one to one." She also plunged into Plato, "who was rather ignored by philosophers then; they said he should only be read as literature." [. . .]

The seeds of this book [*Metaphysics*] lie in *The Fire and the Sun: Why Plato Banished the Artists* (1977) and *Acastos: Two Platonic Dialogues* (1986), of which I'm proud to be the dedicatee. It happened like this. Looking for challenging material for the National Theatre's short Platform Performances, I read her Plato book and wrote asking whether she would now consider writing a piece for actors in Plato's dialogue form, using his key images and arguments, and adding new characters to make her own points.

She replied that it would be impossible. A few months later the first script, "Art and Eros, A Dialogue about Art," dropped through my letter box. It was followed by "Above the Gods, a Dialogue about Religion." These subjects have become two planks of her new book.

[. . .] Working with her on her text was a revelation. I would question something, often a transition or connection. There would be a long pause, as if my question were being fed into some vast complex circuitry in her head. Out would come a precise response—a cut, transposition, or a new sentence deftly inserted at a crucial point.

What was so surprising about "Art and Eros" in performance at the National was how much emotion it contained. The actors—looking as always for the reassurance of character and motive—had at first been intimidated by the apparent dialectical severity of her text. But it played joyfully and communicated excitement, fun, friendship and the drama, nudged by Socrates, of hunting down the truth. [. . .]

Her challenge to the segregating orthodoxies of much current thought lies in the form as well as the content of her book. Like her latest novels, it is capacious and loose-woven, more like conversation than the logic or science to which so much 20th century philosophy has aspired. It is written for the most part in short sentences and defiantly plain language, not the jargon and neologisms of post-structuralism. Its swift, stabbing eloquence often has the clarion urgency of a crusader out to rescue philosophy from assimilation into science and language theory, a betrayal for which she holds Derrida and his disciples most responsible. "I'm talking for the most part about early Derrida," she specifies, "especially *De la grammatologie,* which is still one of the bibles of the scene. Human beings in his picture are either slaves of language, they don't realise they're just using the local code, whose sense is far beyond them; or they're civilised literate persons who can play with language, who know that language is there to enjoy. It's an attractive, amusing doctrine, but it's so unlike what human life is really like, and it entirely abolishes the idea of truth in some of its basic senses. Derrida is a very remarkable writer and a real scholar, but these ideas lead to relativism, and ultimately to determinism."

[. . .] After a thorough work-out with "The Ontological Proof of God," she lists the sort of people who might be unremarked, everyday saints: "Some quiet, unpretentious worker, a schoolteacher or a mother, or better still an aunt. Mothers have many egoistic satisfactions and much power. The aunt may be the selfless unrewarded doer of good. I have known such aunts." She says she's been told it's the funniest thing in the book. It may also be the most revealing picture of the emotional source of her own goodness, which she has channelled and fortified by a lifetime of rigorous thought and free imagination.

22

JOANNA COLES

The Joanna Coles Interview: Duet in Perfect Harmony

Joanna Coles has been a columnist and bureau chief at the London *Times* and recently joined *New York* magazine's staff as features editor. This interview was first published in the *Guardian* (Manchester) on 21 September 1996.

"BELL not working. WE ARE HERE. Knock vigorously." I do, and the cheery face of Professor John Bayley promptly appears at the window, chewing baked beans.

"Come in, come in my dears," he exclaims, opening the front door and waving an oval piece of toast. "I find beans just the thing for lunch don't you? We're not lunch people, we're dinner people, that's when we eat properly, so come in, come in."

He whisks us through a chaotic hall, past a vast, unsteady pyramid of books and into the most eccentric drawing room I have ever seen. There are heaving carrier bags spilling their paper guts across the floor, old stones and sticks, wild piles of books and papers which look as if they may have reproduced on their own the night before. The walls are Georgian Green and though it is midday it's dark, the window unintelligible to the light because of the fig leaves outside creeping across the pane.

As we sit down, Dame Iris Murdoch spirits herself gracefully into the room, and I suddenly notice there's an abandoned glass of red wine tucked away under each armchair, as if perhaps in case of emergency.

Hello, she smiles, her eyes wide and friendly and although I have already explained on the telephone, I explain again that I'm here because there are rumours she has given up writing for good. It is not the easiest of questions to ask such an intelligent and prolific author, and I am worried she may think me rude for even trying. But can it be true?

To my huge relief she smiles. "Well, I'm trying to do something, but, it hasn't, well . . ." and then she starts laughing.

"Just a bit of a block I think," interrupts Bayley, her husband of 40 years, cheerfully.

"Yes, it's not, well, I certainly am trying," she replies.

Now 77, Dame Iris is without question one of the finest writers of her generation, to date producing 26 novels including the hugely acclaimed *The Sea, The Sea, The Black Prince* and *The Red and the Green.* Her last book, *Jackson's Dilemma,* was published in hardback last autumn, but nothing has followed. Has she suffered from this kind of block before? "I think this is a very bad one," she says absently.

"It has occurred before darling," says Bayley, leaning towards her reassuringly. "You've had periods of lying fallow, as one might say, rather like a field. Because what is really rather extraordinary about you darling, if I might say, is that you don't mind being interrupted, and you don't keep pompous writing hours. You simply write whenever you feel like it."

"Perhaps," she says flatly.

I wonder if she still reads a lot?

"Yes, I do." And do you still enjoy writing when you can?

"Well, I enjoy it, when I've found a way out, as it were. But um, otherwise . . ." and she smiles wanly, almost apologetically. "Otherwise I'm in a very, very bad, quiet place."

We are all quiet for a moment before Bayley says to her: "In the past, because of your philosophical mind perhaps, you've tended to get the whole novel worked out in meticulous detail haven't you? It's almost, darling, if you don't mind my saying, like a mathematical theorem. The whole thing worked out in advance."

She falters, "Well I . . ."

"I keep suggesting she should start, in the way an ordinary person would do. You know, Tom and Dick were sitting in a pub, and who should come in but Harry."

"Oh, but I'm afraid I can't do that," says Iris quickly. "At the moment I can't find anything."

Bayley, who retired as Oxford's Warton Professor of English four years ago, heads off to make coffee. "I feel gloomy," says Dame Iris gently. Does she think this will pass, or is it simply old age?

"I think I just haven't yet got anything which will help me," she whispers, adding bravely: "I expect something will turn up."

Did she find it difficult to live up to her reputation? "Well, the books I've written in the past I've done quite quickly, and known what to do and been geared up by them. But I'm afraid at the moment that I'm just falling, falling . . . just falling as it were. But I may get better. I hope so."

There is a copy of *Conversations with Isaiah Berlin* lying open at her feet. What else is she reading at the moment? "Um, well, quite a lot of things, but I haven't found anything which would be really useful to me. I find I haven't got anything at the moment, and this is really rather startling to me. I feel as though maybe the whole thing has packed up. But I hope, I really do believe actually, I could get on and find myself in a happier state, but I don't think so at the very moment. I'm just wandering, I think of things and then they go away forever."

Bayley returns bearing a tray with a pottery jug of coffee, and to make room we remove another tray smothered in old corks, crisp autumn leaves, several pebbles, old notes, a large stone and some photographs. "Simple but effective," says Bayley, nodding at the jug, "as long as you don't mind a few grounds in the mouth!"

"You must pour," says Iris, patting his arm. "You must pour."

"Pour? Oh, I thought you meant paw!" And he starts scrabbling at the air as if he's a cat, and we all laugh. Their relationship is not only touching, it's still fresh and young, making sense of what marriage is for. How, I ask, do they spend their days together?

"I've slipped out of the university now," says Iris. "But I do every day try and collect something or other to myself." Then she gives me a beautiful, generous smile. "Your arrival may help me."

"I wouldn't be surprised," says Bayley, spooning two sugars into each mug. "Sometimes pictures start her off. We went to the National Gallery yesterday."

"I do like pictures," says Iris.

"We discovered yesterday, didn't we darling, that the thing one must do is go in the Orange Street entrance, because you arrive among just the right sort of pictures to warm you up. Instead of being suddenly confronted with these ghastly old masterpieces, there are some very nice Dutch portraits, charming."

He beams at the memory and distributes a packet of McVitie's half-coated digestives.

"One must have the dark chocolate, the milk ones are not the same. Is the coffee all right?"

I abandon my list of prepared questions and ask Bayley about the trilogy he's been writing since he retired. "Oh it's rather frivolous," he says dismissively. "I'm not a natural novelist like Iris. The third one, *George's Lair,* has just come out, but it can't be described as making a big splash."

"Oh it's jolly good," protests Iris loyally. "It's absolutely good." "It's quiet, narcissistic entertainment for me," he explains hurriedly. "I suppose I might have taken to woolwork!"

I wonder what they make of the current vogue, where just about everyone seems to be writing a novel? "It's partly the new feminists," says Bayley, brandishing his biscuit, "who are, quite rightly, wanting to find out who they are—a faintly ridiculous phrase I know, but there's some truth to it. I had a pupil who said 'I've written a novel to find out who I really am.'"

Dame Iris laughs at this and he continues. "Writing means you do catch an insight into your limitations, but (nodding at Iris) I don't think you bother about who you are at all darling. In fact you once said to me you didn't think you had much of an identity!"

"Well yes," she nods. "At present . . ."

"Your identity goes into your work."

"Writing came immediately to me," says Iris suddenly. "I had a wonderful education, I went to excellent schools (Badminton) where they knew what was possible. And as time went on, I knew with passion when I finished a novel that I wanted to do the next one."

Then she stops and remarks clearly: "I am in a place from which I am trying to get out."

We all pause, nonplussed, until Bayley eventually breaks the silence by asking me if I have written a novel. I confess gloomily that I haven't.

"It's well worth trying," he says encouragingly.

"Try and find the time," says Iris. "Do. Do."

"Henry James found it solitary, but then he would wouldn't he?" Bayley giggles. "He thought you had to make a choice between living and writing. But I'm often struck by how Iris isn't the least bothered about whether she should live or write. And you never seem to mind giving it up for a bit. You did that book on philosophy [*Metaphysics as a Guide to Morals*]. I sometimes quite resent that book, because it interrupted the novels."

"Oh I'm at peace with that," says Iris dismissively. "I don't know whether I should write another non-fiction book." She looks at me kindly: "I'm afraid you've arrived in a low situation."

"This is American-style coffee," says Bayley suddenly. "They make it weak over there so they can drink it all the time."

"I don't feel we're getting anywhere," says Iris.

We wander out to the garden, an uproarious spread of wild mint, goldenrod, Michaelmas daisies and some old cut flowers, still in their vases. "I was very lucky," says Iris as Bayley disappears into the kitchen. "I met a man I couldn't say no to, and I couldn't be persuaded to throw him away."

He returns with a flat cap on which he insists on wearing "for without it, I look like Humpty Dumpty." Despite Dame Iris's current problems, they seem utterly at ease with each other. "We've done all the things we want to, and now we just have a quiet life," says Bayley.

"Actually . . ." begins Iris. "Yes, you're more restless than me," concedes her husband. And I wonder if they missed having children? "Iris has never shown the slightest interest in being a mum," says her husband.

"And I'm not sure, but you could say the best women novelists didn't have children. Jane Austen, George Eliot . . . I mean the really top notch ones."

As Iris poses obediently for photos, he beckons me over to the kitchen table, where there appear to be two of everything, two honey pots, two mustard pots, two jam pots and seven jars of coffee. "We've been to see doctors you know and they say the old brain's very crafty. It can come up against a block and for a bit things seem a bit strange, but then it finds its way around things again."

23

ROBERT WEIL

Memories of Iris

Robert Weil, executive editor at W. W. Norton & Co., has edited recent books by John Bayley and Peter J. Conradi. This article was first published in the *Partisan Review* in 1999.

Iris Murdoch, the renowned philosopher and beloved novelist, died in Oxford on February 8, 1999 of complications of Alzheimer's disease. Self-effacing and modest despite her genius, she eschewed the praise and publicity which have aggrandized many contemporary writers. Yet this most private of people would have fully approved of the very public way in which her husband, John Bayley, chronicled her inexorable decline in his two memoirs, *Elegy for Iris* and *Iris and Her Friends.* In fact, like many characters in her more than two dozen novels, Murdoch would have preferred to go by example, because she had always maintained that moral values could only be communicated through individual and personal behavior.

Aware of Iris's philosophy, John Bayley decided in the fall of 1997 to defy conventional sensibilities about illness, and deal with Iris's incapacity strictly on their own terms. Deeply influenced then by the works of Leo Tolstoy, Bayley was bringing his own Tolstoyan drama to life, making Iris's death as visible as that of his literary mentor who, in 1910, ran away from home at the age of eighty-two, his whereabouts not even known to his wife, Countess Sophia.

Writing in unsparing yet rhapsodic detail about the ravages brought on by Alzheimer's, Bayley, also a most private man, was following Tolstoyan precedent in redefining society's fear of disease and mental illness, echoing the words of Ivan Ilyich, who had "searched for his accustomed fear of death and could not find it." Bayley's dramatic decision not only to come forward with a public announcement of his wife's illness, but also to write joyously and spiritually about his experiences in caring for her reflects his estrangement from a late twentieth-century society where old age is feared and where death has been sanitized by our mainstream culture.

I first met Iris in September 1994 on a routine publishing trip to London, where I received an unexpected phone call from Natasha and Stephen Spender (whom I had just signed up for what would become his last two books) for what was described as a "simple dinner" with "just a few friends," among them Iris Murdoch and John Bayley, as well as Antonia Fraser and Harold Pinter. Fearing that I would be perceived as a neophyte at best, I tried to allay my anxiety by running out and buying a few Murdoch works that were readily available. I was apprehensive an imperious Dame Iris Murdoch might grill me on the contents of her novels.

Indeed, I was seated next to Iris, and did, in fact, speak with her for over three hours of passionate conversation, but my fear of Murdoch as an intimidating interrogator bore no resemblance to this deeply inquisitive, radiant woman of seventy-five. Dressed modestly and looking like a kindly headmistress of a boarding school, Iris completely beguiled me with the most improbable admixture of wondrous curiosity and barbed wisdom. There was a seductive, yet wholly ineffable, manner to her being that could effortlessly hypnotize and reassure a dinner companion. She wanted to know everything about me, about my upbringing, my favorite writers, and particularly my parents' stories as refugees from Nazi-occupied Europe. It was these accounts culled from my family's past life on the edge—innocent individuals caught in the maelstrom of evil—that fascinated her the most, and she mentioned her own work with Jewish refugees in the 1940s.

I would not see Iris again for another three years, until October of 1997, and by then I already knew from the published accounts that her situation had markedly changed for the worse. Having just signed up John's novel *The Red Hat*, I visited the couple at their eccentrically decorated Oxford home, where Alp-like piles of books threatened to collapse at any moment, expecting to pay something of a sympathy call. I assumed that Iris's condition would be politely ignored as John reminisced, perhaps over tea, about the Spenders' memorable dinner party, and discussed the publication plans of his novel. Instead, the scene before me was one that I will never forget. There was Iris transfixed by the television set, intrigued by the trajectory of a golf ball as it swerved its way into the hole. When she addressed me, which was often, she smiled and laughed, occasionally asking questions that were nonsensical as well as repetitious. Although her condition could no longer be hidden, there was a profound joy and merriment that pervaded the Murdoch-Bayley household, an unspoken reaffirmation of the marriage vows through both sickness and health. There was no gloom, no shame, and John was sprightly and ebullient, discussing how he had to make various accommodations over the previous few years. Rather than regarding her as a victim, incapable of sentience or emotional needs, John doted on Iris as if this were their honeymoon, and she his newly won bride. Like Orpheus, he acted as if he could do the impossible, and transport his beloved back from a dark underworld that had robbed her of her sanity. And responding to his melodious words and playful behavior, Iris rarely demonstrated the irritability that frequently complicates Alzheimer's, her abundant smiles always communicating emotions when her words became unintelligible. Following John's example, I engaged Iris on her own cognitive level, with the most basic questions, like which dish on the menu she would like to order. And it was that afternoon that the idea of the first memoir was first discussed.

Following my visit, I would call John and Iris as often as two or three times a week from New York. Such calls extended far beyond the discussion of the manuscript-in-progress, for I felt that I was quickly becoming a personal friend and family member. Routinely, we would talk after he and Iris had enjoyed one of John's home-cooked dinners, and virtually no conversation with John ever ended without these seven words: "Would you like a word with Iris?" The first time I thought it was strange to be invited to talk with someone whose thoughts were scattered and frequently incomprehensible, but it wasn't long before I looked forward to these many "chats" with Iris.

"Iris, it's Bob, it's Bob from New York," I would intone loudly.

"Ah," she would exclaim with child-like delight, as if she had become accustomed to my voice on the telephone without comprehending who I really was.

If it were Monday evening, I would perhaps ask her if she had had a good time at their friends' home in Wales.

"Did you have a nice weekend with Peter and Jim?"

"We had a nice weekend, thank you," she would respond, able to key in to specifics of very basic questions, frequently ending any statement with the words, "Thank you."

"Did you have fun with the dog, Cloudy?"

She would pause and then say, "Cloudy, yes," and giggle a bit as if recalling the shaggy dog who would snuggle with her so affectionately.

More frequently, I would merely ask her about the weather, specifically whether it had rained or if it had been hot, as well as about their dinner. "Did you like the spaghetti, did you eat all of your food?" I asked with the apprehension of a parent.

She would pause, as if in deep thought, and more often than not, would reassure me with a chuckle or a "yes I did" that she had cooperated in eating one of John's home-cooked meals.

Occasionally she corrected me, as in the time she was with John on a vacation in France.

"Did John take good care of you on the trip, is he a good husband?"

"No, John is a perfect angel," she reproved, and after that, I would almost always ask her if John was indeed "a perfect angel."

Particularly, the word "love" elicited a small cry of joy, and she seemed very comforted by the reassurance that her admirers and friends all over the world genuinely loved her.

The danger in all this attention being paid now to Iris's last few years is that we are inclined to overlook her prodigious output, and only memorialize her for her tragic passage into senility. This would be a horrendous trivialization of a remarkable career, and Iris's essence—her extraordinary struggle to depict the individual battle between good and evil—can be found in such novels as *The Nice and the Good* and *The Red and the Green,* or in her own comments that she provided to other writers. "I believe," she once told the novelist Rachel Billington, "we live in a fantasy world, a world of illusion. And the great task is to find reality."* And reviewing Murdoch's *The Good Apprentice* in *The New York Times Book Review*, Harold Bloom noted: "Miss Murdoch's only consistent spirituality is grimly parallel to Freud's, since her novels insist that religious consciousness, in our postreligious era, must begin with the conviction that only death centers life, that death is the only valid representation of a life better than the life-in-death we all suffer daily."†

Iris's death, in fact, came suddenly on a Monday afternoon with John at her bedside. Forced by her rapid physical decline to place her only a few weeks before in an Oxford nursing home that specialized in Alzheimer's, John had not anticipated how immediately her death would come, although he had alerted me the night before that Iris was no longer eating. Upon hearing the news from colleagues on February 8, I sifted through old files at home to find the last lucid conversation I had had with Iris last fall. Although generally unable to communicate any more on the phone, she had surprised me on that last occasion with a rare burst of lucidity.

"How are you, Iris?" I had asked.

"You know," she volunteered, "I'm just a strange person."

"You're not strange at all, you're a wonderful person and you give love to everyone."

"Ah, but my head, I'm not real," she responded.

And after a few minutes of familiar patter, we had our parting words:

"I hope you have a good weekend, Iris."

"I'll try."

"You know, everyone loves you, Iris."

"Ah, but you're a wonderful person, I love you."

And a little over three months later Iris was gone. Yet as Tolstoy observed, "Instead of death there was light."

---

* Rachel Billington, "Crusading in a Fantasy World," *London Times,* 25 April 1983, 9.

† Harold Bloom, "A Comedy of Worldly Salvation," *New York Times Book Review,* 12 January 1986, 31.

REFERENCES

Indispensable references for the study of Iris Murdoch's life and work are: John Fletcher and Cheryl Bove, *Iris Murdoch: A Primary and Secondary Annotated Bibliography* (London and New York: Garland, 1994; new edition forthcoming); Iris Murdoch, *Existentialists and Mystics: Writings on Philosophy and Literature,* edited by Peter Conradi (London: Chatto and Windus, 1997); and Peter Conradi, *Iris Murdoch: A Life* (London: HarperCollins; New York: Norton, 2001). A more personal view of Murdoch's life is offered in John Bayley's two memoirs, *Elegy for Iris* (New York: St. Martin's Press, 1999) and *Iris and Her Friends* (New York: St. Martin's Press, 2000).

INDEX

Aeschylus, 202; *Agamemnon*, 151, 153

Alzheimer's disease, xxvii, 251–53, 255

America, 174–80

Amis, Kingsley, 172, 232

androgyny, 30

anti-Semitism, 73

Apollo, 77, 148, 152, 153, 187

archaeology, 98, 128, 151

Aristotle, 99

art, 50, 137, 141–42, 161, 174, 241

art history, 98, 128, 151

art, contemporary, 117

Athenaeum Club, 1, 5

Atlas, James, 219

Austen, Jane, xxi, 15, 28, 31, 64, 94, 197, 226, 249; *Emma*, xxii, 150, 224

Australia, 40, 178

Austria, 20

authorial intention, xvi, 101, 173, 186–89, 193

autobiography in the novel, 222

Ayer, A.J., 87

Badminton School, 6, 148, 235, 248

Bakhtin, Mikhail, xvi, 201, 203, 206

Balzac, Honoré de, 15, 95, 190; *Cousine Bette, La*, 170

Barrie, J.M.: *Peter Pan*, 87–88

Barthes, Roland, 101, 110, 117

Bayley, John, xxiv–xxv, xxvii, 129, 222, 223, 229, 245–50, 251–55; *Elegy for Iris*, xxii, xxvii, 251; *George's Lair*, 248; *Iris and the Friends*, xxvii, 251; *Red Hat, The*, 252

Beauvoir, Simone de, 2, 32, 36, 58; *deuxième sexe, Le*, 5, 32

Beazley, John (Sir), 151

Beckett, Samuel, xxi, 4, 28, 34, 36, 46, 75, 111, 114; *Murphy*, 4, 28, 114; *Waiting for Godot*, 4, 114; *Watt*, 28, 114

Beckmann, Max, 228

Belgium, 20

Bellamy, Michael, xxii

Berkeley, George, 79

Berlin, Isaiah, 247

Bible, 3

Bigsby, Christopher, xxvi, xxvii

Billington, Rachel, 254

black studies, xvii, 62, 83

Bloom, Harold, 255

Bodleian Library, 191

Bonhoeffer, Dietrich, 43

Bove, Cheryl, 178

Bradley, Francis Herbert, 211

Brans, Jo, xxvi

Britain, 122; Civil Service, 239

Britten, Benjamin, 120

Brockway, James, 169

Bronte, Emily, xxi, 94, 226; *Wuthering Heights*, 28, 61

Bronzino, Agnolo, 228

Brussels, 242

Buddhism, xx, 41, 43, 62, 76, 99, 106, 136–37, 160, 212, 227

Buddingh, Cees, 170

Bukovsky, Vladimir, 242

Burroughs, William S.: *Naked Lunch*, 29

Byatt, A.S., 30, 232; *Possession*, 230

Cambridge University, 98; Newnham College, 218

Camus, Albert, 113

Canada, 178

capitalism, 62

Carey, John, 149

Carroll, Lewis: *Alice in Wonderland*, 129

Cary, Joyce, 56; *Horse's Mouth, The*, 56, 64; *Mister Johnson*, 56; technique, 56

Catholic church, 43

Catholicism, 143, 195

cats, xxvi, 155

Catullus, 150

censorship, 141

character, xxiii, 2, 8, 10, 12, 31, 42, 51, 80, 81, 84, 102, 114, 134, 156, 177, 185, 224, 227

Chatto and Windus, 167, 229

Chaucer, Geoffrey, 63

Chevalier, Jean-Louis, 72

children, xx, 23, 217, 229, 249

Chile, 122

China, 127

Christianity, xx, 7, 27, 43, 49, 62, 99, 106, 136, 137, 160, 209–17, 237

Church of England, 7, 43; liturgy, 213

Cicero, xxvi, 150

cinema, 4

class, 41

classical mythology, 201, 203

Coleridge, Samuel Taylor, 226

Coles, Joanna, xxvii

comedy in the novel, 25, 37, 54, 59, 72, 77, 118, 133, 171, 202, 206

comedy, Greek, 202–3

Communism, 18, 19, 143, 211

Communist Party, 122, 220

Compton-Burnett, Ivy, 86

computers, 222

conferences, 232

Conrad, Joseph, 31, 84

Conradi, Peter, 171, 191, 200; *Iris Murdoch, The Saint and the Artist*, 200

Conservative Party, 6

contingency, 46, 84, 127, 134, 136, 202, 212, 213

Cornford, Christopher, 232

courage, 242

Coward, Noel, 197

critics and criticism, xxiv–xxv, 15, 45–46, 52, 66, 76, 77, 85, 102, 106, 138, 156, 173, 174, 182, 191, 192–93, 202

critics and criticism, Marxist, 35

Dante Alighieri, 3, 225

death, 137, 195, 252, 255

Delhi, 232

Delphi, 148

Derrida, Jacques, 244; *De la grammatologie*, 244

Descartes, René, 79, 243

desire, 145

determinism, 101, 140, 244

dialogue, 39, 198
Dickens, Charles, xxi, 14, 21–22, 28, 37, 39, 45, 53, 64, 94, 102, 191, 197, 199, 224, 226; *Edwin Drood*, 112; *Our Mutual Friend*, 68
didacticism, 138
Dionysus, 153
Dipple, Elizabeth, 147
discipline, 163
dogs, xxvi, 155
Dostoevsky, Fyodor, xxi, 28, 51, 58, 64, 118, 171, 191, 197, 202, 224, 226; *Brothers Karamazov, The*, 202, 224; *Possessed, The*, 202, 205
Dover, Kenneth, 151
Drabble, Margaret, 171
drama, xvii, xxiv, 4, 16, 28, 48, 58–59, 105, 228
drama in the novel, 59, 133
dreams, 132, 164
Dublin, 192

Easter Rising (Ireland, 1916), 191
Eckhart, Meister, 212
editing, 238
education, 6, 31, 61, 160, 161
egoism, 59, 137, 200, 226, 244
Eliot, George, xxi, 14, 31–32, 45, 64, 94, 197, 226, 249; *Middlemarch*, 84
Eliot, T. S., 3, 7
enfants du paradis, Les, 127
England, 94
Eros, 154
ethics, 52
Europe, 220, 233, 234, 235
existentialism, xix, 5, 20, 25, 46, 63, 79, 97, 98, 109–10, 140, 157, 227–28

experiment in the novel, xxii, 29, 34, 47, 63, 64, 190

fantasy, 7, 100, 115, 158, 226, 255
feminism, xvii, 31–32, 48, 61, 82–83, 248
Flaubert, Gustave, 95, 226; *education sentimentale, L'*, 192
form in art, 10, 50, 101, 116
form in the novel, 10, 47, 127, 133
Foster, Malcolm, 56
Fowles, John, 190
Fraenkel, Eduard, 151, 153
France, 98, 232
Frankfurter, Felix, 220
Fraser, Antonia, 252
freedom, xix, xxvi, 25, 31, 63, 101, 110, 111, 122, 139–47, 228
freedom, political, xix, 141, 144
Freud, Sigmund, 2, 26, 89, 131, 146, 158
friendship, 163

Gaelic language, 195
Gandhi, Indira, 235
Genet, Jean, 28
Gifford Lectures, 152
Glover, Stephen, xvi
Golding, William, 21, 64, 67; *Lord of the Flies*, 57
good and evil, 180, 235
goodness, 200, 241
Gothic, The, 85, 86
Greek language, 5, 148
Greene, Graham, 66

happiness, 165
Hardy, Thomas, 230
Harvey, Andrew, 232
Healey, Denis, 4
Hegel, G. W. F., 54, 59, 79, 211

Heidegger, Martin, 211
Hemingway, Ernest, 224
Henry, Aline, 75
Heusel, Barbara Stevens, xvi
Heyd, Ruth, 49
Hinduism, 41, 160, 213
Hitler, Adolf, 62, 227
Holt, Heleen ten, 169
Homer, xxi, 15, 31, 63, 64, 149,
    197, 202; Iliad, xxii, 150, 224;
    Odyssey, 150
homosexuality, 74, 233
hope, 234
Horace, xxvi, 149
housework, xxvii, 222
human rights, 111
Hume, David, 21, 79, 243
humility, 160

Ibsen, Henrik, 197
Iceland, 127
idealism, 234
imagination, 57, 100, 102, 203, 221,
    226
incest, 204
indeterminacy, xxvi
Index, 122
India, xxvii, 40
intellectuals, 18
Iran, 108, 111
Ireland, 19, 76, 94–96, 194–96, 233
Iris Murdoch Society, 201
Irish Republican Army, 191, 195, 233
irony, 196
Ishiguro, Kazuo: Pale View of Hills,
    A, 230

James, Henry, xxi, 15, 28, 31, 64, 67,
    80, 94, 175, 176, 226, 249; Aspern
    Papers, The, 170; Europeans,
    The, 177; Golden Bowl, The, 175

Jancar, Joze., 231
Japan, xxvii, 40
Jesus Christ, 211, 214
Johnson, Samuel, 173–74
Joyce, James, 34, 63–64, 196;
    Ulysses, 96
Jung, Carl Gustav, 135, 236
juries, 90
justice, 109, 134, 142, 212, 226, 237

Kafka, Franz, 34, 80
Kant, Immanuel, 99, 107, 111, 128,
    152, 238, 243; Fundamental
    Principles of the Metaphysics of
    Mind, The, 79
Kaye, Danny, 4
Kennedy, Alan, 58, 68
Kermode, Frank, xv
Kundera, Milan: Unbearable Light-
    ness of Being, The, 230
Kustow, Michael, 243

Labour Party, 6, 235
Laclos, Choderlos de: liaisons dan-
    gereuses, Les, 170
language, 2, 4, 90, 149, 177
languages, 148, 150, 161, 168, 195
Larkin, Philip, 93, 171
Latin, 148
law, 109
Lawrence, D. H., xxi, 31, 44, 52, 102,
    115, 182, 224, 226, 230; Lady
    Chatterley's Lover, xxi, 102, 185
lawyers, 90
Le Gros, Bernard, 77, 78
letters, 222, 238
liberalism, 110–11, 144
literature, 2, 3, 47, 112, 202
Locke, John, 21
Lodge, David, 190
logical positivism, 90

London, 86
Louvre, The, 87
love, xix, 8, 25, 53, 119, 140, 163, 237

MacDonagh, Donagh, 93
magic, 100, 105, 146, 186–87, 236
Mann, Thomas, 225
marriage, 163
Marxism, xvii, 97, 160, 210, 220, 233, 235
mathematics, 5
Mathias, William, 120
McCarren Act, 220
McKellen, Ian, 60
meditation, 49, 160
Mehta, Ved, 57
Merleau-Ponty, Maurice, 79
metaphysics, 213
Meyers, Jeffrey, xxii, xxvi
migration, 178
Mill, John Stuart: *Utilitarianism*, 79
Miller, Jonathan, xxvii
Milton, John: *Paradise Lost*, 181
Modern Languages Association, 201
morality, xxvi, 99, 107, 108, 109, 111, 133
morality in art, 76, 117, 134, 158, 225
morality in literature, 224
morality in the novel, xxvi, 3, 10, 42, 92, 107–14, 138, 156, 197, 199, 223–25, 230
Morin, Michele, 76, 78
Mozart, Wolfgang Amadeus: *Così fan tutte*, 174
Murdoch, Irene Alice, née Richardson (IM's mother), 7, 95, 129, 196, 209, 219, 229
Murdoch, Iris: articles; "Against Dryness", 9, 10, 62, 110, 143;

"Idea of Perfection, The", xxiv; "Nostalgia for the Particular", 147; "Sovereignty of Good over Other Concepts, The", 20; "Structure in the Novel", xxv; "Vision and Choice in Morality", 143; characters, xv, 7, 11, 22–25, 29, 39, 47–48, 49, 51, 54, 61, 62, 65, 68–69, 72, 74–75, 81–82, 117, 127, 131, 135, 146, 155, 170, 184, 190, 198, 204, 221, 222–23, 229, 236, 240; characters, American, 175–78; characters, female, 161, 207; characters, homosexual, 233; characters, Jewish, 73; childhood, 19, 33, 76, 96, 129, 194, 209, 219, 239; education, 19, 32, 33, 148, 201, 220, 248; family, 19, 76, 94, 95, 129, 130, 196; first person narrative, 47, 71, 81, 170, 205, 208; influences, xxi, 15, 28, 36, 46, 64, 197, 203; non-fiction; *Fire and the Sun, The*, xxiv, 55, 78, 99, 151, 243; *Metaphysics as a Guide to Morals*, 152, 242, 243, 249; *Sartre, Romantic Rationalist*, xxi, 17, 21, 33, 35, 48, 77, 227; *Sovereignty of Good, The*, 43, 151, 157; novels; *Accidental Man, An*, xviii, xx, 37, 147, 161, 170, 175; *Bell, The*, 3, 7, 12, 23, 26, 168, 190, 192, 205; *Black Prince, The*, xvi, xxv, 47, 50, 65, 67–69, 71, 76–77, 81, 84–85, 103–4, 105, 118, 147, 152–54, 186–90, 207, 228; *Book and the Brotherhood, The*, xviii, 176, 190, 233; *Bruno's Dream*, xv, 23, 164, 223; early unpublished, 33; *Fairly Honourable Defeat, A*, xvi, xviii, xix,

Murdoch, Iris (*continued*)

  xxv, xxvi, xxvii, 50–51, 54, 73–75, 108, 117, 135, 165, 179–85, 236; *Flight from the Enchanter, The*, xviii, 7, 24–25, 26, 37, 75, 112, 147; *Good Apprentice, The*, 169, 175, 178, 179, 185–86, 200, 203, 206, 239, 255; *Henry and Cato*, 39, 42, 43, 164, 175, 206, 228; *Italian Girl, The*, 16, 23–24, 26, 81; *Message to the Planet, The*, xviii; *Nice and the Good, The*, 21, 22, 37, 49, 155, 163, 168, 192, 206, 228, 254; *Nuns and Soldiers*, 104, 135, 175, 206, 207, 232, 239; *Philosopher's Pupil, The*, xxvi, 124–28, 133, 155, 170, 190, 199, 201–7; *Red and the Green, The*, 94, 191, 233, 254; *Sacred and Profane Love Machine, The*, xviii, 49, 147, 155, 190, 207, 228; *Sandcastle, The*, 6, 7, 22, 37, 116, 117, 167, 173; *Sea, The Sea, The*, xviii, xxv, xxvi, 81, 100, 105–7, 115, 117, 125, 130, 162, 178, 239; *Severed Head, A*, 7, 12, 22, 23, 24, 26, 66, 134, 228; *Time of the Angels, The*, 21, 22, 62, 86; translations, 168, 173; *Under the Net*, xviii, 4, 7, 12, 21, 28, 50, 56, 75, 81, 101, 105, 112, 116, 117, 147, 168, 190, 192; *Unicorn, The*, xviii, 22, 23, 26, 85, 86, 161, 162, 163, 194, 206; *Unofficial Rose, An*, xviii, 12, 50, 51, 92, 207; *Word Child, A*, xviii, xxv, 42, 46, 49, 54, 70–73, 81, 85, 87, 91–92, 130, 161, 179, 180; operas; *Servants, The*, xxiv, 120–23; plays, 123; *Acastos*, xxiv, 243; *Black Prince, The*, xxiv, 228; *Italian Girl, The*, xxiv, 16, 17, 60; *Servants and the Snow, The*, xvii, xxiv, 48, 60, 120, 121; *Severed Head, A*, xxiv, 16–17, 60, 228; *Three Arrows, The*, xvii, xxiv, 48, 60; plot, 85; poetry, 150; reading, 14, 27, 36, 56, 63, 64, 201, 230, 239; religion, xx, 7, 27, 43, 49, 62, 76, 133, 136, 142, 160, 182, 209–17, 227; settings, 41; style, 149; subject matter, 40, 46; technique, xxii, 12, 14, 22, 27, 38, 47, 54, 57, 65, 71, 81, 85, 126, 129, 191, 198, 204, 220, 223, 246; travels, 40; work habits, 222

Murdoch, Wills John Hughes (IM's father), 7, 33, 95, 129, 130, 196, 209, 219

music, 4, 161, 229, 239

myth, xxiii, 7, 10–13, 21–23, 53, 127, 134, 136, 137, 151–53, 175, 187, 201

mythology, Greek, 152

Nabakov, Vladimir: *Pale Fire*, 29

names, 223

National Gallery, 247

National Theatre, 243

necessity, 46, 122, 126

New Theatre, Cardiff, 120

Nietzsche, Friedrich, 153

novel, xxvi, 29, 34, 47, 63, 85, 92, 101, 133, 138, 182, 197, 199, 230

novelists, 1, 2, 8, 31, 131, 171

novels and novelists, contemporary, xxii, 2, 10, 14, 27, 31, 34, 36, 63, 201, 230

novels and novelists, English, 34, 94

novels and novelists, French, 31, 34

novels and novelists, historical, 190
novels and novelists, nineteenth-
    century, 27, 34–35, 44, 62, 102,
    226
novels and novelists, Russian, 226
novels and novelists, twentieth-
    century, 44
nuclear weapons, 6

O'Connor, Flannery, 198
Oedipus myth, 23
ontological proof, 212, 216, 244
opera, 120
optimism, 45, 46
Oxford analytical school, 20
Oxford University, 4, 19, 20, 32, 55,
    98, 99, 122, 128, 151, 157, 204,
    220, 232, 233; Somerville College,
    218; St Anne's College, 219, 243

painters, 134, 232
painting, 2, 128, 136, 158, 228, 248
Pasternak, Boris, 31
pessimism, 37, 46, 92
Peter Pan (statue), 87
philosophy, 2, 7, 19, 20–21, 57, 78,
    90, 98, 109, 110, 122, 125, 128,
    151, 225, 236, 242
philosophy in the novel, xviii, xix, 3,
    12, 20–21, 36, 46, 58, 89, 124,
    173, 182, 225, 240
philosophy, linguistic, 92, 211
philosophy, moral, 79, 90–91, 99,
    125, 151, 157, 199, 211, 216
philosophy, political, 144
philosophy, pre-Socratic, 236
Pinter, Harold, 252
Plato, 55, 74, 78, 89, 99, 111, 128,
    132, 142, 145, 146, 151–52, 202,
    211–13, 235, 243; Republic, 224;
    Symposium, 79

Platonism, xv, xix, 25, 55, 92, 108,
    140, 151, 212, 216
plot, 12, 17, 31, 71, 105, 114, 230
poetry, 4, 50, 64, 84, 93, 105, 149,
    172
poetry, contemporary, 27
Poland, 143
political pamphlets, 18, 48
politics, xvii, xxvi, 6, 111, 149, 210,
    233, 235
politics in art, 17, 138
politics in drama, 17, 48
politics in the novel, xvii, 48
pornography, 226
postmodernism, 117
Powys, John Cowper, 230
pragmatism, 157
Price, Simon, xxvi
Priestley, J.B., xxiv, 17, 60, 228
propaganda, 17, 18, 48
Proust, Marcel, xxi, 27, 31, 44, 64,
    80, 95, 226; À la recherche du
    temps perdu, 224
psychoanalysis, 53, 59, 88, 131, 136,
    177, 179, 180
psychology, xxiii, 115, 131, 146
public schools, 6
publication and sales, 168
publishers, 199, 222
publishers, American, 167
Puritanism, 95
Pushkin, Alexander Sergeyevich:
    Queen of Spades, The, 170

Queneau, Raymond, 28, 46, 75;
    Pierrot mon ami, 4; Zazie dans le
    métro, 28

racial policy, 6
Radcliffe, Ann, 86
radio, 239

readers, 38, 119, 152, 156, 166, 180, 181, 185, 187, 192, 201, 228, 230, 234
reading, 226
realism, 7, 29, 52, 72, 76, 80, 86–87, 157, 174, 184, 207, 226
refugees, 130, 231, 235, 242, 252
relativism, 107, 108, 244
religion, xx, 8, 26, 42, 45, 62, 99, 100, 117, 136, 139, 140, 143, 159, 164, 209–17, 227, 236, 237
religion, fundamentalist, xx, 159
religions, mystery, 152
religious communities, 205
Rembrandt, Harmensz van Rijn, 87, 134
revenge, 145
Richardson, Samuel, 64
Robbe-Grillet, Alain, 36, 80, 112; gommes, Les, 112; jalousie, La, 112
Rowse, A. L., 86
Royal College of Art, 16, 231–32
Rozanov, Vasily Vasilievich, 203
Rubens, Bernice, 232
Russell, Bertrand, 220
Russia, 24, 122

Saint Augustine, 212
Saint Paul, 214
Sartre, Jean-Paul, xxi, 2, 3, 17, 20, 21, 35, 46, 54, 58, 77, 110, 140, 227, 240, 242; chemins de la liberté, Les, 46, 48, 78; être et le néant, L', 98, 242; Existentialisme et humanisme, 79; mots, Les, 46, 75; nausée, La, 46, 78
satire, xvii, 196, 202
satyr plays, 202
Saunders, James, 17
scepticism, 140
Schlick, Friedrich Albert Moritz, 204

Schopenhauer, Arthur, 131, 136, 152
science and technology, 45, 62, 211, 240
Scotland, 93, 94
Scott, Walter, 39, 199
Scottish Nationalists, 32
sculptors, 232
Seth, Vikram, 232
sex, 25, 230, 241
sex differences, 30
Shakespeare, William, xxi, 3, 15, 31, 63, 64, 80, 84, 101, 102, 103, 127, 172, 173, 191, 197, 202, 224, 225; Hamlet, 47, 67, 107, 152; King Lear, 73, 135; Midsummer Night's Dream, A, 74; Othello, 103; Tempest, The, 74, 105, 125, 174
Shaw, George Bernard, 196
singing, 229, 239
Snow, C. P., 64
social commentary in the novel, xvii, 2, 17–18, 48, 197
socialism, 19, 220, 235
Socrates, 7, 243
Solzhenitsyn, Aleksandr, 31
Spanish Civil War, 220
Spark, Muriel, 63
Spender, Natasha, 252
Spender, Stephen, 252
spiders, xxvi, 223
Stanford University, 175, 179
Steeple Aston, 139, 232
Stendhal, 64, 95, 226; rouge et le noir, Le, 87
stoicism, 135
structuralism, 51, 90, 102
Swift, Jonathan, 196
swimming, 127, 239
symbolism, 13, 23, 66–67, 69, 75–76, 239

Tacitus, xxvi, 150
Taoism, 236
Tate Gallery, 117
teaching, 20, 38, 55, 78, 99, 129, 204, 232, 243
television, 45, 116, 119, 230, 253
Thatcher, Margaret, xvii, 235
theatre, 16, 49, 60, 64, 72, 104, 121, 129, 172, 228
theft, 237
theology, 216
theory, literary, 52
theory, philosophical, 52, 90
Tibet, 100
Titian, 228; Flaying of Marsyas, The, 229
titles, 75, 168, 173, 221
Tolstoy, Leo, xxi, 28, 31, 64, 80, 84, 102, 103, 118, 157, 158, 171, 197, 224, 226, 251; Anna Karenina, 82, 157; War and Peace, 102, 183
tragedy, xxvii, 25, 47, 59, 72, 172, 202
tragedy, Greek, 203
translation, 149
travel writing, 41
Treasury (Great Britain), 128, 218, 220
truth, xvii, 237
truthfulness, xxviii, 2, 7, 18, 50, 53, 118, 134, 158, 159, 174, 190, 225, 238, 242
Turgenev, Ivan, 64

unemployment, 159, 161
United Nations Relief and Rehabilitation Administration (UNRRA), 20, 130, 218, 220
United States of America, 40, 111, 176, 220
universities, 239
University College, London, 16

University of California, Berkeley, 179
utilitarianism, 211

Vassar, 220
Vietnam, 18
Vietnam War, 17, 18, 175
Virgil, 150
visions, 164

Wales, 94, 195
Waugh, Evelyn, 171
weapons, 223
Weil, Robert, xxvii
Weil, Simone, 49, 76, 135, 137
Welsh National Opera, 121
Whitehead, A.N., 235
Wilde, Oscar, 87
Wilson, A.N., 232
Wilson, Angus, 64; Middle Age of Mrs Eliot, The, 61
Wittgenstein, Ludwig, 4, 5, 7, 52, 98, 152, 211
Wolff, Maria, 168
women artists, 5
women writers, 30, 83, 229, 249
women's education, xvii, 5, 31, 48, 82
women's rights, xvii, 5, 32, 48, 61, 82–83, 111, 207
women's studies, xvii, 62, 83
Woolf, Virginia, 63, 64
Wordsworth, William, 57
work, 142, 144, 159, 161, 239
World War One, 129, 219
World War Two, 19, 97, 122, 128, 151, 219, 227
writers, black, 208
writers, Irish, 19, 196
writers, Russian, 31

Yugoslavia, 18